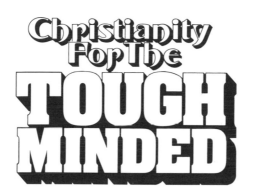

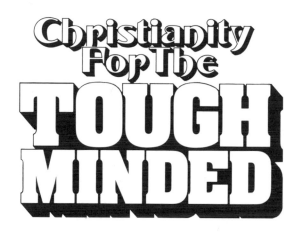

Christianity For The TOUGH MINDED

Essays in Support of an Intellectually Defensible Religious Commitment

Edited
with Introduction and Preliminary Essay on
God's Existence

by

John Warwick Montgomery

BETHANY FELLOWSHIP, INC.
Minneapolis, Minnesota

Library of Congress Cataloging in Publication Data
Montgomery, John Warwick,
Christianity for the Tough-minded
1. Apologetics—20th century—Addresses, essays, lectures.
I. Montgomery, John Warwick, ed.
BT1105.C55
239
73-4842
ISBN 0-87123-076-3

*Throughout this volume, drawings have been reproduced
with the kind permission of the Back to God Tract
Committee.*

Printed in United States of America

"The tough-minded and the tender-minded, as William James described them so brilliantly, are perennial types, perennially antagonistic . . . . Respect for the facts of experience, opon mindedness, an experimental trial-and-error attitude, and the capacity for working within the frame of an incomplete unfinished world view distinguish [the tough-minded] from the more impatient, imaginative, and often aprioristic thinkers in the tender-minded camp."

—Herbert Feigl, *Logical Empiricism*

To
TOM STARK
in whose fertile cerebrum the idea for this
book germinated

Contents

7

Introduction

Most books on Christianity are written for Christians. This one is not. The essays comprising the present work have Christians as their authors, but they are Christians with an all too uncommon perspective: once among the religiously undecided, troubled, or antagonistic themselves, they have become convinced that the claims of Christianity are not only relevant but in fact true, and they write in an effort to show those who stand where they once stood that the contemporary objections to the Christian faith are vastly overrated. In all cases (with the possible exceptions of the editor, one of his former students at a Canadian university and professional peers who have graciously supplied appendix material) the contributors are full-fledged members of the "now" generation—graduate students or recent alumni of graduate degree programs at the Trinity Evangelical Divinity School.

Religious arguments, admittedly, have a grim reputation, and they generally deserve it. Canadian humorist Stephen Leacock thus describes an archetypical religious discussion in his classic, *Sunshine Sketches of a Little Town*:

> Mallory Tompkins was a young man with long legs and check trousers who worked on the Mariposa *Times-Herald*. That was what gave him his literary taste. He used to read Ibsen and that other Dutch author—Bumstone Bumstone, isn't it?—and you can judge that he was a mighty intellectual fellow. He was so intellectual that he was, as he himself admitted, a complete eggnostic. He and Pupkin used to have the most tremendous arguments about creation and evolution, and how if you study at a school of applied science you learn that there's no hell beyond the present life.
>
> Mallory Tompkins used to prove absolutely that the miracles were only electricity, and Pupkin used to admit that it was an awfully good argument, but claimed that he had heard it awfully well answered in a sermon, though unfortunately he had forgotten how.
>
> Tompkins used to show that the flood was contrary to geology, and Pupkin would acknowledge that the point was an excellent one, but that he had read a book—the title

9

of which he ought to have written down—which explained geology away altogether.

Mallory Tompkins generally got the best of the merely logical side of the arguments, but Pupkin—who was a tremendous Christian—was much stronger in the things he had forgotten. So the discussions often lasted till far into the night, and Mr. Pupkin would fall asleep and dream of a splendid argument, which would have settled the whole controversy, only unfortunately he couldn't recall it in the morning.

It will be noted that the utter insanity of this religious interchange stems from two considerations: (1) the arguments of the "eggnostic" ("the miracles were only electricity"; "if you study at a school of applied science you learn that there's no hell beyond the present life") are masterpieces of absurdity, and (2) the Christian defender of the faith manages, with no little effort, to exceed his opponent in sheer nincompoopishness by the few things he remembered (the possibility of "explaining away geology altogether") and the vast number of "things he had forgotten." But readers of the book in hand have a refreshing surprise in store for them: its authors focus attention only on the genuinely trenchant arguments currently being directed against the Christian faith, and they remember a great deal.

* * *

"But who cares?" is the predictable response of some who come across this volume. "Religion isn't my bag." "Live and let live is my motto." "If it makes *you* feel better, fine; I can get along without it." "What you believe doesn't make any difference as long as you're sincere." "There are lots of religious roads going up the mountain and they all get to the same place in the end." Et cetera.

The trouble with this line of thought (or, better, non-thought) is that it is utterly unrealistic. In the first place, as theologian Paul Tillich correctly observed, religion is *everybody's* bag, whether one recognizes it or not, since every individual without exception has an "ultimate concern"—a commitment to some value above others. This value (whether the God of Christianity, the goal of fame and fortune, passion for a sportscar or a blonde, or sheer deification of self) is a religious commitment: a god. The question is not: Should I bother choosing a religion? It is rather: What is my religion at present and does it qualify as a proper ultimate concern? Am I engaged in an idolatry no different in principle (though perhaps considerably more sophisticated in practice) than the activities carried on by primitive tribes?

Secondly, the religions of the world are mutually exclusive; the basic tenets of one contradict the fundamental convictions of the others, so all of them cannot possibly be correct. As Boston University philosopher Edgar Sheffield Brightman used to say: "A universe in which Roman Catholicism and Christian Science could both be right would be a madhouse." If this is true of positions within the broad expanse of "Christendom," how much more is it the case when one considers the major religions of the world? Tantristic faiths (Hinduism, Buddhism) hold to the transmigration of souls, a process that will allegedly lead to Nirvana for those who separate themselves from all desire; Christianity diametrically opposes such attenuation of desire, and asserts that God's kingdom and eternal life are immediately open to every man who accepts God's forgiveness in Christ. Islam makes salvation dependent upon the fulfilling of the Quranic law; Christianity offers salvation as a free gift of God's grace to those who realize that they cannot save themselves. The Christian religion accepts the exclusive claim of Christ: "I am the Way, the Truth, and the Life; no man comes to the Father but by me"; all other religions reject this claim in varying degrees. Surely the issue as to who is right— if anyone—in this cacaphony of religious affirmations is of more than routine importance.

Thirdly, the acceptance of one religion over another is of immense practical consequence. A Charles Addams cartoon in *The New Yorker* several years ago depicted a Victorian living room in which two middle-aged ladies were having tea. Said the lady of the house: "My parents objected to my marrying Herbert because of our religious differences." In the background Herbert was seen stealthily crossing the room, holding an axe in one hand and leading a goat with the other. His religion? One was left in doubt—but with a profound sense of disquiet! Religious practices are not automatically good—or even neutral. Ferdinand Duchêne, a former Justice of the Court of Appeals of Algiers, received the Grand Prix Littéraire de l'Algérie for his account of the ghastly effects of Quranic teaching on the status of women in Muslim lands: treated like chattel, they have little hope in this world or the next. Or consider examples even closer to home: the consequence of demonic religious commitment to Nazi blood and soil on the part of an entire generation of German youth; and the results of a not dissimilar totalitarian involvement (though it uses the language of the far left rather than the far right) among those who, while declaring that "religion is the opiate of the people," drug themselves with the Marxist world-view. Arthur Koestler and other notables who extricated themselves with the greatest of difficulty from this latter commitment rightly saw its true character when they described it in a book titled, *The God That Failed.*

* * *

The search for a veracious religious orientation is, then, a matter of utmost importance. It is no less than the search for reality itself. How tragic to spend years—to say nothing of an entire lifetime—in the worship of "gods that fail." And how miserable, how less than human, to pass one's life in a self-deception that misses reality entirely. The recent Broadway musical *Cabaret* is a telling indictment of mankind's willingness to fool itself into creating dream worlds in order to avoid the world that is. This modern morality play is set in the Germany of the early thirties, and shows Everyman in the *personae* of a hopelessly naive Jewish merchant who will not leave the country for his own safety ("I understand the German people—why, I am German myself!"), an elderly woman who loves him but prefers to live out her declining years in misery without marrying him because to marry a Jew would jeopardize the "success" of her ancient and crumbling rooming house ("we do what we must"), and a young English girl, who throws away the certainty of happiness with a boy, and even aborts her child by him, in order to retain her illusionary career as a "singing star" in the cheap cabaret that she has come to substitute for reality. As the M.C. sings—who appropriately wears a death mask in the final scene—"Life is a cabaret, my friend; life is a cabaret." This is precisely the kind of chimerical world a vast number of people settle for, and it is hard to distinguish it from Huysmans' *Là-Bas*, or from the country described in an old play as "the londe of Rumbelowe, three myle out of hell." As Socrates well put it: "The unexamined life is not worth living."

The present book should offer its serious readers an unparalleled opportunity for Socratic examination of the religious question—unless, to be sure, the path has already been closed off by one's fallacious methodological commitments. Two misconceptions are wide-spread enough to warrant some remarks at the outset. They are: the conviction that nothing can be "proved" anyway (skepticism), and the view that the only proof worthy of consideration is of the mathematical-deductive variety (rationalism).

The trouble with skepticism is that no one can apply it consistently. An hilarious scene in Molière's comedy, *Le Mariage Forcé*, makes the point better than direct argument. An elderly gentleman who contemplates marriage with an inconstant young thing and who suspects that he is in for big trouble consults a philosopher of the skeptical school on the matter. The dialogue runs as follows (we have taken the liberty to abbreviate the scene somewhat):

SGANARELLE.—Professor, I need your advice in a small matter and I have come here for that reason.

MARPHURIUS.—My dear sir, I beg you to change your manner of speaking. Our philosophy prohibits entirely the enunciation of unqualified propositions; one must speak of everything with uncertainty; judgment is always to be suspended. Therefore, you must not say, "I have come," but: "It *seems* to me that I have come."

SGANARELLE.—It seems to me.

MARPHURIUS.—Exactly.

SGANARELLE.—Great scott! It ought very well to seem that way, since it is the case.

MARPHURIUS.—That does not follow. One must doubt everything.

SGANARELLE.—I'm here to tell you that I wish to be married, and that the girl is very young and very beautiful.

MARPHURIUS.—It isn't impossible.

SGANARELLE.—Will I be making a wise or unwise decision to marry her?

MARPHURIUS.—Either the one or the other.

SGANARELLE.—Well, what do you think? What would you do in my place?

MARPHURIUS.—I have no idea. Do what you please.

SGANARELLE.—I am losing my patience. (*To himself:*) I'll make him change his tune, the philosophical oaf! (*He trounces Marphurius with his cane.*)

MARPHURIUS.—What insolence! To have the audacity to beat a philosopher of my station!

SGANARELLE.—I beg you to change your manner of speaking. One must doubt everything, so you should not say that I have struck you, but that it seems to you that I have struck you.

MARPHURIUS.—I have the very marks of the blows on my person!

SGANARELLE.—It isn't impossible.

The inability of the skeptical philosopher to speak to the issue at hand and the reduction of the whole business to personal preference (a situation having remarkable parallels with

Jean-Paul Sartre's refusal, in *Existentialism and Human Emotions*, to give advice to a young Frenchman undecided as to whether he should join the Free French forces in World War II) finally and inevitably boomerangs: skeptical incapacity to recognize the objectivity of other people's situations prevents one from defending oneself against identical treatment. Selective skepticism proves impossible, and total skepticism cannot be carried out in practice. Even the most relativistic and skeptical person objects when you maltreat *him* and claim he can't prove it; and the solipsist, just like anyone else, looks both ways before crossing the street.

As for the notion that the only "true" proof of anything is mathematical-deductive in form, it is sufficient to note that the only people who seriously maintain this are those who do not understand what pure mathematics and deductive logic actually involve. Whitehead and Russell in the *Principia Mathematica* showed that pure mathematics is a special case of deductive logic and that both derive from tautological, definitional axioms. This means that the "certainty" of mathematical-deductive proof is built-in, and does not derive from the investigation of the world at all. Logic and mathematics never inform us as to what the world consists of; they tell us how to relate together the facts of the world as we discover them by independent observation. The assertion "2 + 2 = 4" can refer to fairies or to faculty members; its certainty rests on axiomatic definitions, not on whether faculty members or fairies actually exist. To determine the latter, there is no substitute for the investigation of the world by observation of facts and the collection of evidence. As the philosopher Wittgenstein shrewdly observed, logic and mathematics are but a kind of "scaffold" displaying the shape or form of universal relationships; to find what the building actually consists of, you must come into direct contact with it by observing it and by examining the testimony of others who have seen what you have not.

The book in hand endeavors to put its reader into immediate contact with the kind of evidence that has led innumerable critical thinkers to an acceptance of the Christian faith. Not only does such evidence exist; the data are available for consideration by anyone who is willing to examine them. Christianity is radically different from the welter of religious options of past and present in that it does not demand a "leap of blind faith"—an amputation of the head—as prerequisite for inner confirmation of its message. True, as with any life commitment (marriage is an obvious example), Christianity's subjective attestation comes only with the personal *entrée* into it, but that entrance can be made with full confidence that the evidence warrants it. To appropriate Christianity subjectively is to respond in the most reasonable manner to the powerful objective evidence of its truth. Christian faith, as the great theologians have emphasized, is a personal commitment (*fiducia*) thoroughly grounded in factual truth (*notitia*). The Christian believer, far from being a wooly-minded mystic, is a man who—unlike most of his fellows—insists on conforming his personal religious predilections to what is religiously the case, rather than making the world a reflection of his own subjective religious needs. He is dead-set against idolatry; he refuses to re-make God in his own image.

* * *

And if the wide-ranging evidence presented in the following pages leads the reader to the threshold of Christian conviction—what then? How does one "come to faith"? Someone has said that becoming a Christian is both the easiest and the hardest thing in the world to do. It is the easiest because it requires nothing on the part of the individual: Christ did everything necessary for man's salvation when on the cross He suffered indescribable agony to expiate the sins of each one of us. But at the same time the acceptance of this is the hardest thing in the world because it requires a man to admit that he is in fact incapable of saving himself—that he does not have what it takes to merit a relationship with God and eternal life. The last thing one wants to give up is his illusory capacity for self-salvation, and this basal egocentrism, more than any other single thing, keeps people from God's Kingdom. Like the rich young ruler in the Gospels, they turn sorrowfully away from Christ not because His claims lack sufficient evidence but because, were these claims to be accepted, control of one's destiny would no longer rest with one's own resources, but with Christ alone.

To become a Christian, then, requires the heartfelt prayer: "Lord, be merciful to me a sinner." Whenever that prayer rises from the depths of the soul to the God who died for sinners and rose again, the heavens open and life changes. Copernican revolutions occur and God becomes the proper center of human life. A personal relationship is established between God and the believer which grows as God the Holy Spirit literally takes up residence in the believer's heart. This relationship is sustained and deepened as the Christian increases his understanding of Christ through contact with the Bible—God's inspired revelation of His will and purpose—and through contact with other believers in the church, the community of faith. Since "faith comes by hearing and hearing by the Word of God," faith grows as it is nourished by Holy Writ and by those believing communities where that Word is preached in its purity and entirety.

Thus can the tough-minded become tender-hearted without any loss of that intellectual sharpness which is, in fact, one of God's most precious gifts. All that one loses in becoming a Christian is egotistic self-deception; and when one has experienced that "loss," one finds it to be an inestimable gain. The mind clears, the universe swings into proper perspective. The contributors to this book join its editor in offering that greatest of all experiences to every one of its readers.

JOHN WARWICK MONTGOMERY

Strasbourg, France
7 July 1972

Acknowledgements

The following essays have appeared in other periodicals and appear here with the permission of their authors and of the editors from whose publications they were taken. The present book has in some cases afforded the authors an opportunity for making minor revisions and corrections in their original texts.

"Is Man His Own God?": *Journal of the Evangelical Theological Society*, XII (Spring, 1969).

"Science and Christianity: Toward Peaceful Coexistence": *The Technograph*, LXXXIII (December, 1967 and January, 1968).

"A Critique of Bertrand Russell's Religious Position": *Bulletin of the Evangelical Theological Society*, VIII (Autumn, 1965).

"Some Weaknesses in Fundamental Buddhism": *Evangelical Missions Quarterly*, VII (Fall, 1970).

"Passover Plot or Easter Triumph?": *The Gordon Review*, Summer, 1967; *Journal of the American Scientific Affiliation*, XXI (March, 1969).

"A Sample of Scrollduggery": *America*, September 3, 1966.

"Computer Analysis and the Pauline Corpus: A Case of Deus ex Machina": *Bibliotheca Sacra* (January-March, 1973).

Part One

PHILOSOPHY AND SCIENTIFIC METHOD

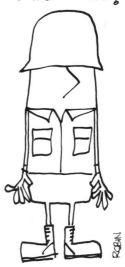

Is Man His Own God?*

John Warwick Montgomery

Currently making the rounds on American college campuses is the question, "How are you going to recognize God when you get to heaven?" Answer: "By the big 'G' on his sweatshirt." This litany has more metaphysical profundity than meets the eye, for it reflects the contemporary philosophical dilemma as to the meaningfulness of God-language—a dilemma to which we shall be addressing ourselves shortly. But it is essential to make one basic point at the very outset: in the philosophy of life of every person without exception, someone or something is invested with the sweatshirt lettered "G." There are no atheists; everyone has his god. In the language of Paul Tillich (who was ironically called an atheist by some of his less perceptive critics), all of us have our "ultimate concerns," and the sad thing is that so few of them are truly ultimate or worthy of worship. As one of William James' "twice-born" (having come to Christian belief as an adult), I am especially concerned that idols be properly identified and that only the true owner of the cosmic sweatshirt should wear it. As a modest contribution to that end, we shall first consider how much ultimacy ought to be attributed to three prominent alternatives to biblical theism, and then devote ourselves to the crucial arguments in behalf of the Christian view of God.

THE UNREALITY OF MAJOR NON-THEISTIC POSITIONS

Pantheism à la Spinoza

I recall but one occasion when my old Greek professor at Cornell was drawn into a religious discussion, and—in a state

---

* An invitational presentation at DePaul University, Chicago, February 5, 1969, in debate with humanist Julian J. Steen, dean of the Chicago School for Adults. The debate was sponsored by DePaul's theology department; Professor Robert Campbell, O.P. served as moderator. This same essay was also presented at Harvard University on February 14, 1969 as one of a series of "Christian Contemporary Thought Lectures."

of obvious discomfort—he defended his unorthodoxy somewhat as follows: "But do not conclude that I am an atheist. Far from it. For me the universe as a whole, with all its mystery, is God, and I reverence it." This viewpoint (which can, of course, be stated in many different ways) has perhaps best been set forth and defended by Spinoza. In Part One of his *Ethics*, the philosopher endeavors to show that the universe is a single, all-embracing unity and that that unity is God. This is proved by the fact that the universe obviously consists of some thing—Spinoza calls it Substance—and this Substance "is in itself and is conceived through itself"; now since God is properly defined as "a being absolutely infinite" and Substance is infinite and unique, it follows that Substance is God.

The fallacy in this piece of geometrically-modeled legerdemain has been well stated by C. E. M. Joad in his *Guide to Philosophy*: "If we assume that Substance in the original definition means simply 'all that there is,' then the initial definition contains within itself the conclusion. Such a conclusion is not worth proving. It is, indeed, merely a tautology—that is to say, an asserting of the same thing in two different ways." Pantheism, in other words (and this applies equally to all forms of it, whether derived from Spinoza or not), is neither true nor false; it is something much worse, viz., entirely trivial. We had little doubt that the universe was here anyway; by giving it a new name ("God") we explain nothing. We actually commit the venerable intellectual sin of Word Magic, wherein the naming of something is supposed to give added power either to the thing named or to the semantic magician himself.

Humanism

If the universe cannot be meaningfully deified, why not man himself? Can we not regard as strictly literal the question posed in the title of this presentation, "Is Man His Own God?" and answer it affirmatively? For the humanist, man is himself the proper "ultimate concern," and human values are the only eternal verities.

But which "human values" do we mean? Anthropologists such as Ruth Benedict have discovered a most bewildering variety of human value systems, styles of life, and ethical norms. And what is worse, these morals and mores are often entirely incompatible. Some peoples reverence their parents and others eat them. Among cannibals it is doubtless both good ethics and good table manners to clean your plate.

How is the humanist going to decide among these competing value systems? He has no absolute vantage point from which to view the ethical battle in the human arena. He is in the arena himself; or, to use beatnik poet Kerouac's expression, he is "on the road"—not in a house by the side of the road where he can watch the world go by and arbitrate it. All value systems that arise from within the human context are necessarily conditioned by it and are therefore relative. Out of flux, nothing but flux. As Wittgenstein correctly observed in the *Tractatus Logico-Philosophicus*: "If there is any value that does have value, it must lie outside the whole sphere of what happens and is the case . . . . Ethics is transcendental."

* * *

Yet a transcendental perspective is exactly what the humanist does not have. He is therefore left to *consensus gentium* (majority values), cultural totalitarianism (the values of one's own society) or sheer authoritarianism (*my* values, not yours). But, sad to say, fifty million Frenchmen *can* be wrong; the ethical perspective of an entire society can be cruelly immoral; and the individual who considers himself the true barometer to moral worth may simply be suffering from overactive glands or an advanced stage of messianic complex.

To establish absolute ethical values for human action is both logically and practically impossible apart from transcendence. To move the world Archimedes rightly noted that he would need a fulcrum outside the world. The assassination of biblical revelation in the 18th century left man without a clear conception of or confidence in God, and God's resultant death in the 19th century (in the work of Nietzsche and others) set the stage for the dehumanization of man in the 20th. Nietzsche recognized full well that apart from God only man remains to establish his own value; and the stronger has every right under such conditions to impose his self-centered value system on the weaker—and eliminate him if he does not learn his lessons well. The anti-Semitism of the deists of the 18th century Enlightenment (as definitively researched by Arthur Hertzberg in his 1968 publication, *The French Enlightenment and the Jews*), the Nietzschean transvaluation of values, will-to-power, and antichristic treatment of the weak, and the National Socialist extermination of racial and political minorities demonstrate only too clearly what happens when man becomes the measure of all things. It is curious that humanists presently (and commendably) striving for racial equality in this country do not ask themselves why, in any absolute sense, their goals are more justifiable than the genocide practiced by an equally passionate and idealistic generation of young people in the Germany of the 1930s and 1940s. As for me, I'm for absolute racial justice, and I'm unwilling to see it—or any comparable value—left at the mercy of relativistic humanism. If man is his own god, then religion is *really* in trouble. Personally, I'd be willing to join a Man-is-dead movement!

Agnosticism

High on the popularity poll of non-theistic ultimate concerns today is agnosticism. What is seldom recognized, however, by either its advocates or its opponents, is that the term agnosticism embraces two very different positions. The first might be called "hard-boiled" agnosticism: "I know that I am unable to know that there is a God"; the second, "soft-boiled" agnosticism: "I am not sure whether knowledge of God is possible."

Little time should be spent on hard-boiled agnosticism, since it is tantamount to traditional atheism, and suffers from its basic fallacy: it presumes that one can (apart from any revelation of God, to be sure!) know the universe so well that one can assert the non-existence of God or the non-existence of compelling evidence for his existence. But such comprehensive knowledge of the universe would require either (a) revelation, which is excluded on principle, or (b) divine powers of observation on the part of the atheist or hard-boiled agnostic. In the latter case, atheism and the extreme agnostic position become self-defeating, since the unbeliever perforce creates a god by deifying himself.

As for soft-boiled agnosticism, it is highly commendable *if actually practiced* (which is very seldom). A genuine agnostic of this school will of course bend every effort to see whether in fact evidence does exist in behalf of theistic claims. His view of the universe is open-ended; he is a passionate seeker for truth; and he recognizes that his best energies must be put to this quest, since one's happiness in this world, to say nothing about one's eternal destiny in the next, is directly at stake if God in fact exists and makes demands on his creatures. The true agnostic, then, might be thought of as a person in a room who was not sure whether or not to believe a report that a bomb was planted in the building and would go off in two hours. Because of the cruciality of the *possibility*, he would not sit here in blasé indifference (the usual agnostic posture), but would clear the room and engage in a most diligent search of the premises to determine whether concrete evidence supported the claim or not.

It is now our task to perform a brief, but hopefully constructive, check of the universal premises to see if divine power is there revealed.

THE REALITY OF THE BIBLICAL GOD

Where to look for the footprints of Deity? Virtually anywhere but in the arguments of some modern theologians, clerics, and mystics, of whom it might well be said: "With friends like that God doesn't need any enemies." I refer, for example, to those Anglican canons who parachuted from the top of St. Paul's Cathedral, to "bring the young people back to the church" (eliciting the remark in *Esquire* magazine: "If God isn't dead, maybe he wishes he were"); or the Protestant-Roman Catholic-Jewish death-of-God school; or Aldous Huxley's World Controller, who declared in *Brave New World* that God now "manifests himself as an absence; as though he weren't there at all." Once having stated this small *caveat*, however, not even the sky is the evidential limit. As Jacques Maritain so well expressed it in *Approaches to God*: "There is not just one way to God, as there is to an oasis across the desert or to a new mathematical idea across the breadth of the science of number. For man there are as many ways of approach to God as there are wanderings on the earth or paths to his own heart." We shall consider four such pathways.

God and the World

In his famous 1948 BBC debate with Bertrand Russell, the great historian of philosophy F. C. Copleston succinctly stated the fundamental "argument from contingency" for God's existence:

First of all, I should say, we know that there are at least some beings in the world which do not contain in themselves the reason for their existence. For example, I depend on my parents, and now on the air, and on food, and so on. Now, secondly, the world is simply the real or imagined totality or aggregate of individual objects, none of which contain in themselves alone the reason for their existence. There isn't any world distinct from the objects which form it, any more than the human race is something apart from the members. Therefore, I should say, since objects or events exist, and since no object or experience contains within itself the reason of its existence, this reason, the totality of objects, must have a reason external to itself. That reason must be an existent being. Well, this being is either itself the reason for its own existence, or it is not. If it is, well and good. If it is not, then we must proceed farther. But if we proceed to infinity in that sense, then there's no explanation of existence at all. So, I should say, in order to explain existence, we must come to a being which contains within itself the reason for its own existence, that is to say, which cannot not-exist.

This argument is not only regarded by most philosophical advocates of theism as the keystone of the so-called "classic proofs" of God's existence; it is today reinforced by a most impressive battery of evidence from the physical sciences. For example (one may on the point consult the engineering publications of University of Michigan professor Gordon J. Van Wylen), the second law of thermodynamics states that for irreversible processes in any closed system left to itself, the entropy (loss of available heat energy) will increase with time; thus the universe, viewed as such a system, is moving to the condition of maximum entropy (heat death): *but* (and this is the significant aspect of the matter for our purposes) if the irreversible process had begun an infinite time ago—if, in other words, the universe were uncreated and eternal—the earth would *already* have reached maximum entropy; and since this is not the case, we are driven to the conclusion that the universe is indeed contingent and finite, and requires a creative force from the outside to have brought it into existence.

It should be carefully noted that this *a posteriori* argument from contingency is empirically grounded in testable experience; it is neither a disguised form of the highly questionable ontological argument, which asserts *a priori* that God's essence establishes his existence, nor an attempt at allegedly "synthetic *a priori*" reasoning. And unlike the "causal argument," it does not gratuitously presuppose an unalterable cause-and-effect structure in the universe (a very doubtful assumption in light of Einsteinian physics and the Heisenberg uncertainty principle which requires us to give serious consideration to all event-claims, even those "miraculously uncaused").

But what about the standard rebuttal: "You just beg the

question; now tell us why God exists"? Though this question evidently started Bertrand Russell on the downhill slide into intellectual anticlericalism at an early age, it is not especially profound. We have just seen some of the evidence for the contingency of the universe we live in; to regard this world as eternal is out of the question. But to regard its creator as likewise contingent ("Who created *him*?") *would* beg the question, for it would force us to pose the very same query again and again. Only by stopping with a God who is the final answer to the series do we *avoid* begging the question—and only then do we offer any adequate account for the contingent universe with which we began. Moreover, the "why God?" question suffers an acute case both of artificiality and of absurdity, as philosopher Plantinga has shown in his essay on "Necessary Being" (in his *Faith and Philosophy* [1964]):

> We should note that the question "Why does God exist?" never does, in fact, arise. Those who do not believe that God exists will not, of course, ask *why* He exists. But neither do believers ask that question. Outside of theism, so to speak, the question is nonsensical, and inside of theism, the question is never asked. . . .
> Now it becomes clear that it is absurd to ask why God exists. To ask that question is to presuppose that God does exist; but it is a necessary truth that if He does, He has no cause. And it is also a necessary truth that if He has no cause, then there is no answer to a question asking for His causal conditions. The question "Why does God exist?" is, therefore, an absurdity.

God and Personhood

Robert Benchley tells of the disastrous college biology course in which he spent the term meticulously drawing in his lab manual the image of his own eyelash as it fell across the microscopic field. The catastrophe occurred because he lost track of the necessary distinction between himself as subject (his subjectivity) and the external object to be observed (the objectivity of the outside world). Such results and others no less dire are inevitable when one engages in what Whitehead well termed "extreme objectivism"—an objectivism which even objectifies the subject. A person is an "irreducible I": he can never be fully comprehended as an object. No matter how complete a list you make of your own characteristics—or of the characteristics of that stunning coed you are dating—you and the coed *transcend* the list. Persons are grounded in the clay of the contingent world we discussed above, but at the same time they transcend it; human personhood warrants the designation "semi-transcendent." This semi-transcendent, irreducible character of the human person is the quality that has escaped (and logically must escape) the behaviorist who always treats his subjects as objects; it is to the credit of contemporary psychological (especially psychoanalytic) thought that efforts are now made to get beyond such hyperobjectivism. Indeed, in those cases where human subjectivity and freewill are consistently denied, the deterministic objectivist loses all right to claim volitional action and purpose as an experimenter. His refusal to recognize the "semi-transcendent I" finally results in his own epistemological evaporation.

Now, as philosophical theologians such as Ian Ramsey have shown in considerable detail in recent years, the partial transcendence of the human subject establishes both the possibility of metaphysical assertions and the legitimacy of God-language. We cannot meaningfully talk about the universe around us without presupposing our own subjectivity, and the partial transcendence we possess demands an unqualifiedly transcendent integrating subjectivity to make *it* meaningful. As Ramsey puts it in an essay in his *Prospect for Metaphysics* (1961): "Just as 'I' acts as an integrator word for all kinds of scientific and other descriptive assertions about myself, 'I exist' being a sort of conceptual presupposition for them all, so also may 'God' be regarded as a contextual presupposition for the Universe."

This perspective sheds considerable light on two fundamental problems raised by theistic belief: the existence of evil and the question of meaningful God-talk (the problem of the "sweatshirt," as alluded to at the outset of this essay). Opponents of theism have perennially argued that the natural and moral evils in the universe make the idea of an omnipotent and perfectly good God irrational. But if subjectivity (and its correlative, freewill) must be presupposed on the level of human action, and if God's character as fully transcendent divine Subject serves to make human volition meaningful, then the existence of freewill in itself provides a legitimate explanation of evil. To create personalities without genuine freewill would not have been to create persons at all; and freewill means the genuine possibility of wrong decision, i.e., the creation of evil by God's creatures (whether wide-ranging natural and moral evil by fallen angels or limited chaos on earth by fallen mankind).

As for the argument that a good God should have created only those beings he would foresee as choosing the right—or that he could certainly eliminate the effects of his creatures' evil decisions, the obvious answer is (as Plantinga develops it with great logical rigor in his *God and Other Minds* [1967]) that this would be tantamount to not giving freewill at all. To create only those who "must" (in any sense) choose good is to create automata; and to whisk away evil effects as they are produced is to whisk away evil itself, for an act and its consequences are bound together. C. S. Lewis has noted that God's love enters into this issue as well, since the biblical God created man out of love, and genuine human love is impossible without freewill—without the free possibility of accepting love or rejecting it. Just as a boy who offers himself and his love to a girl must count on the real possibility of rejection, so when God originated a creative work that made genuine love possible, it by definition entailed the concomitant possibility of the evil rejection of his love by his creatures.

By the "sweatshirt" problem we refer to an objection to theism posed by such analytical philosophers as Kai Nielsen and Antony Flew, who claim that God's very uniqueness makes it irrational to say anything about him: since, in the absence of any perfect analogy, he must always be described in negativities, God-talk becomes totally meaningless. The sweatshirt with the big "G," we are told, is necessarily empty. But again note how the understanding of God as transcendent integrating Subject in relation to semi-transcendent human subjects clears the air. Human persons are *likewise* unique—no person is just like another, and the very meaning of "subject" and individual "freewill" entails this irreducible uniqueness. To call God-talk meaningless, then, is at the same time to render man-talk nonsensical! Conversely, if we once accept what is involved in the concept of human subjective existence (and how can we avoid it?) then we simultaneously open the gate to meaningful God-talk. As Ramsey neatly suggests, "We might perhaps then say that we are as certain of God as we are of ourselves."

However, it would be conceding far too much if we were to allow that talk about God involves only negatives—the so-called "death by a thousand qualifications." Here we find ourselves immediately drawn into discussion of

God in Christ

The following parable, formulated by philosophers Flew and Wisdom (*New Essays in Philosophical Theology* [1955]), is a good statement of the view that God-claims are too vague to be sensible and offer no adequate empirical evidence in their behalf:

> Once upon a time two explorers came upon a clearing in the jungle. In the clearing were growing many flowers and many weeds. One explorer says, "Some gardener must tend this plot." The other disagrees, "There is no gardener." So they pitch their tents and set a watch. No gardener is ever seen. "But perhaps he is an invisible gardener." So they set up a barbed-wire fence. They electrify it. They patrol with bloodhounds. (For they remember how H. G. Wells's *The Invisible Man* could be both smelt and touched though he could not be seen.) But no shrieks ever suggest that some intruder has received a shock. No movements of the wire ever betray an invisible climber. The bloodhounds never give cry. Yet still the Believer is not convinced. "But there is a gardener, invisible, intangible, insensible to electric shocks, a gardener who has no scent and makes no sound, a gardener who comes secretly to look after the garden which he loves." At last the Sceptic despairs, "But what remains of your original assertion? Just how does what you call an invisible, intangible, eternally elusive gardener differ from an imaginary gardener or even from no gardener at all?"

This parable may echo the religious claims of many sincere people, but it has little to do with the Christian affirmation of God. Why? Because central to the Christian position is the historically grounded assertion that *the Gardener entered the garden*: God actually appeared in the empirical world in Jesus Christ and fully manifested his deity through miraculous acts in general and his resurrection from the dead in particular. Christian talk about God therefore becomes in the most rigorous sense affirmative, for when asked to "define God" or "tell us what he looks like," the Christian simply points to Christ. Dr. Jowett was supposed to have been asked by an effusive young lady, "Do tell me—what do you think about God?" and his reply was: "That, my dear young lady, is a very unimportant question; the only thing that signifies is what he thinks about me." The Christian knows what God thinks about him—and the human race; he knows what God's eternal value system is (and how desperately the human race needs that knowledge, as we saw in our discussion of humanism!); and he knows that in spite of man's self-centered trampling of God's values, God's love has reached down to earth. How does he know this? Because God tells him this in Christ.

Now it cannot be stressed too strongly that this claim to divine intervention in history is solidly grounded in historical evidence. The textual case for the New Testament documents which record Christ's divine utterances and acts is so excellent that Sir Frederic G. Kenyon, director and principal librarian of the British Museum, could write in 1940 in *The Bible and Archaeology*: "Both the *authenticity* and the *general integrity* of the books of the New Testament may be regarded as finally established" (Kenyon's italics). The world's foremost contemporary biblical archeologist, W. F. Albright of Johns Hopkins University, has identified the New Testament materials as primary source documents for the life of Jesus, dating all of them (including John's Gospel) "between the forties and the eighties of the first century A.D. (very probably sometime between about 50 and 75 A.D.)" (interview in *Christianity Today*, January 18, 1963). The New Testament writers claim eyewitness contact with the events of Jesus' career, and describe his death and post-resurrection appearances in minute detail. In A.D. 56, for example, Paul wrote (I Cor. 15) that over five hundred people had seen the risen Jesus and that most were still alive. The New Testament writers explicitly affirm that they are presenting historical facts, not religious fables; writes Peter (II Pet. 1:16): "We have not followed cunningly devised myths when we made known to you the power and coming of our Lord Jesus Christ, but were eyewitnesses of his majesty." And if deception and fabrication were here involved, why didn't the numerous religious enemies of the early Christians blast the whole business? F. F. Bruce of the University of Manchester has shrewdly observed in his book, *The New Testament Documents* (5th ed., 1960), that if the early proclaimers of Christ's deity had had any tendency to depart from the facts, the presence of hostile witnesses in the audience would have served as a most powerful corrective.

The central attestation for Jesus' deity is his resurrection, and to deny its facticity isn't easy. To oppose it on historical grounds is so difficult that, if one succeeds, the victory is entirely Pyrrhic: any argument that will impugn the New Testament documents will at the same time remove confidence from virtually all other ancient, and numerous modern, historical sources; the result, then, is a general (and entirely unacceptable) historiographical solipsism. To oppose the resurrection on the ground that miracles do not occur is, as we have noted earlier, both philosophically and scientifically irresponsible: philosophically, because no one below the status of a god could know the universe so well as to eliminate miracles *a priori*;

and scientifically, because in the age of Einsteinian physics (so different from the world of Newtonian absolutes in which Hume formulated his classic anti-miraculous argument) the universe has opened up to all possibilities, "any attempt to state a 'universal law of causation' must prove futile" (Max Black, *Models and Metaphors*), and only a careful consideration of the empirical testimony for a miraculous event can determine whether in fact it has or has not occurred.

Success in opposing the evidence for Christ's resurrection is so hard to come by that some objectors to Christian theism (e.g. humanist Corliss Lamont) are reduced to arguing that the event is trivial. "Even if Christ rose from the dead, would that prove his claims? And would it necessarily mean anything for us?" In a recent public discussion following a lecture I delivered at Roosevelt University, I was informed by a philosophy professor that Christ's conquest of death was no more significant qualitatively than a medical victory over pattern baldness. To which I offered the inevitable reply: "A knock comes at the door. It's the faculty secretary with the message that your wife and children have just been killed in a traffic accident. Your comment would of course be: 'Oh well, what's death? Just like pattern baldness.' " In point of fact, we all recognize the overarching significance of death, and a very large proportion of our individual and societal energies are expended in trying to postpone it (medicine), indirectly overcome it (familial, vocational, and artistic achievement), ignore it (escapist entertainment), or kid ourselves about it (funeral practices). Whether we look to anthropological evidence, psychoanalytic studies (E. Herzog's *Psyche and Death* [1967]), philosophical treatments (Jacques Choron's *Death and Western Thought* [1963]), or literary expressions of the human dilemma (Camus' *La Peste*), the reality of the problem of death for all mankind is displayed with appalling clarity. If Christ did in fact conquer this most basic of all human enemies and claimed on the basis of it to be God incarnate, able to give eternal life to those who believe in him, it would be sheer madness not to take with full seriousness the biblical affirmation that "God was in Christ, reconciling the world unto himself."

God and Human Experience

Contemplation of the centrality of death and man's quest for immortality vis-à-vis the God question leads us quite naturally to a striking recent book which treats the existence of

God from the standpoint of man's sociological experience. I refer to *A Rumor of Angels: Modern Society and the Rediscovery of the Supernatural* (1969) by Peter Berger, a professor of sociology at the New School for Social Research. Berger argues that such human experiences as hope in the face of death and the conviction that there must be a retribution transcending inadequate human justice for the commission of monstrous evil in this life are most sensibly explained in terms of God's existence. Other analogous empirical pointers to the existence of the transcendent are man's affirmation of societal ordering (cf. Voegelin's *Order and History*) and unshakeable conviction that such ordering extends to the universe as a whole (cf. the reassurance given by mothers to their frightened children since the world began, "Everything is all right"); man's humor, reflecting his basic awareness that a radical discrepancy exists between life as he lives it (in finitude) and life as it ought to be (in transcendent rightness); and man's play experiences—his brief transmigrations out of time into realms where finitude is momentarily transcended:

> Some little girls are playing hopscotch in the park. They are completely intent on their game, closed to the world outside it, happy in their concentration. Time has stood still for them—or, more accurately, it has been collapsed into the movements of the game. The outside world has, for the duration of the game, ceased to exist. And, by implication (since the little girls may not be very conscious of this), pain and death, which are the law of that world, have also ceased to exist. Even the adult observer of this scene, who is perhaps all too conscious of pain and death, is momentarily drawn into the beatific immunity.
>
> In the playing of adults, at least on certain occasions, the suspension of time and of the "serious" world in which people suffer and die becomes explicit. Just before the Soviet troops occupied Vienna in 1945, the Vienna Philharmonic gave one of its scheduled concerts. There was fighting in the immediate proximity of the city, and the concertgoers could hear the rumbling of the guns in the distance. . . . It was . . . an affirmation of the ultimate triumph of all human gestures of creative beauty over the gestures of destruction, and even over the ugliness of war and death. . . .
>
> All men have experienced the deathlessness of childhood and we may assume that, even if only once or twice, all men have experienced transcendent joy in adulthood. Under the aspect of inductive faith, religion

is the final vindication of childhood and of joy, and of all gestures that replicate these.

Professor Berger's arguments carry us from the lowlands of sociology to the heights of philosophical ontology, for they conjoin with a very important passage in Norman Malcolm's classic essay on Anselm's ontological proof of God's existence (*Philosophical Review*, January, 1960). Asks Malcolm: Why have human beings formed the concept of "a being a greater than which cannot be conceived"? This is his suggested answer, based, as are Berger's arguments, on "an understanding of the phenomena of human life":

> There is the phenomenon of feeling guilt for something that one has done or thought or felt or for a disposition that one has. One wants to be free of this guilt. But sometimes the guilt is felt to be so great that one is sure that nothing one could do oneself, nor any forgiveness by another human being, would remove it. One feels a guilt that is beyond all measure, a guilt "a greater than which cannot be conceived." Paradoxically, it would seem, one nevertheless has an intense desire to have this incomparable guilt removed. One requires a forgiveness that is beyond all measure, a forgiveness "a greater than which cannot be conceived." Out of such a storm in the soul, I am suggesting, there arises the conception of a forgiving mercy that is limitless, beyond all measure.

The experiences of death, judgment, order, humor, play, and guilt point beyond themelves—as does the very "I" who is conscious of them—and the direction of the signpost is to a Cross where the transcendent God offered "forgiving mercy that is limitless, beyond all measure." In the words of the Apostle (Rom. 4:25), he was "delivered for our offences and was raised again for our justification." Is man his own God? No, for man could never attain such limitless mercy. But God became man to offer that mercy, which no one could buy at any price, as a free gift. The evidence of God's existence and of his gift is more than compelling, but those who insist that they have no need of him or it will always find ways to discount the offer. As Pascal trenchantly observed (*Pensées*, No. 430): "Il y a assez de lumière pour ceux qui ne désirent que de voir, et assez d'obscurité pour ceux qui ont une disposition contraire." This statement is, of course, but a corollary of Jesus' words (Mt. 9:13; 18:3): "I am not come to call the righteous, but sinners to repentance. Except you be converted and become as little children, you shall not enter into the kingdom of heaven."

A Critique of Bertrand Russell's Religious Position

Arnold D. Weigel

Russell is without question "one of the most productive and most brilliant thinkers of our age, mathematical logician, philosopher, journalist and libertarian." [1] There is probably "no figure [who] has . . . dominated the intellectual world so long, so contentiously, and so courageously as Bertrand Russell." [2] In scholarly circles he has won great acclaim through his monumental publication (completed jointly with Alfred North Whitehead), *Principia Mathematica*, first published in 1910. This work conclusively demonstrated that mathematics was a special case of deductive logic, and, in the hands of Russell's pupil Ludwig Wittgenstein, it profoundly influenced the development of contemporary analytic philosophy. [3]

The "brilliant, crotchety, opinionated" [4] Russell has also acquired great notoriety as a "Ban the Bomb" man, especially through such statements as: "I deplore the Russian tests just as I deplored American tests." [5] This venture for peace has given Russell an international popularity, which has been enlarged further by his prolific writing. In 1950 he received the Nobel prize for Literature. [6]

In America, however, Russell is perhaps most remembered for an incident which occurred in 1940 on the campus of the

[1] Morton White, *The Age of Analysis: Twentieth Century Philosophers* (New York: Houghton Mifflin, 1955), p. 22.

[2] Edwin Diamond, "Russell—War, Peace, The Bomb." *Newsweek*, LX (August 20, 1962), 56.

[3] Charles Percy Sanger, "Bertrand Russell—Philosophy," *The Encyclopedia Britannica* (24 vols., 14th ed.; London: Encyclopedia Britannica Co., 1929), XIX, 678.

[4] David Susskind, "Fourscore and Ten," *Newsweek*, LIX (June 18, 1962), 36.

[5] Edwin Diamond, *loc. cit.*, p. 55.

[6] F. W. Dillistone, "Russell, Bertrand Arthur William," *Twentieth Century Encyclopedia of Religious Knowledge*, ed. L. A. Loetscher (Grand Rapids, Mich.: Baker, 1955), II, 987.

College of the City of New York. Russell, who had been hired to teach philosophy, was declared morally unfit by the College authorities because of certain of his educational views, of which the following is representative: "I am sure that university life would be better, both intellectually and morally . . . if most university students had temporary, childless marriages." [7] This incident proved to have damaging effects on the one hand, and limited positive results on the other, for Russell's acquired popularity. While practically every newspaper, periodical, and journal joined in the "chorus of defamation" [8] against Russell, there were some members of the university faculty who sympathized with Russell and who felt that he had been "viciously maligned . . . in large sections of the press." [9] As a kind of honorable recompense for this alleged disgraceful treatment of Russell, one of the sympathizers, Paul Edwards by name, edited most of Russell's religious writings in a book entitled, *Bertrand Russell, Why I am Not a Christian*. It is these religious writings, which display without a doubt a marked "sophisticated naiveté," [10] that will serve as the focal point of this paper.

Because of Russell's unequalled fame acquired through his prolific writings and his outspoken words, there is the danger that his religious writings, in which he sweepingly rejects all religions, including Christianity, will be read uncritically and accepted as the gospel truth. A detailed critique is badly needed in order to prevent students of Russell's religious—or better anti-religious—works from naively accepting him as an authority in the religious field. In spite of his competence in other areas, it is the present writer's opinion, after examining Russell's religious writings, that in the religious sphere he reveals an abysmal lack of competency and proficiency. The present critique,[11] though recognizing Russell's great talents and accomplishments, thus aims to subject his religious writings to

---

[7] Edwin Diamond, *loc. cit.*, p. 56.

[8] Bertrand Russell, *Why I am Not a Christian*, ed. Paul Edwards (London: George Allen and Unwin, 1957), p. 183. For a complete account of the "Bertrand Russell Case" at City College in 1940, see the chapter, "How Bertrand Russell was Prevented from Teaching at the College of the City of New York," pp. 181-220.

[9] *Ibid.*, pp. viii-ix.

[10] Reinhold Niebuhr, "Reason vs. Belief," *The New York Times Book Review*, Sept. 22, 1957, p. 6.

[11] No thorough scholarly critique of Russell's anti-Christian writings has yet been done. Two such attempts were made in 1928. One was written by H. G. Woods, *Why Mr. Bertrand Russell is not Christian* (London: Student Christian Movement, 1928), and the other by Kenneth

rigorous analysis, in the conviction that in religion as in detection, "the truth will out."

RUSSELL'S OBJECTIONS TO CHRISTIANITY

Russell's thesis against religion in general is two-pronged, as may be gathered from the Preface which he writes to Edwards' book: *Bertrand Russell, Why I am Not a Christian.*

There has been a rumour in recent years to the effect that I have become less opposed to religious orthodoxy than I formerly was. This rumour is totally without foundation. I think all the great religions of the world—Buddhism, Hinduism, Christianity, Islam, and Communism— *both untrue and harmful.* . . . I am as firmly convinced that religions do harm as I am that they are untrue.[12]

This argument Russell actually reduces to a single "cause-effect" argument, viz, "All the great religions are untrue; therefore, all the great religions are harmful."

If this is so, then we might justifiably ask Russell why it is that people believe in that which is both "untrue and harmful." To this Russell replies: "Most people believe in God be-

---

Ingram, *The Unreasonableness of Anti-Christianity* (London: Published on behalf of the Catholic Literature Association by the Society of S. S. Peter and Paul, 1928). I have examined both of these books and have found them inadequate. Mr. Woods' book cannot be regarded as definitive for three reasons: (1) It was published in 1928 and Russell has written much on the topic of "anti-Christianity" since then. (2) It does little more than quote Russell's arguments against Christianity; and when the author does occasionally try to refute Russell's position, he operates not from a Christian standpoint but rather from that of humanistic-liberal theology. Significantly, he dedicates his book to the influential but avowedly liberal New Testament scholar of the last generation, F. J. Foakes Jackson, and refers to him as "Magistro meo at amico." (3) A man who in 1928 writes, "Mr. Russell is not a Christian and so is not bound by it, but Christians ought to do something about it" (p. 54), and then in 1958 (in spite of Mr. Russell's consistently non-Christian position during the intervening years) writes an article entitled: "Bertrand Russell, Rationalist and Christian" (*Expository Times*, LXIX [February, 1958], pp. 132-34), certainly displays aberrational judgment. In this article, Mr. Woods himself admits: "I treated the tract [*Why I am Not a Christian*] rather cavalierly and lightheartedly." This is, as a matter of fact, an accurate depiction of his critique. The book by Mr. Ingram likewise does not render the present essay superfluous, for (1) it was also published in 1928 and is now out of print; and (2) Mr. Ingram presents more a philosophical than a theological critique of Russell's writings.

[12] Russell, *op. cit.*, p. xi (italics mine).

cause they have been taught from early infancy to do it, and that is the main reason." [13] There is also a second less powerful reason, which is "the wish for safety, a sort of feeling that there is a big brother who will look after you." [14]

These two bases for religious belief, in Russell's opinion, stem from a common denominator—fear.

> Religion is based primarily and mainly upon fear. It is partly the terror of the unknown, and partly . . . the wish to feel that you have a kind of elder brother who will stand by you in all your troubles and disputes. Fear is the basis of the whole thing—fear of the mysterious, fear of defeat, fear of death. Fear is the parent of cruelty, and therefore it is no wonder if cruelty and religion have gone hand in hand.[15]

Consequently, Russell's basic contention with all religions is that they are based on a belief that is generated through fear, which in essence is bad; therefore, all religions are "both untrue and harmful."

Russell has, moreover, certain specific objections to the Christian religion. These objections are of two kinds: "intellectual and moral." [16] In stating his case against Christianity, Russell says:

> Therefore, I take it that when I tell you why I am not a Christian I have to tell you two different things; first, why I do not believe in God and in immortality; and, secondly, why I do not think that Christ was the best and wisest of men.[17]

Comprehended in Russell's moral argument is his frequently stated claim that the organized Christian Church has been the powerful agent of moral retardation in the world.

Russell rejects a belief in God on the basis of an analytic evaluation of the Thomistic rational proofs for the existence of God. "You know, of course, that the Catholic Church has laid it down as a dogma that the existence of God can be proved

---

[13] *Ibid.*, p. 9.

[14] *Ibid.*

[15] *Ibid.*, p. 16. Russell maintained the same position in 1954 in "Can Religion Cure Our Troubles," when he remarked: "Mankind is in mortal peril, and fear now, as in the past, is inclining men to seek refuge in God" (*ibid.*, p. 169).

[16] *Ibid.*, p. 23.

[17] *Ibid.*, p. 2.

by the unaided reason." [18] Briefly, these arguments may be summarized as follows: (1) *The causal argument.* Every effect has a cause. The world also must have been produced as an effect from a cause, which necessarily must have been the first cause. This "prima causa" must be God. (2) *The nomological argument.* The universe operates according to fixed natural laws. Every law presupposes a lawgiver. Therefore, there is a superior lawgiver, namely God. (3) *The cosmological argument.* We observe design and order in the activity of the universe. This design and order must have some origin. Therefore, God exists as the source and guarantor of this design. (4) *The moral argument.* Within the universe we observe a gradation of goodness. Consequently, we must presuppose an "ens perfectissimum" to account for the gradation of goodness in the universe. This "ens perfectissimum" is none other than God. (5) *The teleological argument.* The universe has a purpose, which is imposed upon it by some higher being. Things are observed to move towards an end, but they do not have this end within themselves—entelechy—as an inner force. Rather this purposive end is ordered by the supreme mind, which must be God.

These traditional Aristotelian arguments do not convince Russell that God exists. Neither does he claim to be able to prove the non-existence of God. When asked of F. C. Copleston in a radio interview what his position was, he replied:

> My position is agnostic. . . . I'm not contending in a dogmatic way that there is not a God. What I'm contending is that we don't know that there is. [19]

Consequently, Russell claims that he cannot believe in God because His existence cannot be proven with absolute certainty.

> The Christian God may exist; so may the Gods of Olympus, or of ancient Egypt, or of Babylon. But no one of these hypotheses is more probable than any other: they lie outside the region of even probable knowledge, and

---

[18] *Ibid.*, p. 3. Cf. Thomas Aquinas, *Basic Writings.* ed. Anton C. Pegis (2 vols.; New York: Random House, 1945), I. 18-24; and also Richard McKeon, *Introduction to Aristotle* (New York: Modern Library, 1947), pp. 243-296.

[19] Russell, *op. cit.*, pp. 144, 157. "The Existence of God," a debate between Bertrand Russell and Father F. C. Copleston, S. J., was originally broadcast in 1948 on the Third Programme of the B.B.C.

therefore there is no reason to consider any of them. [20]

The question of immortality of the soul is another stumbling-block for Russell. He claims that it is a basic Christian tenet to believe in the immortality of the soul. Yet such a belief he cannot accept because "it is rational to suppose that mental life ceases when bodily life ceases." [21] Of course, here Russell is equating "soul" with "mental life." He goes on to argue against a belief in the immortality of the soul on the grounds that such a belief leads to hyper-individualistic Christian ethics, to a breakdown of the natural biological family tie, and to unwarranted superstition.[22] As for himself, Russell states: "I believe that when I die I shall rot, and nothing of my ego will survive." [23] The truth of a belief in the immortality of the soul cannot be proven rationally; therefore, Russell cannot subscribe to it.

From the standpoint of morality, Russell presents two specific arguments against the Founder of Christianity. He denies that Jesus was the wisest and best of persons because he miscalculated the time of his return and he spoke of the "damnation in hell."

> I now want to say a few words upon a topic which I often think is not quite sufficiently dealt with by Rationalists, and that is the question whether Christ was the best and the wisest of men. It is generally taken for granted that we should all agree that that was so. I do not myself.[24]

For example, Jesus says,

> "There are some standing here which shall not taste death till the Son of Man comes into His kingdom," and

---

[20] *Ibid.*, p. 40. in "What I Believe," published in 1925.

[21] *Ibid.*, p. 40. Cf. Bertrand Russell, *Religion and Science* (New York: Oxford University Press, 1961), pp. 110-143, especially the chapter on "Body and Soul."

[22] See Russell, *Why I am Not a Christian*, p. 26. Here Russell makes his position patent when he says: "I think it is clear that the net result of all the centuries of Christianity has been to make men more egotistic, more shut up in themselves, than nature made them." Within this context, he further remarks: "This individualism culminated in the doctrine of the immortality of the individual soul, which was to enjoy hereafter endless bliss or endless woe according to circumstances."

[23] *Ibid.*, p. 43.

[24] *Ibid.*, pp. 9-10.

there are a lot of places where it is quite clear that he
believed his second coming would happen during the
lifetime of many then living.[25]

Therefore, Russell argues that Jesus (whom Russell, as a matter
of fact, doubts ever existed), in advocating that his second coming would be imminent, belied his alleged supernatural wisdom.
Moreover, Jesus spoke of "damnation in hell" and of everlasting
punishment.

There is one very serious defect to my mind in Christ's
moral character, and that is that he believed in hell.
I do not myself feel that any person who is really profoundly humane can believe in everlasting punishment. . .
I must say that I think all this doctrine, that hell-fire
is a punishment for sin, is a doctrine of cruelty.[26]

After having rejected both God and Christ, Russell now feels
compelled to swing his axe upon the organized Christian Church.

You find as you look around the world that *every* single
bit of progress in humane feeling, *every* improvement in
the criminal law, *every* step towards the diminution of
war, *every* step towards better treatment of the coloured
races, or *every* mitigation of slavery, *every* moral
progress that there has been in the world, has been
consistently opposed by the organized Churches of the
world. I say quite deliberately that the Christian religion,
as organized in its Churches, has been and still is the
principal enemy of moral progress in the world.[27]

Why, in summary, is Russell not a Christian? First, he believes that all religion is based on fear and thus is bad. Secondly,
he cannot on rational grounds accept a belief in God or in the
immortality of the soul. Thirdly, he is unable to regard Jesus
as the wisest and best of men. Lastly, he sees the organized
Christian religion as a retardation to moral progress in the world.

AN ANALYSIS OF RUSSELL'S OBJECTIONS

Let us now take up in turn each of Russell's arguments
against Christianity. Our task will be to evaluate each point

---

[25] *Ibid.*, p. 11.
[26] *Ibid.*, pp. 12-13.
[27] *Ibid.*, p. 15 (italics mine).

objectively in an attempt to discover just how valid Russell's anti-Christian arguments are. We shall consider his above stated views against the background of the rationalistic humanism which he presents as an alternative to the Christian religion.

Russell's conviction that all religious belief is a result of fear is a claim that displays what Randall and Buchler have well termed the "sociological fallacy." [28] This fallacy occurs when people try to establish the origin of something, in this case religious belief, by considering it as it actually functions in society, and then on the basis of this sociological investigation use the common elements to evaluate that which has allegedly arisen out of the societal situation. But such an approach is using a descriptive statement as though it were a normative definition. With regard to the distinction between descriptive and normative definition, E. S. Brightman in *An Introduction to Philosophy* rightly points out:

> A descriptive definition would state what common elements actually have been present in those bodies of experience and belief that have called themselves religious. A normative definition would undertake to tell what religion ought to be. A descriptive definition would be based on a study of the facts of religious experience *without attempting to pass judgment on the value of the facts.*[29]

Consequently, Russell's assertion that "all religious beliefs are based upon fear" does not actually *evaluate* belief; it merely *describes a condition* present in *some* people at the time they come to belief in God. Moreover, fear is not even a necessary condition for belief, as other factors such as desire for happiness, freedom, security—only to mention a few—may be equally as determinative as fear. William James, in *The Varieties of Religious Experience*, points out that "if there were such a thing as inspiration from a higher realm, it might well be that the neurotic temperament would furnish the chief condition of the requisite receptivity." [30] Thus origin does not determine value, even if we were to admit (and there would be no way of proving it) that fear is the source of religious conviction. Analogously we may state that most people fear fire, but this

---

[28] J. H. Randall, Jr. and Justus Buchler, *Philosophy: An Introduction* (New York: Barnes and Noble, 1942), p. 271.

[29] Edgar S. Brightman, *An Introduction to Philosophy* (New York: Henry Holt and Company, 1925), pp. 317-18 (italics mine).

[30] William James, *The Varieties of Religious Experience* (London: Longmans, Green and Co., 1904), p. 25.

says nothing about nor does it determine the value of fire. H. G. Woods succinctly notes that psychological reasons "do not explain the origin of . . . beliefs. They help to show *why* men believe. They do not account for *what* they believe." [31]

In opposing the traditional rational proofs of God's existence, Russell is destroying a straw man, not the Christian position. The truth of the matter is that "the modern philosopher can never cogently prove the existence of a God beyond this world. . . . If human reason tries to transcend the limits of the perceptible world or of mathematics . . . its thinking is bound to get entangled in contradictions. . . . Rational conclusions are dependent on certain premises which reason itself is unable to prove." [32]

A rational proof of God's existence is, moreover, actually inconsistent with the Christian faith. Blaise Pascal, the French apologist of the seventeenth century, has well stated in his *Pensées* that "the heart has its reasons which reason does not know. . . . It is the heart which experiences God, and not the reason." [33] This is not to say that reason has no place within the Christian religion; it is, however, to assert that the Christian does not come to a knowledge of his personal God via rationalism. The God which reason can produce is not the personal God of the Holy Scriptures but rather an impersonal God which is Aristotelian and Thomistic. [34]

However, Russell makes the great mistake of assuming that because Aristotelian Christians have been unsuccessful in proving God's existence, no objective case for Christianity is possible. In other words, he narrows the meaning of the word "proof" to rational proof. In point of fact, the word "proof" may be employed in at least two other senses: (1) the historical, and (2) the subjective. These Russell dismisses summarily, though the key to the Christian apologetic lies there. Of the historical, he says:

> I may say that one is not concerned with the historical question. Historically, it is quite doubtful whether Christ ever existed at all, and if he did we do not know anything about him, so that I am not concerned with the historical

---

[31] Woods, *Why Mr. Bertrand Russell is Not a Christian*, p. 23.

[32] Erich Frank, *Philosophical Understanding and Religious Truth* (New York: Oxford University Press, 1952), pp. 38-40.

[33] Blaise Pascal, *Pensees and the Provincial Letters* (New York: Modern Library, 1941), p. 95.

[34] Aquinas, *op. cit.*, [in n. 18], pp. 18-24.

question, which is a very difficult one. I am concerned with Christ as he appears in the Gospels.[35]

Of the subjective, he smilingly states:

I can speak only from observation, not from personal experience.[36]

Therefore, Russell accepts the Christ-event neither as *Historie* ("a happening in the past as an . . . *occurrence*, which is *reported* and which is contained in *objective*, detached terms"),[37] nor as *Heilsgeschichte* ("a happening in the past as an *event*, which is *proclaimed* and which, instead of being the object of detached observation, comes to one as a personal *encounter*").[38] Yet if Russell wishes to say anything significant about the Jesus presented in the Gospels, he cannot afford to overlook both of these aspects of the New Testament proclamation.

The case for Christianity rests, as the Apostles well knew, on the "objective, historical truth of the resurrection of Jesus Christ from the dead." [39] "If Christ was not raised, then our gospel is null and void, and so is your faith" (I Cor. 15:14). The "Christ of the Gospels" can be no different from the Christ of history, for "on the basis of accepted principles of textual and historical analysis, the Gospel records are found to be trustworthy historical documents—primary source evidence for the life of Christ." [40] F. F. Bruce, Rylands Professor of Biblical Criticism and Exegesis in the University of Manchester, points

---

[35] Russell, *Why I am Not a Christian* [in n. 8], p. 11. It is precisely because of Russell's lack of concern for the historical question that he can equate Christianity with "Buddhism, Hinduism, Islam and Communism" (p. xi). For Christianity "is the only religion which purports to offer external, objective evidence of its validity. All other religions appeal to inner experience without any means of objective validation" (John Warwick Montgomery, *The Shape of the Past* ["History in Christian Perspective," Vol. 1; Ann Arbor, Mich.: Edwards Brothers, 1962], p. 140).

[36] Russell, *Why I am Not a Christian*, p. 179, in "Religion and Morals," published in 1952.

[37] Robert Scharlemann, "Shadow on The Tomb," *Dialog: A Journal of Theology*, I (Spring, 1962), 23.

[38] *Ibid.*, p. 23.

[39] Montgomery, *op. cit.*, p. 138.

[40] *Ibid.*, pp. 138-39. Cf. F. F. Bruce, *The New Testament Documents: Are They Reliable?* (5th rev. ed.; London: Inter-Varsity Fellowship, 1960). Also E. J. Barnes, "The Dependability and Value of the Extant Gospel Manuscripts," in Montgomery, *op. cit.*, pp. 341-57.

out that none of the Gospels could have been written later than A.D. 100; therefore, when the Gospels were written, "many were alive who could remember the things that Jesus said and did." [41]

In these sound historical records, "Jesus exercises divine prerogatives and claims to be God in human flesh; and he rests his claims on his forthcoming resurrection." [42] In Mark 2:1-12 Jesus forgives sins and in John 10:30 he plainly states: "I and the Father are one." [43] When Jesus in John 2:19 says: "Destroy this temple, and in three days I will raise it up," he is speaking of his body. "After his resurrection his disciples recalled what he had said, and they believed the Scripture and the words that Jesus had spoken." [44]

Russell discounts the supernatural aspects of Jesus' life as recorded in the New Testament on the ground that miracles are impossible. He says:

> In former days, miracles happened in answer to prayer: they still do in the Catholic Church, but Protestants have lost this power. However, it is possible to dispense with miracles, since Providence has decreed that the operation of natural laws shall produce the best possible results.[45]

But the fact of the resurrection cannot be eliminated on *a priori* philosophico-rational grounds; exceedingly strong historical evidence points in favor of its having happened, and one must start with this historical evidence, not with preconceptions. "Miracles are impossible only if one so defines them —but such definition rules out proper historical investigation." [46] C. S. Lewis has put it well when he says:

---

[41] Bruce, *op. cit.*, p. 13.

[42] Montgomery, *op. cit.*, p. 139.

[43] "In Mark 2:1-12 Jesus forgives sins; in such passages as Matt. 11:27; 16:13-17; John 10:30; 12:45; 14:6-10, Jesus states his divine relation to God the Father. It is also of great significance that the Gospel writers apply to Jesus the ascription *Kyrios* ("Lord") which in the Greek translation of the Old Testament (the Septuagint) had been used as an equivalent of *Adonai* and *Yahweh*, the Hebrew designations for God Himself" (*ibid.*, p. 168).

[44] *Ibid.*, p. 169.

[45] Russell, *Why I am Not a Christian* [in n.8], p. 42.

[46] Montgomery, *op. cit.*, p. 139. Cf. C. S. Lewis, *Miracles* (New York: Macmillian, 1947); and Edward John Carnell, *An Introduction to Christian Apologetics; a Philosophic Defense of the Trinitarian-Theistic Faith* (Grand Rapids, Mich.: Eerdmans, 1948), chaps. xiv-xv.

Remove miracles from the Bible and you relieve it of all its supporting pillars. The Bible teaches that ... [the Apostles] *saw* the resurrected Christ; they *ate* with Him; they put their *hands* upon Him and *felt* Him; they *talked* with Him and were *instructed* by Him. "Then he said to Thomas, 'Put your finger here, and see my hands; and put out your hand, and place it in my side; do not be faithless, but believing.' Thomas answered him, 'My Lord and my God' " (John 20:27-28). This is but a typical sample of the unequivocal manner in which all of the disciples personally and empirically came into contact with the resurrected Christ.[47]

This argument is no proof for the existence of God in the sense of a rationalistic demonstration; "it is an empirical argument based upon the application of historical method to an allegedly objective event." [48] Certainty can never be attained in historical research. Paul Tillich was quite right when he said with reference to the resurrection: "Historical research can never give more than a probable answer." [49] Yet probability must be utilized by anyone investigating a factual problem if his research is to have any meaning at all.

As we pointed out earlier, forced intellectualization of the Christian faith is completely inconsistent with the nature of Christianity. Therefore, the purpose of this argument is not to force anyone into the Christian religion. It is rather to afford a solid objective basis for testing the Christian faith experientially.

How is the test made? By confronting, with no more than "suspension of disbelief," the Christ of the Scriptures; for "faith comes by hearing and hearing by the word of God" and (said Christ) "whoever has the will to do the will of God shall know whether my teaching comes from God or is merely my own" [Rom. 10:17; John 7:17]. The Scriptural Gospel is ultimately self-attesting, but the honest inquirer needs objective ground for trying it, since there are a welter of conflicting religious options and one can become psychologically jaded through indiscriminate trials of religious belief. Only the Christian world-view offers objective ground for testing it experientially; there-

---

[47] Lewis, *op. cit.*, p. 246 (italics mine).
[48] Montgomery, *op. cit.*, p. 139.
[49] Paul Tillich, *Systematic Theology*, II (Chicago: University of Chicago Press, 1951), 155.

fore, Christ deserves to be given first opportunity to make his claims known to the human heart.[50]

It follows then, that when Russell asserts that there is no basis for belief in the existence of the Christian God, he takes a position that cannot be squared with historical evidence. There is a basis: Jesus Christ, who claimed to *be* God and attested his claim by his resurrection.

In criticizing the concept of the "immortality of the soul," Russell commits three serious blunders. First, he holds that those who believe in the immortality of the soul, when they speak of the "soul," refer to a particular aspect of man, namely, the "mental life." Secondly, he presupposes that the Greek idea of the immortality of the soul is a basic Christian tenet. Thirdly, in rejecting belief in the immortality of the soul, he attacks a straw man and not the true Christian position. In general, he mistakenly thinks that immortality is supposed to rest in man himself; and when he finds this notion incredible, he discards immortality entirely.

T. A. Kantonen, in reflecting upon the problem of the immortality of the soul, correctly observes:

> The state of man after death has been the object of endless speculation, philosophical and religious, scientific and popular. . . . Hence the question of life after death has been the question of demonstrating the immortality, the death-defying capacity, of the soul. The body is of little consequence. This way of thinking is entirely foreign to the Bible.[51]

In Scripture, man is a totality and when the words, "soul" (*nephesh* in Hebrew; *psyche* in Greek) and "body" (*soma* in Greek) are used by the Biblical writers, they refer to man *in toto.*[52]

For these various anthropological categories (soul, body, heart, mind, etc.) do not refer to different *parts* of a man

---

[50] Montgomery, *op. cit.*, p. 140.

[51] T. A. Kantonen, *The Christian Hope* (Philadelphia: Muhlenberg [now Fortress] Press, 1945), pp. 27-28. Cf. Matthew 10:28: "And fear not them which kill the body, but are not able to kill the soul: but rather fear him which is able to destroy both soul and body in hell."

[52] John A. T. Robinson, *The Body* ("Studies in Biblical Theology"; London: SCM, 1952), p. 14.

at all, but refer rather to a man as a totality, described from different points of view.[53]

Indeed we should not say that man *has* a soul, but that he *is* a soul; nor consequently that he *has* a body, but that he *is* a body.[54]

Now if the word "immortality" were used in this holistic sense, then the concept would be a satisfactory starting point for Christian doctrinal formulation. For "immortality" as signifying an afterlife is not offensive to the Christian faith, since all it implies is that there is an afterlife of some kind. The problem with "immortality," however, is that it denotes too little for it to be a basic Christian tenet *per se*. Belief in the afterlife must be given a specific content.

Calling belief "in an afterlife" a "basic Christian tenet" is like saying that belief in God is a basic Christian tenet. Christians do believe in God, but so do practically all other religious people in the world. Belief in God cannot be called a "basic Christian tenet" until some content is given to the word "God." ... The same is true of belief in an afterlife.[55]

And this content is neither "immortality of the soul" nor "resurrection of the body," both of which imply a dangerously dualistic anthropological viewpoint, but rather "resurrection of the dead" in a holistic sense as a future hope.[56]

How, then, does the Christian share in this glorious hope for the future? First of all, there is nothing in man himself that will prove that he is immortal.

God alone is immortal in the absolute sense of the word (Gr. *ousiodos*), but through his grace shown at creation he gives immortality to man as well. We are created for immortality: still, our immortality is not our own achievement but a divine gift.[57]

---

[53] James H. Burtness, "Immortality and/or Resurrection," *Dialog: A Journal of Theology*, I (Spring, 1962), 47.

[54] Claude Tresmontant, *A Study of Hebrew Thought*, trans. Michael Francis Gibson (New York: Deselee, 1960), p. 94.

[55] Burtness, *loc. cit.*, p. 46.

[56] The expression that we find employed throughout the New Testament is neither "immortality of the soul" nor "resurrection of the body" but "resurrection of the dead," and the latter has been guaranteed to all believers through Jesus Christ. Cf. Tresmontant, *op. cit.*, p. 105.

[57] Johann Gerhard, *Loci Theologici* (Frankfurt/Hamburg: Zacharia Hertel, 1957), VII, 85; II, 109, quoted by Edward Smits, "The Blessed Immortality," *Dialog: A Journal of Theology*, I (Spring 1962), p. 41.

Consequently, immortality always originates in God and from God. It is not something that springs forth from man. Yet, man has a foretaste of the glorious life with God through Jesus Christ who overcame the barrier of sin between God and man. It is Jesus Christ through the Holy Spirit who daily renews man unto newness of life. "For as the Father has life in himself, so has the Son by the Father's gift" (John 5:26). Therefore, "if Christ is life then the believers will never die (John 6:50; 11:26). . . . The new life is given to the believer already as a down payment here on earth." [58]

Therefore, immortality, properly understood from a Christian standpoint, does not primarily refer to a here-and-now state within man but rather points to a future hope; nevertheless, man presently decides for an eternal relationship either with God or with demonic powers.[59] Oscar Cullmann speaks quite correctly of the Christ-event as a "decisive victory already accomplished . . . but the not-yet-consummated victory at the end." [60] Thus, in a sense we may speak of a conditional immortality—conditional in the sense that the believer while alive already shares in this relational experience with his God, and conditional also in the sense that this immortality of relationship rests upon man's decision while alive here on earth. This immortality, however, is not consummated until the final judgment which is "incontestable and cannot be appealed." [61] It is at the final Judgment when all the dead will be raised

---

Contrast Burtness' statements: "The word immortality does occur occasionally in the New Testament, but it is used to designate a future hope rather than a present possession (Rom. 2:7; I Cor. 15:53 f.), or as an attribute which belongs to God alone (I Tim. 6:16), or as an attribute of the risen Christ (II Tim. 1:10). In no case does it refer to a present aspect of human existence, even when qualified as a gift of God to the believer" (loc. cit., p. 48). In this latter sentence, Mr. Burtness is depriving the believer of that gift of immortality which God has given man at Creation and restored again at the Resurrection: the gift of eternal fellowship with his God in spite of sin.

[58] Smits, loc. cit., p. 44.

[59] "There is no immortality of the soul but a resurrection of the whole person, body and soul, from death. The only immortality which the Bible recognizes is the immortality of a personal relationship with God in Christ" (T. A. Kantonen, op. cit., p. 33). Cf. "The decisive consideration is not, are you a man and therefore an immortal being, but, are you 'in Christ' and therefore assured that not even death can separate you from him?" (Kantonen, op. cit., p. 36).

[60] Oscar Cullmann, Immortality of the Soul or Resurrection of Dead (London: Epworth, 1958), p. 48.

[61] Carnell, op. cit. [in n. 46], p. 350.

(I Corinthians 15) and all the living changed through the gift of glorious resurrected bodies (in a holistic sense) such as that with which Christ made his post-resurrection appearances.[62] Since "this event is not an individualistic affair but a corporate one,"[63] it cannot lead to individualistic ethics.[64]

Properly regarded, immortality and the resurrection of the dead must be blended together.[65] Russell clearly does not understand the nature of "the Christian hope" and therefore his supposed refutations of it have little value. In point of fact, the Christian faith, with its stress on total restoration of the person at the Last Judgment, works well into the psychosomatic monism of contemporary medicine and psychology. Granted, the coming resurrection (like all future events) cannot be empirically demonstrated now, but the Christian has the explicit assurance of resurrection hope from the only One who ever conquered death—Jesus Christ.

Was Jesus the best and wisest of men? Russell would respond with an emphatic "No." Yet, with what justification does he make such a claim, if indeed he wishes to follow the historical portrait of Jesus in the primary records? As we noted earlier, Russell argues (1) that Christ miscalculated his second coming; and (2) that he believed in hell and spoke of "damnation in hell" for all those who refused to believe in him as the true revelation of God to man.

To the first of these claims, three rebuttals may be advanced. First, we have the position adopted by C. S. Lewis, that Jesus was in fact in error but simultaneously admitted his ignorance

---

[62] Matthew 28:16-20; Luke 24:50-53; John 20:26-29; 21:1-23. In these passages Christ appears in an identifiable body.

[63] Burtness, loc. cit., p. 48. "The resurrection of all the dead is the end result of Christ's triumph over death, the manifestation of its cosmic proportions" (Kantonen, op. cit., p. 93).

[64] "In the same way in which the Biblical writers think synthetically rather than analytically in relation to anthropology, they think synthetically rather than analytically about the people of God" (Burtness, loc. cit., p. 49). Cf. James Barr, The Semantics of Biblical Language (London: Oxford University Press, 1961), pp. 12 ff. Also see T. A. Kantonen, op. cit. Contra individualistic ethics, note how many times Christ admonished his followers against leading others into sin and away from himself (see, e.g., Mark 9:42-48; Matthew 5:29-30; Luke 17:1-2).

[65] A disregard or dismissal of the concept of immortality is generally based on what is regarded as a "rational" approach to the afterlife. Yet if I Corinthians 15 is relevant, then the resurrection of the dead and the immortality given to man by God must be blended.

in this matter of his Second Coming. Jesus said: "There are some standing here which shall not taste death till the Son of Man comes into His kingdom" (Matthew 16:28); but he shortly thereafter asserted, "But of that day or that hour no one knows, not even the angels in heaven, nor the Son, but only the Father" (Matthew 24:36; Mark 13:32).

> The one exhibition of error and the one confession of ignorance grow side by side. That they stood thus in the mouth of Jesus himself, and were not merely placed thus by the reporter, we surely need not doubt.[66]

Thus, Lewis argues, in this one matter of the time of the Last Judgment, the Son of Man knew little more about the end of the world than anyone else. His admission of ignorance preserves him from a charge of falsification.

> The facts, then, are these: that Jesus professed himself (in some sense) ignorant, and within a moment showed that he really was.... The answer of theologians is that the God-man was omniscient as God, and ignorant as man. This, no doubt, is true, though it cannot be imagined.[67]

This argument that Jesus accommodated himself to human error is, I believe, highly questionable, for then "one would have to give specific reasons why the accommodation did not extend to all of Jesus' words. Such accommodation would remove meaning from everything Jesus said, and would leave us with no criterion for the interpretation of his teachings." [68] But Lewis' approach at a minimum suggests that Russell's negativistic argument is not (as he would imply) the only possible interpretation.

How then is this apparent contradiction in the words of One who claimed to be God and rose from the dead best explained? If we consult primary documentary material, which indeed we must, then we find that the whole issue hinges upon two matters: (1) the "coming of the Son of Man" and (2) the word "generation" (for in Matthew 24:34 Jesus said: "This generation shall not pass till all these things be done").

Ingram is quite correct when he points out that in the passages of Scripture which Russell quotes there is in fact no explicit

---

[66] C. S. Lewis, *The World's Last Night* (New York: Harcourt, Brace and Company, 1959), p. 98.

[67] *Ibid.*, p. 99.

[68] Montgomery, *op. cit.* [in n. 35], p. 175.

reference made to the "Parousia" at the end of time.[69] In John 14:16 Jesus gives evidence of this fact when he says in connection with his forthcoming departure from the world: "And I will pray the Father, and he will give you *another* Counsellor to be with you forever." The word used here in Greek is not *heteron* (another of a different kind) but *allon* (another of the same kind).[70] Christ was not thinking of his final Coming, but rather he was looking forward to the time of Pentecost when the Spirit of God would come down "from heaven like the rush of a mighty wind" (Acts 2:2). Then there can be no contradiction in Jesus speaking of "some standing here which shall not taste death till the Son of Man comes into His kingdom," for the Spirit of Christ (the Holy Spirit) came at Pentecost—only a few days after Christ's ascension. Since the phrase "Second Coming" is nowhere found in Holy Scripture, we may justifiably regard Christ's final Coming as really a "Third Coming"! And of *that* Coming Christ said: "But of that day or that hour no one knows, not even the angels in heaven, nor the Son, but only the Father."

Arndt and Gingrich, the New Testament lexicographers, point out that the word *genea* (generation) may also be translated as "race" or "contemporaries." [71] Therefore, if we take Christ as speaking of his Coming at Pentecost, his contemporaries *were* still alive to witness the event. Or, on the other hand, if we take *genea* as signifying "race," then Christ's saying in Matthew 24:34 is not false even if it refers to the Last Judgment, for the Jewish race will remain to the end. On that day there will be "tribulation and distress for every human being who does evil, the *Jew* first and also the Greek, but glory and honor and peace for every one who does good, the *Jew* first and also the Greek" (Romans 2:9-10).

Therefore, it is evident that Russell "uses selected material from the Bible to illustrate an independently formulated phil-

---

[69] Ingram, *op. cit.* [in n. 11], p. 14.

[70] *Allos* means "different from the subject who is speaking and yet of the same kind," whereas *heteros* refers to "someone else" (William F. Arndt & F. Wilbur Gingrich, *A Greek-English Lexicon of New Testament and Other Early Christian Literature* [Chicago: University of Chicago Press, 1957], pp. 395, 896). In John 14:18 Christ further assures his disciples that he will not leave them: "I will not leave you desolate; I will come to you." Also cf. John 5:32: "there is another (*allos*) who bears witness to me."

[71] Arndt & Gingrich, *op. cit.*, p. 153.

osophy." [72] He does not inductively attempt to find what the Bible says before criticizing it; rather, his negative evaluation of the Bible is based upon his predetermined categories. But in the, matter of supposed contradictions, even Aristotle recognized (and all proper literary criticism has followed him here) that "one should first test as one does an opponent's confutation in a dialectical argument, so as to see whether he means the same thing, in the same relation and in the same sense, before admitting he has contradicted." [73] In other words, where there is evidence pointing in both directions, let us give the benefit of the doubt to the subject under analysis. And certainly in this case of Christ's "miscalculation" of his return, the evidence is strongly in support of a non-contradictory interpretation.

Russell, in keeping with his humanistic ideal, cannot conceive of eternal punishment befalling man because in his way of thinking man is essentially good. Consequently, he rejects Christ for believing in hell and for speaking of "damnation in hell." Russell, however, does not consider Ingram's important distinction between the ultimate reality of hell and the description of such a place in human terms. "The only issue . . . is whether the state of hell is inevitable or incredible." [74] From a Christian standpoint, hell is inevitable for the unbeliever but it is not incredible for the believer. For at the close of the age, "the Son of Man will send his angels, and they will gather out of his kingdom all causes of sin and all evildoers, and throw them into the furnace of fire" (Matthew 13:41-42). Moreover, Christ says: "Fear him who, after he has killed, has power to cast into *hell*" (Luke 12:5).

Also Peter, one of the Twelve, gives evidence that Jesus himself descended into hell:[75] "He went and preached to the spirits in prison" (I Peter 3:19). There are, to be sure, several difficulties in this passage. In what sense are the words

---

[72] Montgomery, *op. cit.*, p. 136.

[73] Aristotle, *De Arte Poetica*, 1460^b-1461^b.

[74] Ingram, *op. cit.* [in N. 11], p. 47.

[75] Some doubt that I Peter was written by Peter the Apostle. Yet there is much substantiating evidence in favor of his authorship. (1) I Peter 1:12 makes specific reference to the "Holy Spirit sent from heaven," and we know from Acts 2 that the Apostle Peter was present at Pentecost (indeed, he delivered his great sermon there). (2) The reference in 1:8 to "love" is often regarded as Peter's remembrance of Jesus' challenge to him, "Lovest thou me more than these?"

"descend" and "ascend" used in Scripture? These terms are used in reference to the relational aspect in which or without which man lives. If he lives in the fellowship and spirit of God, then relationally he has ascended unto God. But the reverse is true without this relation, and this is equal to a state of hell.[76] The words which Peter uses are "in which spirit"; this would signify that Christ already possessed his glorious spiritual body when he preached even (Gk. *kai*) to "the spirits in prison," i.e., to the spirits which had hitherto rebelled against God and refused to listen to His saving Word. J. H. A. Hart, in *The Expositor's Greek Testament*, says that the significance of this passage lies in the word "even": Christ preached "*even* to the typical rebels who had sinned past forgiveness according to pre-Christian notions." [77] In other words, it is only Christ who can speak of "damnation in hell," for he alone knows what it is like to be there and he alone has returned to tell us, to forewarn us to seek repentance and forgiveness.

Russell says he wishes to take Jesus as he appears in the primary records; what alternative does he have then but to accept Jesus as he truly appears in the Gospels? For "sheer and ultimate rejection of truth, when there is free and unfettered opportunity to accept truth, is hell." [78] Not without reason, as Philip Schaff has pointed out in *The Creeds of Christendom*, has the doctrine of hell been accepted for centuries by the Christian Church.[79]

Moreover, to judge God by an external ethical standard is self-contradictory. What is Russell's standard of perfection and of wisdom by which he evaluates Christ? Whatever standard Russell sets up, he cannot justify it nor can he measure

---

(Merrill C. Tenney, *The New Testament: An Historical and Analytic Survey* [Grand Rapids, Mich.: Eerdmans, 1953], p. 365). (3) Eusebius reports that the epistle was universally accepted as canonical. It is attested to by many of the Church Fathers, who quote from it; e.g., Clement, Bishop of Rome (A.D. 96), Ignatius (A.D. 115), and Polycarp (A.D. 120). Cf. Bruce, *op. cit.* [in n. 40], p. 18.

[76] J. J. Von Allmen (ed.), *A Companion to the Bible* (New York: Oxford University Press, 1958), p. 86.

[77] J. H. A. Hart, "The First Epistle of Peter," *The Expositor's Greek Testament*, ed. W. Robertson Nicoll (5 vols.; New York: Hodder and Stoughton, 1897), V, 68.

[78] Ingram, *op. cit.* [in n. 11], p. 17.

[79] Philip Schaff, *The Creeds of Christendom* (3 vols.; New York: Harper and Brothers, 1877), II, 478, discussing the descent into hell. The history of this doctrine in the Church creeds will be found *passim*.

Christ in accord with it because Christ is infinitely beyond all that the human mind may imagine.

It is ironic that Russell, in making his erratic frontal attack upon the organized Christian Church, should label it the "Emotional Factor." [80] For it is rather obvious that Russell tries to account for the evil in the world by using the organized Christian Church as a scapegoat, and in so doing he forgets about his original intention and substitutes sheer emotion for reasoned argument.

First, he attacks Christianity by what he sees in practice within the organized Christian Church. And quite often these are two entirely different things.

> Even if Mr. Russell's denunciation were wholly accurate, it would be no proof of the falsity of Christianity. It would prove only that Christians had continuously and without exception prostituted the principles of the religion they professed. It would be as illogical not to believe in Christianity because of the crimes committed by Christians, as not to believe in Socialism because there have been Socialists who propagate their faith by persecution and murder.[81]

But the truth is that Russell does not present an accurate picture when he claims that Christianity is the greatest enemy of moral progress in the world. Kenneth Scott Latourette, generally regarded as the greatest living Church historian, says:

> If mankind is viewed as a whole, never has Christ been as great a force in the human scene and never has Protestantism played as large a part in the human drama.[82]

Furthermore, says Latourette:

---

[80] Bertrand Russell, *The Basic Writings of Bertrand Russell, 1903-1959* (London: George Allen and Unwin, 1961), pp. 592-95. It is here that the rationalist Russell "becomes . . . erratic and disposes of all professional 'rationalism' " (Ingram, *op. cit.*, p. 19.).

[81] *Ibid.*, p. 20.

[82] Kenneth Scott Latourette, "Protestantism's Amazing Vitality," *Christianity Today*, VI (March 2, 1962), 3. Mr. Latourette is Sterling Professor Emeritus of Missions and Oriental History at Yale University. He is also author of the great classic, *A History of the Expansion of Christianity* (7 vols.; New York: Harper and Brothers, 1937-1945). This series, especially Vol. VII (titled, *Advance Through Storm*), should be consulted for compelling evidence of Christianity's remarkable growth and positive cultural contributions.

Never has the Christian faith been as widely accepted at it is today. Indeed no other religion has ever had as extensive a geographic spread as has Christianity in the twentieth century. . . . A century and a half ago Protestantism was confined almost entirely to Northwestern Europe. Today it is the prevailing form of the faith in the United States, Canada, Australia, New Zealand, and South Africa, and it is increasing by leaps and bounds in Latin America, the Philippines, Africa south of the Sahara, India and Indonesia.[83]

If Russell's moral condemnation of the Church were true, then we should rightly conclude that all these nations are morally degenerate. Though this is of course *possible*, common sense makes us doubt that such is the case. It is probably much truer to say that moral uplift, rather than moral degradation, goes hand in hand with the spread of Christianity.

"The Christian understanding of history does not necessarily deny progress."[84] As a matter of fact, historical evidence points in the opposite direction, as Latourette vividly expresses.

Moved by their faith, Christians devised new methods and programmes for the education of the masses. They brought into being hundreds of colleges and universities. . . . Christians also were the initiators and supporters of measures and movements to reduce the sufferings attendant on wars and to eliminate war by devising and operating institutions and measures for the peaceful adjustment of friction between nations and for international co-operation for the welfare of mankind. By its symbol and name the Red Cross bore witness of its Christian origin. It came into being through the efforts of a Protestant layman of Geneva, Henri Duvant.[85]

Moreover, when Russell engages in his negativistic arguments against the organized Christian Church, what is his standard of moral decay? He cannot justify it here any more than he can when he judges Christ.

Therefore, Russell's arguments against the institutionalized Christian Church cannot be proven empirically nor established historically—the former because empirically there is no way of proving that any progress or hindrance thereof is due solely

---

[83] Latourette, *Christianity Today*, VI (March 2, 1962), 4.

[84] *American Historical Review*, LIV (January, 1949), 272 ff.

[85] Kenneth Scott Latourette, *A History of Christianity* (New York: Harper and Brothers, 1953), pp. 1336-1337.

to one factor such as the Christian Church, and the latter because there is much positive evidence in behalf of Christianity's claims to be in fact "the light of the world."

RUSSELL'S RATIONALISM VIS-A-VIS THE CHRISTIAN WORLD-VIEW

If Russell rejects Christianity, what is his alternative? It is a rationalistic humanism based on the good life inherent within man, inspired by love and guided by scientific knowledge. The pursuit of this good life will, he claims, free the world of all its evils.[86] His motto is basically this: "Conquer the world by intelligence, and not merely by being slavishly subdued by the terror that comes from it." [87]

The knowledge in which Russell trusts is solely "scientific"; it is knowledge acquired by means of the scientific method. Nevertheless, he "does not always appear to grasp the essential fact that we have assumed the existence of a world and man, and then occupied ourselves with solving the problem of the relation between them, which is called knowledge." [88] In other words, implicit in his philosophy there is a faith—yet a faith which he nonetheless refuses to admit. He seems to believe that belief can only properly be generated by the scientific method!

To be sure, the scientific method is a most valuable way of obtaining information, but it is not the only way. It is not at this point, however, that Russell makes his greatest mistake. His great blunder occurs when he places his faith in science as a religion, for a "scientific faith" cannot be justified by the scientific method. Science starts with *a priori* presuppositions, such as "the world is of real space, of real time, and of real matter"—and such presuppositions cannot be verified by means of the scientific method.[89] Furthermore, "science is analytic; its laws are statements about the relations of the

---

[86] Russell, *The Basic Writings of Bertrand Russell*, 1903-1959, pp. 376-390.

[87] Russell, *Why I am Not a Christian* [in n. 8], p. 16. According to Russell, in order for us to overcome the evil in the world, we must resort to intelligence; it is only intelligence that can give us an honest and frank picture of the universe.

[88] T. C. Hammond, *Reasoning Faith: An Introduction to Christian Apologetics* (London: Inter-Varsity Fellowship, 1943), p. 94.

[89] Montgomery, *op. cit.* [in n. 35], p. 266-67.

parts which analysis has revealed." [90] Science is a description of the laws of phenomena and of situations as they actually exist, not as they ought to be or become. This fact becomes vividly clear in the *Kinsey Reports* on the sexual habits of Americans,[91] which (popular opinion notwithstanding!) are only descriptive in nature and *not* normative. Even though many worship science as a "sacred cow," science can never properly assume the status of a religion because it has no intrinsically justifiable axiology. Anthony Standen, himself a scientist, in his book *Science is a Sacred Cow* well expresses science's limitations in the field of value; e.g., "If a scientist became really objective about freedom, he would not even be able to say what it is." [92] In light of such considerations, science must be rejected as a legitimate religion.

Furthermore, rationalists will usually argue that God could not be infinitely good or wise because, first of all, if He were good, He would not have created an evil world; and, secondly, if He were wise, He would not set man in control of the world because He would have seen that man would make a hell of it. Yet, strangely enough, rationalists will "claim that men are naturally good at heart and will do the right thing if only they are educated properly." [93]

Here can be seen the inconsistency of rationalism. Rationalists, when arguing their own position, paint the world in far rosier colors than the facts warrant; but they paint it black when arguing against God's existence! They regard the Biblical doctrine of original sin as preposterous.

> The rationalist who disbelieves in original sin is much more satisfied with man than the Christian. He violently opposes the idea that we are "miserable sinners." He bases his code of morality on man's essential goodness. Yet—when it suits him to do so—he turns completely round and urges that a good God could never have created such a revolting biped as man.[94]

---

[90] Brightman, *op. cit.* [in n. 29], p. 10.

[91] Donald Porter Geddes (ed.), *An Analysis of the Kinsey Reports on Sexual Behaviour in the Human Male and Female* (New York: Mentor Books, 1954).

[92] Anthony Standen, *Science is a Sacred Cow* (New York: Dutton, 1958), p. 219.

[93] R. E. D. Clark, *Scientific Rationalism and Christian Faith; with particular reference to the writings of Prof. J. B. S. Haldane and Dr. J. S. Huxley* (London: Inter-Varsity Fellowship, 1945), p. 81.

[94] *Ibid.*, p. 82. Cf. Arnold S. Nash, *Protestant Thought in the Twentieth Century: Whence & Whither?* (New York: Macmillan, 1951), p. 113.

The fundamental idea at the root of the rationalistic ethic is that externals only are at fault. This Russell illustrates when he argues that the institutionalized Christian Church is the cause of much evil in the world. Christians, on the other hand, maintain that the problem lies basically within man himself —as sinner—and that the nature of man leads him to follow wrong motivations and pursue immoral ends. Neither education nor the creation of better living conditions is going to make the world a utopia. Rationalists such as Russell offer numerous remedies as panaceas to overcome chaotic world conditions. "Many of them are excellent indeed, but not one of them goes to the heart of the problem—*not one of them will make bad men good.*" [95] For it would seem that "every social development of natural good in history breeds a corresponding evil which neutralizes it." [96]

Russell argues, as does Marx, that religion is the opium of the masses. If so, then it seems to be a far less intoxicating opiate than rationalism, which is virtually blind to the reality of things.

> The Christian is at least sufficiently wide awake to diagnose what is wrong. He has no need to blind himself to the truth about man and about man's history. He believes that there is something fundamentally wrong about human beings.[97]

Rationalists are often very anxious to do something about world conditions, but they are never ready to go to the root of the problem: man in his sinful condition. "The fact is that the man who will not or cannot mend himself likes to project his sins on other people." [98] Yet the truth of the matter is that

> the best contribution that men can make to the welfare of the world in which they live is, surely, to return to the only known ethical system which undermines the sin of self-righteousness—to repent of sin and accept the good news that God showed His love to man in the Cross of Christ. But to do this is not primarily to moralize on

---

[95] Clark, *op. cit.*, p. 87. Cf. Carl F. H. Henry, *Contemporary Evangelical Thought* (New York: Harper and Brothers, 1957), pp. 140-143. Ethics cannot be decided upon until the problem of God is settled. Also cf. Edward John Carnell, *A Philosophy of the Christian Religion* (Grand Rapids, Mich.: Eerdmans, 1952).

[96] Clark, *op. cit.*, p. 87.

[97] *Ibid.*, p. 88.

[98] *Ibid.*, p. 89.

how other people should behave: it must start with you and me.[99]

This, then, is the solidarity of the Christian faith which Russell so superficially maligns: it alone is rooted in a realistic view of man, and it alone offers a historically grounded and experientially satisfying answer to the human predicament.[100]

In order to understand the real Russell, we should not overlook his childhood religious experiences—which consisted mainly of Unitarian indoctrination by his Victorian grandmother.[101] During this period Russell, in a quiet, reflective manner, came to rebel against his grandmother's moralistic asceticism. This does not, of course, justify Russell's present-day anti-Christian position nor does it account for his adherence to humanistic and scientific rationalism. But herein probably lies the formative source of Russell's religious orientation. For the Unitarians are non-conformists who, as Williston Walker points out, set themselves against all "creeds of human composition." [102] Thus their rejection of Jesus Christ as divine; and thus also their substitution of faith in man's rationality for faith in God's grace.[103]

Yet it is indeed a pity that a man of Russell's stature, with such keen perceptivity and superior intelligence in mathematical logic, should permit his mind to be so warped in religious matters as to blind him to reality. Clearly, he wishes to encounter the world as it really is:

> We want to stand upon our own feet and look fair and square at the world—its good facts, its bad facts, its beauties, and it ugliness; see the world as it is, and be not afraid of it.[104]

---

[99] *Ibid.*, p. 96.

[100] See n. 50 above.

[101] I am not using Russell's childhood religious experiences to explain away his adult position; I am merely citing them to point up his reaction against moralistic legalism. Granting the legitimacy of Russell's rebellion against a perversion of Christianity is not, however, to approve his wholesale rejection of the theological baby along with the legalistic bath water! Russell's article, "My Religious Reminiscences," is found in *The Basic Writings of Bertrand Russell*, 1903-1959 [in n. 80], pp. 31-36.

[102] Williston Walker, *A History of the Christian Church* (rev. ed.; New York: Charles Scribner's Sons, 1959), p. 443.

[103] Leo Rosten (ed.), *A Guide to the Religions of America* (New York: Simon and Schuster, 1955), p. 143.

[104] Russell, *Why I am Not a Christian* [in n. 8], p. 16.

The answer to this problem of seeing the world and humanity "fair and square" lies not in rationalism, as we have been at pains to point out, but in the Cross of Jesus Christ, in the Person of the One who recognized the true condition of man as a "miserable sinner," and who on the Cross at Calvary overcame the world, sin, and death, and concretized man's hope in eternal life—not through any abstract rational arguments but by sacrificing his very life on the Cross and by rising again for man's justification. This is humanity's only true faith and hope; to accept it is indeed, to use the Pauline phrase, "a reasonable service," but to reject it as a result of carelessly warping its content and message, is assuredly tragic blindness.

Religion Without Revelation?

A Critique of Julian Huxley's Evolutionary Humanism

Esther Lo

The title of this essay probably seems familiar. Except for one telling difference, it is precisely the title of one of Julian Huxley's books. My addition of the final question mark is meant to indicate that I have doubts—grave doubts—about his brand of religion. In the following pages I shall present a resumé of Huxley's philosophical position and credit his work for its positive values. Then I shall attempt to spell out the reasons for my skepticism, for the fact that I find his religion, literally, incredible.

HUXLEY'S BRAND OF RELIGION: EVOLUTIONARY HUMANISM [1]

Evolution As an All-embracing Process

Huxley uses the term "evolution" in a comprehensive sense. "All reality, in fact," he asserts, "is evolution, in the perfectly proper sense that it is a one-way process in time; unitary; continuous; irreversible; self-transforming; and generating variety and novelty during its transformation." [2] This overall process is comprised of three main phases: the inorganic or cosmological; the organic or biological; and the human or psycho-social. In the first phase, on a slow time-scale, loose clouds of hydrogen atoms gradually coalesced into stars and planets. "Nowhere in all its vast extent," says Huxley, does the universe show "any trace of purpose, or even of prospective significance. It is impelled from behind by blind physical forces, . . . in which the only overall tendency we have so far been able to detect is that

---

[1] Julian Huxley has written several works to explain his religious system. The more significant ones, which will be dealt with in this essay, are *Evolution in Action* (New York: Harper & Row, 1953), *Religion Without Revelation* (New York: The New American Library, 1958), and *The Humanist Frame* (New York: Harper & Row, 1961).

[2] *Evolution in Action*, p. 2.

summarized in the Second Law of Thermodynamics—the tendency to run down." [3] In the biological phase of evolution, there is the origin and evolution of living species by mutation and natural selection, culminating in the appearance of man and the emergence of mind. Organisms are built as if purposefully designed but the purpose is only apparent. Only natural selection operates in relation to the future—the future survival of the individual and the species. [4] The psycho-social phase of evolution is restricted to man. It operates by the mechanism of cultural tradition, which involves the cumulative self-reproduction and self-variation of mental activities and their products. Instead of a succession of successful bodily organizations, there is now a succession of successful idea-systems. [5]

The Place and Function of Religion

Huxley's philosophy differs from Marxist materialism, which considers mental or psychological activities in general to be essentially epiphenomena, the result of "objective" material events. Huxley asserts the *real* importance of mental or spiritual factors in the cosmos. Spiritual forces, however, are only a particular product of mental activity and so are as much a part of nature as material forces. The capacity for experiencing the sacred is a fundamental capacity of man on account of the construction of the normal human mind. Religious experiences are the outcome of human minds in the strange commerce with the outer reality and in the still stranger and often unconscious internal struggle between their compartments. But they are nonetheless real. [6] Huxley's outlook is thus not merely naturalistic as opposed to supernatural, but monistic as opposed to dualistic.

Religion has a function similar to that of art. For Huxley, the function of religion is to enable man to cope with the problems of meaning and destiny. Religion always involves the emotion of sacred mystery experienced by men confronted with the numinous, the sense of right and wrong and feelings of guilt, shame or sin. Religion is always concerned in one way or another with the relation between the individual and the community, and with the possibility of man's escaping from the imprisoning

---

[3] *Ibid.*, p. 5.
[4] *Ibid.*, p. 7.
[5] *The Humanist Frame*, p. 16.
[6] *Religion Without Revelation*, pp. 186-187.

immediacies of space, time and selfhood by relating himself to some broader frame of reference, or in some self-transcending experience of union or communion with a larger reality.[7]

Evaluation of Present Religions

Huxley thinks that the raw materials of which religions are formed consist of actual religious experiences, numinous, holy, mystical or transcendent. And the particular form each takes is primarily the result of its experientially-dependent framework of belief, with its attending ethical codes and ceremonious rituals. Three general types are distinguishable: religions erected on the magic hypothesis, on the spirit hypothesis, and on the daimonic or god hypothesis. On the magic hypothesis, man projects his experience of sacred power onto external objects or events. On the spirit hypothesis, sacred power is supposed to reside in the spirits of the dead. And on the god hypothesis, man projects the sacred power behind phenomena and clothes it in the garb of personality.[8]

Analogous to the development of a human individual from the infantile phase of emotion to the child's phase of awareness of personality and then to the rational adult stage, so religions, based on man's primal experience within himself, evolve from the magical to the daimonic and then to the mythological mode of thinking.[9] Though apparently successive in origin, these three modes of thought remain entangled throughout much of history. Furthermore, in the evolution of religions, there is a tendency to move from variety to unity, from the natural to the supernatural, from the material to the spiritual and the more highly ethical.

Now Huxley says that the magic hypothesis evidently can no longer be seriously entertained. On the other hand, the spirit and god hypotheses involve a basic dualism between the natural and the supernatural, whereas the discoveries of physics, general biology and psychology now necessitate a naturalistic hypothesis, in which there is no room for the supernatural.[10] Any belief in the supernatural must introduce an irreparable split into the universe that prevents man from grasping its real unity. Moreover, belief in supernatural beings and exclusive claims to revelation and salvation produce harmful psycholog-

---

[7] *The Humanist Frame*, p. 41.

[8] *Religion Without Revelation*, p. 183.

[9] *Ibid.*, pp. 53-56.

[10] *Ibid.*, p. 187.

ical effects and erect formidable barriers against progress, against the possibility of moral, rational, or religious improvement. Thus theistic religions have reached the limits of their usefulness as an interpretation of the universe and of human destiny. They are no longer adequate to deal with the phenomena, as disclosed by the advance of scientific knowledge.

Evolutionary Humanism As the New Religion

Having denied the usefulness of present religions, Huxley essays to affirm something new. He sees the function of religion in the modern technological world to be that of providing an ideal or goal for future development and for practical action. Therefore, according to Huxley, the world needs a single new religious system to replace the multiplicity of conflicting and incompatible religious systems that are now competing for the mind of man.[11] This religious system should believe in knowledge. Specifically, it should use our increased knowledge of the mind to define man's sense of right and wrong more clearly so as to provide better moral guidelines for human existence, and to focus the feeling of sacredness on worthier objects than gods, spirits, and magical objects. Science will be the ally of the new religion instead of its rival for it can provide a "scientific" theology, a scientifically-ordered framework of belief, that will enable the new religion to be a self-correcting system, open to transformation and progress. Also this new religion should accept the basic and universal mystery—the mystery of existence in general and that of the mind in particular.[12] It must have a background of reverence and awe in its belief-system and must seek to keep alive man's sense of challenge and wonder in all his dealings with the existing world.

For Huxley, the new religion is found precisely in the kind of humanism he offers. Evolution is its center and circumference. Evolutionary biology reveals man's place in nature as the highest form of life produced by the evolutionary process on this planet, the latest dominant type and the only organism capable of further major advance and progress.

Whether he knows it or not, whether he wishes it or not, he is now the main agency for the future evolution of the earth and its inhabitants. In other words, his destiny is to realize new possibilities for the whole terres-

---

[11] *The Humanist Frame*, p. 41.
[12] *Ibid.*, p. 42.

trial sector of the cosmic process, to be the instrument for further evolutionary progress on this planet.[13]

Man's most sacred duty and, at the same time, his most glorious opportunity, is to promote the maximum fulfillment of the evolutionary processes on this earth. This includes the fullest development of his own inherent possibilities, both as an individual and as a race. Man should aim at a continued increase of those qualities which have made for progress in the biological past—his capacities for reason, imagination, and conceptual thought which overflow into love of beauty, desire for truth, urge to creation and fuller expression, and the desire to participate in some larger enterprise. It is true that human nature always contains the possibilities of evil, waste, and frustration, but it also contains the possibilities of good, of achievement, and of fruition. The religion of evolutionary Humanism stipulates that we must think in these fulfilling terms.

Huxley's evolutionary humanism, by pointing out the right destiny of man, is a "religion without revelation." It can unify man because evolution is a cosmic process and to further evolutionary progress is the duty of the whole human race. Derived from science, this religion will progress with science. Through it, man's feelings of mystery, sacredness, wonder and awe are preserved as the indispensable modes of human fulfillment. Huxley regards evolutionary humanism to be the gospel for modern man.

HUXLEY'S CREDITABLE INSIGHTS

Huxley shows considerable acumen when he stresses that religion is of great importance to man in dealing with the question of destiny. Man certainly needs some supporting framework for his present existence and a purpose or goal toward which to strive. He rightly recognizes that the capacity for the feeling of sacredness or wonder is innate in man and not to be neglected. He has correctly observed that religious feelings are often of great value to those who experience them.

Huxley also shows insight when he says that there is an urgent need for resolving the conflicts between men. Prejudices accompanying differences in religious beliefs certainly disturb the human peace, often with disastrous results. The world certainly needs a religious system which stresses the brotherhood of all men.

---

[13] *Religion Without Revelation*, p. 193.

Some theologians today have a split mentality in accepting the theories of science on the one hand and on the other gratuitously removing religion to a realm untestable by history or science. These Christians certainly create a dreadful split in the universe and make the Christian faith to seem irrational. In contrast, Huxley's proper stress on religion being consonant with the facts of the real world grounds religious claims on a surer footing.

Huxley's stress on the importance of individual fulfillment is of great value. The dignity of the individual human being certainly needs to be safeguarded in view of certain ideologies which, by placing priority on the class, the nation, or the human race, relegate the individual to a means to an end.

Undoubtedly Huxley must also be applauded for his attempt to unify the various disciplines. With staggering comprehensiveness, his system incorporates theories of science, comparative religion and psychology. It is certainly a heroic endeavor when a biologist ventures from his field of specialization to answer questions of human destiny by synthesizing a vast amount of knowledge. Huxley's great sincerity and concern for truth in this task make it all the more noteworthy.

A SKEPTIC'S RESPONSE

Evolution As a Fact

It is doubtful whether the word "evolution," which originated in biological science and has a fairly well-defined meaning, should be made to cover all the vast changes occurring in the inorganic universe, where the nature and scope of the processes are often so different from those of biology. As G. G. Simpson points out, even more dubious is the usage of this same term to describe the ideological and cultural changes that occur in the human society where mental and social, not biological, forces come into play. At first sight it would appear innocuous enough to use a single term in various ways in the same context. However, by some kind of word-magic, "evolution" for Huxley becomes an all-embracing natural evolutionary process, continuous, unified, and exhibiting the same basic principles throughout. Moreover, while noting that evolution is "blind and purposeless," Huxley writes that there is "a trend toward sentience, mind and richness of being." Despite his recognition that man's advance will be psycho-social rather than biological, Huxley discusses analogies between biological evolution and cultural evolution. At last, in acquiring philosophical and mythological overtones,[14] evolution actually achieves the status of a propelling force, the guarding of which becomes for Huxley a "sacred duty."

Most scientists do assert that organic evolution has occurred in the past. Yet certain significant voices have been raised recently among biologists that would qualify this. Professor Kerkut of the Department of Physiology and Biochemistry at the University of Southampton is one of them.

> There is a theory which states that many living animals can be observed over the course of time to undergo changes so that new species are formed. This can be called the "Special Theory of Evolution" and can be demonstrated in certain cases by experiments. On the other hand there is the theory that all the living forms in the world have arisen from a single source which itself came from an inorganic form. This theory can be called the "General Theory of Evolution" and the evidence that supports it is not sufficiently strong to allow us to consider it as anything more than a working hypothesis.[15]

Even more embarrassing to Huxleyan evolutionists may be W. R. Thompson's article which appeared as the introduction to Darwin's *Origin of Species* in Everyman's Library. There he presents the fallacy of the so-called evidences for a general organic evolution. While these cautionary voices do not totally deny evolution, they ought at least to make one extremely suspicious of a humanistic religion to which pan-evolutionism is foundational.

Derivation of Ethical Norms from Evolution

The values that Huxley derives in part, at least, from the trend and character of evolution are intelligence, self-awareness, co-operation, and the greater importance of the group than that of the individual. Several biologists and philosophers, however, set forth their reasons for rejecting evolutionary ethics. The famous geneticist, T. Dobzhansky, asserts:

> Attempts to discover a biological basis of ethics suffer from mechanistic oversimplification. Human acts and aspirations may be morally right or morally wrong, regardless of whether they assist the evolutionary process

---

[14] Stephen Toulmin, "Contemporary Scientific Mythology," in *Metaphysical Beliefs* (London: SCM Press, 1957), p. 18.

[15] G. A. Kerkut, *Implications of Evolution* (Oxford: Pergamon Press, 1960), p. 157.

to proceed in the direction in which it has been going
or whether they assist it in any direction at all. Moral
rightness and wrongness have meaning only in connection with persons who are free agents. . . . This new evolution, which involves culture, occurs according to its
own laws, which are not deducible from, although also
not contrary to, biological laws.[16]

In a fair treatment on the issue of ethics and the theory
of evolution,[17] Anthony Quinton suggests that there are some
values, such as survival, efficiency, and independence of the
environment, which evolutionary considerations can establish
to be "valuable" for evolution. But these are of a subordinate
and defeasible nature and of an *ex post facto* character, while
the human characteristics relevant to ethics and social policy
are socially acquired and not genetically inherited. Thus evolutionary biology neither furnishes nor aids the discovery of a
criterion for the justification of judgments of value.

G. G. Simpson also differs with Huxley when he says that
no ethical conclusions can be drawn from nature. "All trend
ethics demand the postulate that the trends of evolution, or
some particular one among those, is ethically right and good,"
he declares. "There is no evident reason why such a postulate
should be accepted."[18] For example, any identification of
ethical norms with survival begs the question: Why is survival
good? Furthermore, any selection of specific biological trends
as normative equally begs the question, for it depends on prior
criteria of selection.

In this connection, it is instructive to observe how men
have variously perceived the values thought to be inherent
in evolution. Spencer saw in evolution a justification for laissez-
faire capitalism, Nietzsche for political absolutism, Marx for
dialectical materialism, and Huxley for the message of the
UNESCO charter. In fact, such wildly differing conclusions
depend largely on prior ethical commitments that lead one
to select particular aspects of evolution as definitive. The values
to which J. Huxley subscribes—the sacredness of individual

---

[16] T. Dobzhansky, *The Biological Basis of Human Freedom* (New
York: Columbia University Press, 1956), pp. 132, 143, quoted by I.
G. Barbour, *Issues in Science and Religion* (Englewood Cliffs, N.J.:
Prentice-Halls, 1966), p. 411.

[17] A. M. Quinton, "Ethics and the Theory of Evolution," in *Biology
and Personality*, ed. by I. T. Ramsey (Oxford: Basil Blackwell, 1965).

[18] G. G. Simpson, *The Meaning of Evolution* (New Haven, Conn.:
Yale University Press, 1949), p. 304.

persons, the importance of inner harmony, beauty, truth, and love, for example—stem less from his analysis of evolution than from the heritage of the Western humanistic tradition. In general, naturalistic ethics in the twentieth century are either more ruthless (e.g., Stalinism) or more arbitrary (e.g., atheistic existentialism) than Huxley's genteel goodwill. Evidently his is but one of the more traditional options. One is even tempted to ask whether Huxley's ethics could be preserved in the absence of the theistic framework which gave rise to the western humanistic tradition.[19]

Inadequacy of Present-Day Religions

For Huxley to present a new religion he needs to show how present religions are inadequate. He rightly dismisses the magical mode of religious thinking as untenable. However his analysis of the evolution of religion has great difficulties. His analogy of the development of religions to that of a developing individual is in fact exceedingly tenuous, if not outright false. Hans-Joachim Schoeps concludes his chapter on the origin of religion by confessing that "we know, in fact, nothing certain about the origin of religion and its primitive stages. . . . All evolutionary constructs are unproved and unprovable. Nor can they help us to any conclusion, because every historical religion must obviously be understood in terms of its own tenets and its own peculiarities." [20]

Huxley's arguments against theism are no less flawed than his approach to the history of religions. To begin with he asserts that the discoveries of physics, general biology, and psychology now necessitate a thorough-going naturalistic outlook. In making this kind of statement he is speaking not as a scientist but as a prophet—as a metaphysician. Surely, to be able to give a naturalistic explanation of events in the universe is not to preclude interpretations on a different plane or from a different perspective. In the past Newton and Laplace could describe the universe in scientific laws and retain belief in God. Today there are Christians who subscribe to theistic evolution as scientists. Believing in a personal God is not incompatible with intellectual honesty and scientific objectivity.

Huxley further accuses the theists for being dualists, for

---

[19] Cf. Barbour, op. cit., p. 143.

[20] Hans-Joachim Schoeps, *The Religions of Mankind*, trans. by Richard and Clara Winston (Garden City, N.Y.: Doubleday & Co., 1966), p. 9.

introducing an irreparable split into the universe that prevents men from grasping its real unity. But there is no *a priori* reason that the universe must be made of one "world stuff" and that there is not a real, ontological dualism on account of God's existence and the immortality of human spirits.

Third, Huxley rejects supernatural religions because of the harmful effects they engender. But surely the abuse of a position does not invalidate the position itself. In all fairness, one should point out that Christianity, for one, has brought much good to the world.

Huxley confesses that he finds much in the universe to be inexplicable—the mystery of the existence of the world, mind, and purpose, for example. Indeed, he cannot explain on his system how blind and purposeless forces can result in order, in mind, and in the spiritual dimension. But he is content to regard these mysteries as given. "We accept the universe." He refuses to consider the possibility that theism may, after all, be correct. But perhaps God, too, is a "given." Huxley believes that man has a capacity to experience the numinous. May it not be that traditional religion is right in asserting that this capacity has been created for communion with the Creator? It is interesting to note the similarity between Huxley's version of man's "sacred duty," namely, to ensure the right direction of evolution as the cosmic process, and the duty of man as prescribed by the God of Judaism and Christianity:

> And God blessed them, and God said to them, "Be fruitful and multiply, and fill the earth and subdue it; and have dominion over the fish of the sea and over the birds of the air and over every living thing that moves upon the earth." [21]

One wonders whether the mandate in the Bible is not more specific and more satisfying, when rightly understood.

A FINAL WORD

Huxley denies religions based on the god-hypothesis and on revelation. In their place he proposes to establish the new religion of evolutionary humanism. Yet his religion, based as it is on pan-evolution and an evolutionary ethic, is ill-founded. It leaves unexplained the mysteries of existence and mind, but refuses to countenance the "mystery" of a Creator-God.

In fact, there are indications that a Creator may really

---

[21] Gen. 1:28. (R.S.V.)

exist. There is a case for theism because God has revealed himself in our world. Precisely at this point Christianity differs from other religions in saying that God actually became man in history. Christians believe that the man Jesus is the revelation of God the Creator.[22] His life, death, and resurrection were attested by eye-witnesses who wrote their case for theism in the New Testament and later died for the God-man of their faith. In the New Testament and in the words of Jesus one finds ethics and an approach to religion that transcend by their divine origin Huxley's human guesses. One finds there clues to the nature of mind and purpose, and a solution for the mystery of existence in a God who creates, communicates, and in love condescends to save man from his hellish predicament. Christianity offers what Huxley's evolutionary humanism can never attain because it is truly religion *with* revelation.

---

[22] Jn. 1:1-14; Heb. 1:1-3.

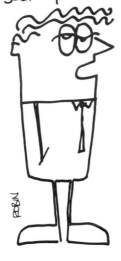

Science and Christianity: Toward Peaceful Coexistence

James R. Moore

One invariably jars the emotional status quo of an intellectual community when discussing the traditional warfare between science and Christianity. Whether you are disinterested or doctrinaire, permit me therefore to instigate a bit of controversy by presenting the front-line action in what has been an intriguing and variegated battle of wits between secular scientists and philosophers of science and Christian theologians. As a kind of war-correspondent, I shall cover two significant skirmishes: the first is the issue of the miraculous and the second, the existence of God. Related in this order, these battles (which still disrupt the minds of many students) will reveal the philosophical essence of most scientific objections to the Christian faith. Simultaneously, as an ambassador of peace, I shall attempt to describe the conditions which make possible the peaceful coexistence of science and Christianity.[1]

SCIENCE AND MIRACLES

The point in dispute can be put in six Anglo-Saxon syllables: can miracles occur? In all fairness to those who would answer in the negative we ought first to consider their anti-supernatural arguments.

---

[1] W. A. Whitehouse correctly observes that "important common ground may be obscured by attempts to map out the provinces of science and theology so that the two kinds of enterprise may enjoy peaceful coexistence" ("Theology and the Natural Sciences," in *The Scope of Theology*, ed. by Daniel T. Jenkins, Meridian Books [Cleveland: World, 1965], p. 154). Thus I do not intend "coexistence" in the political sense of non-aggression between mutually-opposed armed camps. Rather the attempt will be made to negotiate for a veritable harmony which permits the disciplines to occupy common ground—not to establish a DMZ.

James Harvey Johnson of the Thinkers Club begins the polemic:[2]

> Religious beliefs are against common sense. There is no god, just because priests say so. There are no angels, devils, heavens, hells, ghosts, witches, nor miracles. These superstitious beliefs are promoted for the purpose of making the gullible believe that by paying money to the priest class they will be favored by one of the gods. There is nothing supernatural—nothing contrary to natural law.

If you are even slightly perceptive you have already determined that Johnson's organization is misnamed. Common sense arguments carry no weight because they are totally uncritical. Furthermore, Johnson's crass indictment of organized religion reveals a baleful ignorance of religious history and psychology. But though this approach to the miraculous collapses as a valid argument, we must still evaluate the truth of the conclusion which Johnson reaches: "There is nothing supernatural—nothing contrary to natural law."

We turn to fairer intellectual climes in the writing of A. J. Carlson, Nobel prize-winning geneticist and humanist spokesman:[3]

> By supernatural we understand information, theories, beliefs and practices claiming origins other than verifiable experience and thinking, or events contrary to known processes in nature, . . . contrary to facts now known, or rendered untenable, as possibilities, by known facts . . . science and miracles are incompatible.

This plausible statement merits consideration together with the view of eminent New Testament scholar, Rudolf Bultmann:[4]

> The whole conception of the world which is presupposed in the preaching of Jesus as in the New Testament generally is mythological; . . . the conception of the intervention of supernatural powers in the course of events;

---

[2] "Religion is a Gigantic Fraud" published by The Thinkers Club, Box 2832, Dept. RG, San Diego, California. The days of the hidebound village atheist which this pamphlet tokens are virtually past.

[3] "Science and the Supernatural" (first given as the William Vaughan Moody Lecture at the University of Chicago in 1937, appearing in *Science* magazine for February 27, 1937, and currently published in pamphlet form by the American Humanist Association, Department St., Humanist House, Yellow Springs, Ohio), pp. 5-8.

[4] *Jesus Christ and Mythology* (New York: Charles Scribner's Sons, 1958), p. 15.

and the conception of miracles, ... This conception of the world we call mythological because it is different from the conception of the world which has been formed and developed by science ... modern science does not believe that the course of nature can be interrupted or, so to speak, perforated by supernatural powers.

Here, surprisingly enough, we find a humanist and a Christian theologian in accord on an issue so often in debate between their respective schools of thought. However Bultmann tells us that he has given up the miraculous as mythological because "modern science does not believe"; scientist Carlson simply tells us why that is the case. The fact that Bultmann has jumped on the scientist's bandwagon accounts in large measure for his abandonment of the historic Christian view of the miraculous. (The popularity of Bultmannian thought in contemporary theology doubtless accounts in turn for the recent de-escalation in the age-long warfare of science with Christian theology.)

Finally, together with eminent repudiations of the miraculous and over against simple-minded anti-supernatural argumentation, we must consider David Hume's classic, philosophical argument.[5] As we shall see, it forms the backbone of each argument cited above.

A miracle is a violation of the laws of nature; and as a firm and unalterable experience has established these laws, the proof against a miracle, from the very nature of the fact, is as entire as any argument from experience can possibly be imagined. .... Nothing is esteemed a miracle if it ever happens in the common course of nature. It is no miracle that a man, seemingly in good health, should die on a sudden; ... But it is a miracle that a dead man should come to life; because that has never been observed in any age or country. There must, therefore, be a uniform experience against every miraculous event, otherwise the event would not merit that appellation.

Taken in context with Lessing's historical criticism and Kant's philosophical criticism, this argument was very often thought to constitute Christianity's *coup de grâce* during the 18th and 19th centuries.

The pattern is now obvious: Bultmann's theology depends squarely on the scientific attitude voiced by Carlson, and Carl-

---

[5] *An Enquiry Concerning Human Understanding* (LaSalle, Ill.: Open Court, 1958), pp. 126-27.

son's analysis rests on Hume's philosophical underpinning. (Compare Carlson's statement that "supernatural" denotes phenomena apart from "verifiable experience" and "contrary to known processes in nature" and "to facts now known" with Hume's understanding of a miracle as "a violation of the laws of nature" and contrary to "firm and unalterable experience.") Therefore the critical mind must question Hume; the entire anti-miraculous edifice clearly rests on his philosophical foundation.

According to Hume, a miracle is any event which does not occur. ("Nothing is esteemed a miracle if it ever happens in the common course of nature.") C. S. Lewis criticizes Hume in this way:[6]

> Now of course we must agree with Hume that if there is absolutely "uniform experience" against miracles, if in other words they have never happened, why then they never have. Unfortunately, we know the experience against them to be uniform only if we know that all the reports of them are false. And we can know all the reports of them to be false only if we know already that miracles have never occurred. In fact, we are arguing in a circle.

In other words, Hume's fallacy stems from his view of natural law as an immutable causal scheme discoverable within the "uniform experience" of mankind. One can know that all experience is uniform only if he has prior knowledge of inviolable natural law. And inviolable natural law cannot be known apart from the uniform experience in which it is discovered. A vicious circle indeed.

Leaving the question of uniform experience aside, may we not still admit the existence of an immutable system of natural law? Is it not man's discovery of natural law that which ultimately permits such a magnificent achievement as a visit to the moon?

Men of the Newtonian epoch viewed the universe as a closed playing field in which scientists knew all the rules. Natural law was understood to be a structure latent in the universe which was being progressively uncovered. When exposed and

---

[6] *Miracles: A Preliminary Study* (New York: Macmillan, 1947), p. 105. A remarkably lucid and incisive book, *Miracles* was written for "the reader who has difficulty in finding use for miracles" by the late Professor of Mediaeval and Renaissance Literature at Cambridge University.

mathematically formulated, natural law allegedly enabled scientists and philosophers to *prescribe* what could and what could not happen. Werner Heisenberg's observation on Newtonian physical theory applies as well in principle to the traditional mind-set of other scientific disciplines:[7] "For once the main reasoning of classical physics had been accepted as the *a priori* of physical investigations, the belief arose, through an obvious though false extrapolation that it was absolute, i.e., valid for all time, and could never be modified as the result of new experiences."

However, with the advent of the Einsteinian era, heralded by Planck's work on black-body radiation and the publication of Einstein's *Special Theory of Relativity* in 1905, scientists were confronted with the vicissitudes of so-called natural law in an uncharted and unobstructed universe. J. W. N. Sullivan makes this point *in extenso* in his book, *The Limitations of Science*:[8]

> What is called the modern "revolution in science" consists in the fact that the Newtonian outlook which dominated the scientific world for nearly two hundred years, has been found insufficient. It is in process of being replaced by a different outlook, and, although the reconstruction is by no means complete, it is already apparent that the philosophical implications of the new outlook are very different from those of the old one.

Today scientists will admit that no one knows enough about "natural law" to say that any event is necessarily a violation of it. They agree that an individual's non-statistical sample of time and space is hardly sufficient ground on which to base immutable generalizations concerning the nature of the entire universe. Today what we commonly term "natural law" is in fact only our *inductive and statistical descriptions of natural phenomena*. These tried and true theories, many of which are sufficiently certain to permit space travel, for example, must

---

[7] *Philosophic Problems of Nuclear Science* (Greenwich, Conn.: Fawcett Premier Books, 1966), p. 24. This is an excerpt from a lecture originally published in *Naturwissenschaften*, XXII (1934).

[8] *The Limitations of Science*, Mentor Books (New York: New American Library, 1963), p. 138. For a helpful, semi-technical survey of the implications of research in modern physics for philosophy and physical theory, see the lectures given at Oxford University in Trinity Term, 1958, published as *Turning Points in Physics*, Harper Torchbooks (New York: Harper & Bros., 1961).

always be brought before the bar of the facts they are alleged to describe.

Can miracles occur? The key to the answer is the very experience which Hume maintained was absolutely uniform. There is no a priori method of determining whether miracles have occurred, or that experience is absolutely uniform. Rather, the way to determine that anything happens is to investigate specific, alleged events in their own right. Observation is of the essence of scientific method and the collective experiences and investigations of mankind must be decisive both in validating scientific theories and in verifying the occurrence of miracles. Therefore not only *may* miracles occur, but they also *may have* occurred. In either case determining whether miracles occur is the duty of scientific and historical investigation rather than of philosophical speculation.

If miracles are not intrinsically impossible events, what then distinguishes events that merit the appelation "miracle"? The significance of events that are normally called miracles does not lie in the fact that they violate a rigid, universal framework of natural law, but in the fact that they are *contextually unique*—and that their uniqueness lends prestige or authority to a miracleworker. By contextually unique it is meant that the events were extraordinary and unparalleled (ambiguous, perhaps, but suggestive words) within the culture or epoch in which they occurred. Miracles are events whose explanation transcends man's knowledge of the natural world at the time of their occurrence and, perhaps (who can say?), at later dates in history. The prestige or authority gained by a miracleworker thus depends both on the historical context in which the events took place and on the causal connection observed between his claims, commands, and pronouncements and the events themselves. Again: a miracle may be understood to be a unique event of extraordinary significance within a certain historical context, the apparent result either of a discernible or of an inscrutable causal agency.

Before proceeding with the second episode of conflict between Christianity and science it has been necessary to clarify the meaning of the word "miracle." As we shall see, the occurrence and definition of miracles is an issue logically prior to belief in the Christian God. That is to say, without a wide-open worldview—a philosophical outlook eminently hospitable to modern science—one will insensibly narrow his field of vision to whatever he considers normal, casually overlooking any unusual events that may be connected with the revelation of God to man.

SCIENCE AND THEISM

The time was when virtually all scientists believed in God. Whether of the Cartesian or Newtonian schools, God was First Cause, providentially sustaining his creation by constant supervision on the one hand and sitting outside his universe while watching the cosmic clock tick on the other. But when the extension of the mechanical idea reached its climax in the work of Laplace, who believed he had demonstrated the inherent stability of natural law in the universe, the providential elements in the world-order were eliminated.

> While God was thus being deprived of his duties by the further advancement of mechanical science, and men were beginning to wonder whether the self-perpetuating machine thus left stood really in need of any supernatural beginning, Hume's crushing disposal of the ideas of power and causality along another tack were already disturbing the learned world with the suspicion that a First Cause was not as necessary an idea of reason as it had appeared and Kant was preparing the penetrating analysis which frankly purported to remove God from the realm of knowledge altogether.[9]

It was not many years later, after the emergence of Darwinian evolution, that Nietzsche could express the idea that "God is dead," the truth of which had been plaguing the consciences of scientists for decades. Whereas man had once thought himself to live at the center of a finite, providential universe, the work of men such as Copernicus, Newton, Laplace, Hume, Kant and Darwin had, in the course of 400 years, not only removed man from the center of the cosmos, but had also explained away providence and had shown man himself to be a chance product of the inexorable forces of natural law. In such a situation the pressure upon honest scientists to give up belief in a supernatural God was irresistible. Only man, whose acumen had revealed and understood his origin and role in the natural order, is a worthy object of veneration.

The compelling force in this historical overview, the "idea of progress," has carried over into the Einsteinian era in which we live. It seems to scientists that a strong correlation exists between man's religious ideas and his scientific knowledge. From some kind of primitive animism to a high monotheism, science has prospered while the number of gods has been re-

---

[9] Edwin A. Burtt, *The Metaphysical Foundations of Modern Science*, Anchor Books (Garden City, N.Y.: Doubleday, 1954), pp. 298-99.

duced to one (at least in the West); today an easy extrapolation informs the scientist that further progress will be indicated by a reduction in the number of gods to zero.

Even though man's notion of natural law has been overhauled and the possibility of Laplacean order has once and for all been eliminated by quantum physics, scientists still cannot resist the logic of John Hick's eloquent analysis:[10]

> The sciences have cumulatively established the autonomy of the natural order. From the galaxies whose vastness numbs the mind to the unimaginable small events and entities of the subatomic universe, and throughout the endless complexities of our own world which lies between these virtual infinities, nature can be studied without any reference to God. The universe investigated by the sciences proceeds exactly as though no God exists.

But does the atheistic conclusion follow? Because science has neither discovered something nor has found use for it in its investigations, does it follow that that "something" is nonexistent? And is there a distinct and necessary correlation between religious ideas and scientific progress? To both general questions the answer is no.

Yet is not asking the scientific mind to believe in a God totally absent from the phenomenal world an invitation to intellectual hari-kari? Scientists work with the "stuff" of the world and their belief in the theories and laws which describe its reality is predicated on intimate acquaintance with objective data accruing from careful experiment. To plunge into a morass of fuzzy-minded, non-evidential religious belief is, for the thoughful scientist, to embrace a disconcerting inconsistency between daily life and religious practice—disconcerting because the dichotomy of the secular (scientific) and the sacred (religious) is an unsupported presupposition that he must question.

Here then is the dilemma: it appears that the scientist can say nothing about God; he can neither disallow nor affirm God's existence. Under pressure from a religious environment and from his own natural misgivings, the result is frustration—frustration often issuing in outright verbal warfare against religion in general and Christianity in particular.

However, the mention of presuppositions brings us to the level of discussion where problems and solutions are most read-

---

[10] *Philosophy of Religion* (Englewood Cliffs, N.J.: Prentice-Hall, 1963), pp. 37-38.

ily elucidated. Since everyone brings presuppositions to an inquiry and since those who cannot or will not admit them are most likely to distort their data, the scientist at once exposes his presuppositions to all criticism: (1) knowledge is possible; (2) the universe is orderly; (3) men will report the results of research honestly. But because the scientist has chosen presuppositions with minimal factual content, assumptions which we all make in order to live in this world, he has fairly escaped criticism.

These presuppositions are used to justify investigation of the universe. Theories and models are constructed imaginatively and checked inductively in attempts to render the resultant data intelligible. Finally a world-view is constructed from the processed data. Observation, correlation, experimentation—this in short is the method followed by scientists in search of truth.

The Scientific Mind and Theological Method

If scientists cannot blindly affirm the existence of God without commiting intellectual suicide and if they understand the presuppositions and procedure employed in their quest for truth, what reasonable synthesis of mind and method can they expect which will allow them to arrive at scientific truth about God? Philosopher Paul Schlipp frankly states what synthesis they cannot expect:[11]

> There can be no "science" of God. God may be a claim of (more or less) reasonable faith; He may be a (more or less valid) metaphysical hypothesis (and all metaphysics is purely speculative); He may even be the answer to someone's "religious" need. But, in the very nature of the case (i.e., because He is thought of as infinite, whereas man and all man's knowledge are only finite), He cannot be the object of scientific analysis and investigation.

But is Schlipp correct? Must science be short-circuited in the search for God? Let us see if theologians have grounded their endeavors in scientific method—whose grass appears to be decidedly greener than prairies of blind faith and speculative metaphysics.

On the one hand we have theologians who have swallowed Schlipp's statement. In the temple of the mind where Einstein

---

[11] "Science, Theology and Ethical Religion," *Zygon: Journal of Religion and Science*, I (June, 1966), 189-90.

held his "gedanken experiments"[12] these men sacrifice their intellects on the metaphysical altar they have erected to G O D —a linguistic symbol which is meant to denote "being" that is totally indiscernible, either by tangible, historical contact *or* by a theoretical thought experiment.[13] The irrationality of this approach to God is apparent when we consider the parallel situation of a physicist who believed in the existence of completely undetectable particles which he called "glerps?" The evidence he submits for the particles' existence is nothing more than his intuitive or mystical feelings. Therefore who knows whether his belief was elicited by anything more impressive than indigestion? The lesson we learn is that the Christian theologian, too, must also be able to distinguish "the Lord" from both gastronomical pie and metaphysical pie in the sky. In the last analysis only the application of scientific method will rescue theologians and physicists from the snare of senseless speculation and muddy-minded mysticism.[14] Let us see why this is true.

Theoretical construction must be subject to specific, factual investigation if it is to contribute to man's world-view and if, in fact, it is to make sense. Whether they are the specious utterances of philosophical idealism or the speculations of scientific occultism, propositions which purport to say something that may be true or false but which cannot be checked in the real world are in reality nonsensical. We might even admit them as genuine assertions if they could be checked *in principle*, such as in a gedanken experiment. But because there are no conditions under which the utterances could conceivably be

---

[12] Edwin L. Goldwasser, *Optics, Waves, Atoms and Nuclei* (New York: W. A. Benjamin, 1965), pp. 195-96.

[13] See, for example, Paul Tillich, *Systematic Theology* (3 vols.; Chicago: University of Chicago Press, 1951), I, 235-49, and John Macquarrie, "How Can We Think of God?" in *New Theology No. 3*, ed. by Martin E. Marty and Dean G. Peerman (New York: Macmillan, 1964), pp. 47-52.

[14] Carl F. H. Henry illustrates this well in a capsule summary of contemporary theology: "from the objective-transcendent personal God of Judeo-Christian theology, . . . neo-Protestant interpreters have moved in recent generations to the nonobjective-transcendent personal God (Barth and Brunner), to the nonobjective-transcendent impersonal Unconditioned (Tillich), to the nonobjective-mythological-transcendent personal God (Bultmann), to nonobjective-nontranscendent religion." If all objectivity has been lost then modern man has perforce lost all means of impartial evaluation of Christianity; he is then in the lamentable religious position where "no reason can be adduced for choosing one faith or set of religious beliefs over its opposite, or, for that matter, for choosing any at all on rational grounds" (*Frontiers in Modern Theology* [Chicago: Moody Press, 1966], pp. 148-149.).

true or false—because they are compatible with any and all conditions or evidence—they are uninformative and nonsensical (i.e., without cognitive sense) except to the extent they reveal the psychological state of the speaker—that he is either duped, unbalanced, or given to playing "language-games" which float free from reality. The lesson is the same: if one is to make sense when speaking of God or of subatomic particles he must be certain that his statements can be checked objectively. Checking is accomplished in some fashion by means of scientific method.[15]

Thus, on the other hand, many Christian theologians have refused to yield to Schlipp's pronouncement. They have left the speculative ivory towers of theologizing and have embraced the down-to-earth methodology of the modern scientist. They believe in a God who has revealed himself objectively in the space-time world and has objectively attested the veracity of that revelation. They have discovered and assimilated the facts connected with that revelation through scientific method.[16]

Three factors account for this development:

1. The facts themselves are of such a nature as to compel investigation. That God should appear on the human scene in the remarkable way in which he did is even more electrifying than the events that led to the discovery of the Double Helix by Watson and Crick.

2. Christian theologians realize that they must make cognitive sense when speaking of the existence of God. Therefore they rest their belief on the evidence for the God whom men have seen, heard, and touched.

3. Absolute ethical and spiritual truths cannot be derived from the human situation because every human being is caught

---

[15] Cf. Kai Nielsen, "Can Faith Validate God-Talk?" in *New Theology No. 1*, ed. by Martin E. Marty and Dean G. Peerman (New York: Macmillan, 1964), and Antony Flew and Alasdair MacIntyre, eds., *New Essays in Philosophical Theology* (New York: Macmillan, 1964), *passim*. On the "language-game" see Fredrick Ferré, *Language, Logic and God* (New York: Harper & Row, 1961), pp. 58-61. The Princeton philosopher, Walter Kaufmann, distinguishes between the statements "God exists" and "God *really* exists" and concludes that the latter has no clear meaning whereas the former may be a meaningful component of the universe of Judeo-Christian discourse (language-game) (*Critique of Religion and Philosophy*, Anchor Books [Garden City, New York: Doubleday, 1961], pp. 173-181.).

[16] For an excellent and comprehensive study of the scientific theologian's methodology see John Warwick Montgomery, "The Theologian's Craft: A Discussion of Theory Formation and Theory Testing in Theology," *Journal of the American Scientific Affiliation*, XVIII (September, 1966), 65-77, 92-95, reprinted in the same author's *Suicide of Christian Theology* (Minneapolis: Bethany Fellowship, 1970).

up in the flux of life. There is no absolute frame of reference within the human domain from which one can gain a comprehensive, absolute perspective on the universe. If one wishes to arrive at final truth in religion, one must seize upon an objective revelation of the God who speaks to man—the God whose statements constitute absolute ethical and spiritual truth. Notice here that the facts themselves, the logical priority of facts for theory construction, and the search for truth—all factors in any scientific inquiry—are central to belief in the Christian God. Therefore, *contra* Schlipp, there can be a "science of God." [17] There is hope for the scientific mind in a theological method which yields a rational basis for belief in God—a belief perhaps akin to a scientist's acceptance of his empirical data as recorded in a laboratory manual or as generalized by a "natural law." What then is this evidence which has brought Christians and Christian theologians to a scientific belief in God?

Data on Deity

Superstitious men point to an object—an icon—and call it god. Better informed individuals identify God with an idea or an ideal. Yet in each case the kind, quality, and amount of data available for evaluating the truth of the theistic claim rule scientific investigation out of the question. Christians point to a man and say that he was God, one whose life and deeds offer a considerable body of data for a scientific investigation of the claim. Of course in one sense this is nothing unusual; throughout history scores of pretenders to deity have left us with valuable data with which to evaluate their claims or the claims of others for them. But whereas the historical data regularly disprove these claims, the Christian claim stands remarkably confirmed.

In a series of unusual events nearly 2000 years ago in the land of present-day Israel, Christians say that God entered human history in a unique person known by his contemporaries as Jesus of Nazareth. It is claimed that this self-professed God-man spoke absolute ethical and spiritual truths and attested his identity and pronouncements by performing miracles and, ultimately, by returning to life after a brutal murder at the hands of the religious and political authorities. The historical data for these "laws" of Christianity were collected by eyewit-

---

[17] Cf. Austin Farrar's *A Science of God* and his criteria: "Some solid and relevant facts"; "An effective and reliable method of studying them"; and "The ability to form appropriate theories."

nesses at the time of the events and were subsequently recorded in a "laboratory manual" of primary source documents. In investigating Christian theism, therefore, one begins with these pre-collected historical data which constitute the New Testament. He finds them to be free of systematic error; he is assured of their historicity in the same way that he may learn of certain events that occurred during World War II by reading Dwight D. Eisenhower's *Crusade in Europe.*

The centrality of miracles to the Christian God-claim is now evident. First century men were in many ways as skeptical as modern scientists would be if confronted with a pretender to deity.[18] However, it is recorded that Jesus went about doing remarkable things which we call miracles—deeds which won him a tremendous following from the ranks of his monotheistic countrymen.[19] It also seemed miraculous that throughout the course of his public life his ethical and moral character was entirely compatible with his claim to be God.[20] And when asked for an ultimate sign of his authority and deity Jesus replied that he would cap his brief career by returning to life from the dead.[21] The documents record the circumstances surrounding the resurrection and post-resurrection appearances of Jesus in clinical detail. Taken in context with Jesus' claims, character and other miracles, the resurrection can be considered the final vindication of Christian theism.[22]

Experiment

In the historical person of Christ, God may be known. It is, in fact, at this point, in Him, that science and faith meet, and it is also here, as we encounter the historical

---

[18] See Luke 5:17-26; John 7, 8; John 20:24-31 for examples of first-century skepticism.

[19] Cf. John 11:45-48. That Jesus regarded Himself as no less than Jehovah of the Jews is patent in the New Testament; see John 8:56-59.

[20] Cf. John 5:17-24; 10:22-39; 14:9. One of the most startling aspects of Jesus' public image was that friend and foe alike confessed his blameless innocence: Pilate and Herod, Luke 23:14, 15; Judas, Luke 27:4; Malefactor, Luke 23:41; Roman centurion, Luke 23:47; Peter, Acts 3:14; I Peter 3:18; Stephen, Acts 7:52; John, I John 3:5; Paul, II Corinthians 5:21.

[21] John 2:18-22, Matthew 12:38-40.

[22] Beginning with St. Paul (I Corinthians 15:14), men of all ages have recognized this fact. Frank Morison, for one, set out to disprove the resurrection and the sheer facticity of the event drove him to God and thus to answer the only question for which he could not conceivably rationalize an answer, viz., *Who Moved the Stone?* (London: Faber and Faber, 1944).

Christ, that we see most clearly both the value and the limitations of scientific method. It is possible to approach Christ as a scientist. We may study the New Testament records of His life and work as a historian, or as a philosopher, or as a sociologist, or as a doctor, or as a psychologist, and it may be expected that all such studies will be of relevance and value.[23]

The application of scientific method to history has these features. But it also has at least one drawback: experimentation *qua* science in efforts to establish and experience personally the identity of a historical figure is impossible. If we had lived in Jesus' day we might have "experimented" by becoming his personal friends—perhaps even his disciples. In a personal relationship with him his true character would be revealed far more clearly than by the data of any historical narrative. But what about today? Is it possible to conclude our scientific search for God by actually making his acquaintance?

We must remember who Jesus claimed to be and what ultimate attestation he offered for his claim. Jesus claimed to be no less than God in human flesh—a claim to be attested by his resurrection. If it can be historically determined that Jesus actually returned to life then his claim is made good and, moreover, he lives today. He may not be visibly present to his seekers, but his promise, "I am with you always," can be accepted on his established authority. Thus Frank H. T. Rhodes, Professor of Geology at the University College of Swansea writes,[24] ". . . if there is any possibility that the Christian claim of a personal God may be true, the detached scientific approach must be utterly inadequate to make His acquaintance: I must participate as a person in whatever encounters there may be with Him." Indeed,

> there is no way to get around the fact that, just as we come to know another human person not by calculation but by a relationship of trust, so too we cannot know God apart from trust and the practical obedience it implies. This is more than an article of . . . Christian faith; it is a fundamental requirement of a truly *scientific theology.*[25]

---

[23] Frank H. T. Rhodes, "Christianity in a Mechanistic Universe," in *Christianity in a Mechanistic Universe and Other Essays,* ed. by Donald M. MacKay (Chicago: Inter-Varsity Press, 1965), p. 46.

[24] *Ibid.,* p. 47.

[25] Harold O. J. Brown, "A Theology of Trust," *Christianity Today,* April 11, 1969, p. 5.

Part Two

ETHICS AND SOCIETY

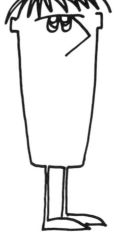

What About Situation Ethics?

Joseph Blasczyk

Moral decisions are a part of life. We are faced every day with situations which call for them. How are we to know what the right choices are? Is there some standard or code which is to be followed? Or must we merely do what we hope is right? A basis for action has recently been suggested by Joseph Fletcher, Bishop John Robinson, Paul Lehmann, and others. These men have rejected the notion that right decisions can be based on an absolute standard or code. They suggest that the rightness or wrongness of an act is a function of the circumstances attending the situation. Thus according to them it may be right, for example, to lie in one situation, and wrong to lie in another.

In his book, *Situation Ethics*, Joseph Fletcher maintains that love is the sole criterion to be used in judging the rightness or wrongness of actions. In any situation, he says, we are to maximize love, to do the most loving thing. And the loving thing will be the right thing. This is not to say that one throws out all rules and principles. According to Fletcher, we are to carry principles from our community and its heritage into situations with us. These principles are then to be used as illuminators of the situation, but not as directors. They are to be kept in a position subservient to love and only to be used if they serve love's purposes. Thus if it is more loving in a given situation to lie, one would be right in lying.

This method of solving ethical questions is called situation ethics. It is a theological issue which has been hotly debated within Christian circles. In 1956, situation ethics was labeled "the new morality" by the Roman Catholic Church. Fletcher, however, does not consider it new. He traces its roots to historic Christianity in the teachings of Jesus and Paul. Jesus sums up the law in Matthew 22:35-40 by saying, "You shall love the Lord your God . . ." and "You shall love your neighbor as yourself." This, says Fletcher, is the essential spirit of all the particular laws of the Old Testament and is what we must concern ourselves with. Again, Paul in Romans 13:8 states, "owe no one anything except to love one another" and in Galatians 5:14, "the whole law is fulfilled in one word, 'You shall love your neighbor as yourself.'" Fletcher wholeheartedly endorses Augustine's concise ethical maxim: "Love with care and what you will, do." "Augustine was right," says Fletcher, "to make love the source principle . . . upon which all other virtues hang. . . ." [1]

The only absolute in situation ethics is love. It alone is universal and intrinsically right. Particular laws are not intrinsically right or wrong. Particular laws cannot provide adequate answers for the diversified situations which call for ethical decision.

What about Fletcher's ethic? Is it reasonable? Is it Christian? Since love is the only admissible absolute in situation ethics one might well test for soundness at this crucial point. If any decision of consequence is determined in love, one surely needs a clear conception of love by which to judge.

IS FLETCHER'S ETHIC REASONABLE?

Sorry to say, Fletcher seems confused here. Dr. John Lachs, professor of philosophy at the College of William and Mary, illustrates this confusion by laying out "an astonishing series of half-developed and contradictory indications" of love given by Fletcher:[2]

> Love is first said to be something we do: it is thus (1) an action or a way of behaving (p. 61). This definition is quickly revised: Love becomes (2) a characteristic of certain human actions and relationships (p. 63). Again, it is (3) the purpose behind the action (p. 61). Towards the end of the book it becomes (4) the motive behind the decision to act (p. 155). Elsewhere love is (5) an attitude of persons, (6) a disposition to act in certain ways, (7) a preference for certain values, and (8) good will or a cognitive predisposition to take certain attitudes (pp. 79, 61, 104, 105). And it is also said to be (9) a relation, (10) a formal principle, and (11) a regulative principle (pp. 105, 60, 61).

---

[1] Joseph Fletcher, *Situation Ethics* (Philadelphia: Westminster 1966), pp. 78-79.

[2] John Lachs, "Dogmatist in Disguise," *The Christian Century*, November 16, 1966, p. 1403.

Now, clearly, love cannot be all of these things at the same time. As Lachs points out, if it is (1), it is not (2); if it is (9), it is not (4), (5), and (6). Also, if it is (3), it cannot be (10) or (11). Lachs also contends that Fletcher is confused about what really makes an action right: the action itself, the intentions behind the action, or the consequences of the action. According to explanation (1), the rightness of an act seems to be found within the act itself; according to (3), (4), (5), and (8), rightness is linked with the intentions; in (9), it is linked with the consequences.

Hence, Graham B. Blaine, Jr., Chief of Psychiatry at Harvard University, says that "It is this very confusion about the definition of love that makes the new morality virtually useless as a system of ethics." [3] Fletcher himself is aware of the confusion. In his book, he confesses that love "is 'a semantic confusion' which we are tempted to 'drop altogether' and 'throw away ruthlessly.' [But] instead of doing that, . . . he exalts it to the place of supremacy in his system." [4]

The extent of personal responsibility is another of Fletcher's muddled concepts. He claims that we are to act responsibly in love, considering the effect of our action on others. But what "others"? Who is our neighbor? Vernon Grounds asks,[5]

> Is he only the man who confronts me now in this fleeting encounter? Or does the law of neighbor-love eventually embrace my total environment with all its interlocking, ongoing relationships and obligations, long range no less than immediate? And how in the exercise of love do I, with all my prejudices and passions, all my limitations of insight and foresight, manage to calculate the effects of an action? In responsibly loving one person, am I being irresponsibly unloving to a multitude of other persons, some not yet visible on my horizon, some perhaps unborn?

Father Herbert McCabe (who has debated Fletcher) asks for a limiting factor on the number of consequences to be considered. Suppose one tries to consider all possible consequences. How can he know those consequences that are acci-

---

[3] Graham B. Blaine, Jr., *Youth and the Hazards of Affluence: The High School and College Years* (New York: Harper and Bros., 1966), p. 123.

[4] Vernon Grounds, "The New Morality: What is Wrong with the New View of Right?" *His*, November, 1967, p. 25.

[5] Grounds, *op. cit.*, p. 25.

dental and unforeseeable? Can the moral value of an act change as history reveals new consequences? And if acts are neither good nor bad in themselves, how can we label the consequences either good or bad? [6] This confusion too renders the new morality unreasonable and unworkable.

IS FLETCHER'S ETHIC "CHRISTIAN"?

Fletcher claims to be presenting a Christian ethic. In *Situation Ethics* he affirms, "From this point on, we will be speaking of Christian situation ethics." Yet in an article he claims that God's Spirit is given to all men regardless of Christian commitment. "The Christian situationist says to all men, to all who care about others, whether they are Christians or not: your love is like mine, like everybody's. Love . . . is the Holy Spirit working in us." [7] Supposedly a Christian ethic will agree with Christian teaching, especially that of the New Testament. But one becomes rather suspicious of Fletcher's Christianity when he compares Fletcher's claim with the New Testament. The New Testament declares that the Holy Spirit is given to Christians only in a personal relationship with the living Christ. [8]

But suspicion of Fletcher's "Christian" ethic turns to outright disbelief under closer inspection. Grounds notes that the Christian concepts of guilt, grace, sin, and forgiveness are conspicuously lacking in Fletcher's work. And in a decision-provoking situation where two of God's particular revealed laws may conflict, the laws are not even brought into the picture. Contrast this with the description of a situation given by the noted University of Hamburg professor, Helmut Thielicke. He describes the believer's predicament under a Nazi-like government in which he is called on to lie in order to save the lives of thousands of innocent people. Thielicke says, [9]

> In such extreme cases, untruth cannot be regarded as a "commanded" way of escape, for if we regard it as a commanded way, what we have is again an evasion of the conflict situation, and this is always wrong. It is rather that in such cases a man is prepared to accept the guilt of untruth or of forging papers (when he illegally

---

[6] Herbert McCabe, "The Total Context," *Commonweal*, LXXXIII (January 14, 1966), 440.

[7] Vernon Grounds, "The New Morality: What is Wrong with the New View of Right? (Part II)," *His*, October, 1967, p. 8.

[8] Rom. 8:9, 14, 16; I Cor. 12:12, 13.

assists persecuted Jews, for example). He is willing to take this guilt upon himself not in the name of the tragics, but in the name of forgiveness.

This understanding, says Grounds, is the Christian position. It is in the experience of such "boundary-situations that a believer discovers the anguish of his own sinful predicament and the glory of divine grace." [10]

Fletcher maintains that the Christian is given complete freedom from all particular laws and is thus freed to act lovingly in any situation. But this gives man too much credit. Christian teaching presents man as pathologically selfish and utterly unable to meet God's standard of righteousness.[11] Even after one becomes a Christian he is still imperfect in thought and in deed.[12] St. Paul's epistle to the church at Rome therefore points up the need for law to define evil, to show Christian and non-Christian his errors. In his letter to the church at Galatia Paul teaches that law is the factor which brings selfish men to forgiveness in Jesus Christ. Far from being free from law, men need law to distinguish right from wrong and to map the condition in which they are forgiven.

Lachs concludes that "situation ethics cannot become universal so long as human nature remains what it is now." Since "most people are neither willing nor able to deliberate and decide with the care and rational foresight demanded any genuine morality and because in any situation there are many ways to do wrong and only one way to do right (said Aristotle), one's chance of doing right is not very good. Though following a code—the Ten Commandments for example—does not guarantee that the right thing will be done in every case, "it does insure that the person who unflinchingly acts by the code will do the right thing much more often then if he acted out of instinct or private inspiration." [13]

In place of Fletcher's view of morality, I suggest a view which is consistently Christian. God's particular and revealed laws in Scripture are absolutes for moral conduct. Furthermore these revealed laws are in fact the practical outworkings of

---

[9] Helmut Thielicke, *Theological Ethics*, ed. by William H. Lazareth (Philadelphia: Fortress Press, 1966), I., 615.

[10] Grounds, *op. cit.*, November, 1967, p. 24.

[11] Jer. 17:9; Rom. 3.

[12] Phil. 3:12-14.

[13] Lachs, *op. cit.*, p. 1402.

His pure love. That is, they are statements of how true love acts.

This is not to say that mere conformity to law is a sufficient condition for moral action. It is not. One must have the right attitude as well as perform the right act. Here it seems Fletcher's emphasis on love is correct. Aquinas noted that chastity without love is no chastity at all but its corpse.[14] However, it is not love alone, but love plus law. The law helps to properly direct our love. It is "because God wants to see us exercising love towards Himself and towards men . . . He has given us clear indications of the way in which such love, if genuine, should show itself." [15]

Both the spirit and the letter are necessary for true morality.[16] In the New Testament, in Luke 6:46, Jesus says, "Why do you call me 'Lord, Lord,' and do not what I tell you?" John, known as the apostle of love, declares in his first epistle that lawlessness is sin.[17] Law, then, may be considered the invisible skeleton, the framework, which gives strength and form to love.

What is one to do in situations where two laws of God conflict? There is, for example, the ethical problem in regard to Christian resistance in countries under National Socialist occupation. In Nazi Germany one was called on to lie in order to save innocent lives. First, while these situations do occur, they are the rare exceptions. They do not negate law but constitute the exceptions which prove the rule. One must call on God for guidance. Then he must act, attempting to maximize love, but realizing, as Barth has stated, that the action is "a matter of excusing an evil (because unlawful) act." [18]

The New Testament is replete with practical instruction in the form of concise commands. In the epistles we read: "therefore, putting away falsehood, let everyone speak the truth with his neighbor," and "if your enemy is hungry, feed him; if thirsty, give him drink," and "Children, obey your parents

---

[14] Cited by Herbert McCabe, "The Validity of Absolutes," *Commonweal*, LXXXIII (January 14, 1966), 433.

[15] Oliver G. Barclay, (ed.), *A Time to Embrace: Essays on the Christian View of Sex* (Chicago: Inter-Varsity, 1967), p. 54.

[16] Mt. 5:17-28.

[17] I John 3:4.

[18] Cited by Joseph Fletcher, "Love is the Only Measure," *Commonweal*, LXXXIII (January 14, 1966), 430.

in everything, for this pleases the Lord." [19] However, we do not have in the New Testament or in the entire Bible a complete list of right actions to fit every situation. On some matters God has chosen to be silent. Here again one must rely on God's Spirit for guidance through the general principles laid down in Scripture and seek that guidance in fervent prayer.

Jesus did indeed say that all particular laws were summed up in the law of love.[20] But consider carefully his words: he declared that the first and great commandment is to love God and a second one like the first is to love one's neighbor as oneself. In so stipulating, Jesus linked love and law inseparably. Let us not therefore think that we can consider the matter of loving one's neighbor without first loving God. And what if we love God and seek to live lovingly with our neighbors in every situation? "For this is the love of God, that we keep his commandments." "By this we know that we love the children of God, when we love God and obey his commandments." [21]

---

[19] Eph. 4:25; Rom. 12:20; Col. 3:20.
[20] Mt. 22:35-40.
[21] I John 5:2-3.

God of War

Ronald A. Iwasko

"The Lord is a man of war: the Lord is His name" (Exodus 15:3).

War is an unpleasant business. Some members of our society decry war as immoral. The memories of two World Wars, the Korean conflict, and the more recent Viet Nam fiasco turn our stomachs. Scenes of bandaged mothers and burned or wounded babies intensify the anguish. The thought of God as a God of war turns us off. And a command from God to annihilate men, women, and children is unthinkable.

But here it is, the command to exterminate the Canaanites: "And when the Lord your God gives them over to you, and you defeat them; then you must utterly destroy them; you shall make no covenant with them, and show no mercy to them." [1] This statement is in stark contrast to God's own command at Sinai forty years before, "Thou shalt not kill" [2]! How less moral can one get? Does not this make the morals of such a God suspect? What then of the One who has been pictured as the Moral Governor of the universe? Is He not at best inconsistent? Can He be trusted? Or perhaps morality is to be judged on the basis of the attendent situation rather than by an absolute standard; God Himself appears to operate that way. And what of all this in light of Jesus' teaching about turning the other cheek? Maybe we ought to just chalk it up to another Bible blunder and forget it. Instead let's examine the Scripture more closely.

THE VIEW OF THE OLD TESTAMENT WRITERS

Scientific historical procedure demands that we place strong emphasis on the testimony of those nearest the action, both spatially and temporally. When we do, it is particularly note-

---

[1] Deut. 7:2.
[2] Ex. 20:13.

worthy that no voice of protest is raised against God or His earthly representatives, either for ordering the extermination of the Canaanites or for other similar commands. True, this may reflect a nationalistic spirit, but this is hardly in keeping with the high moral ideals evidenced elsewhere by the writers of the Old Testament which fostered sharp criticism of their own people.

Israel usually obeyed the voice of God (e.g., Joshua 6:21 "Then they utterly destroyed all in the city, both men and women, young and old . . ."). In other cases, failure to obey was not conditioned by moral objections to God's law, but by other factors such as greed.[3] The penalty for disobedience was judgment upon Israel itself.

But what about the commandment "Thou shalt not kill"?

THE SIXTH COMMANDMENT

Long before the giving of the Decalogue on Mt. Sinai, God emphasized the sanctity of man's life. Prof. Murray states,[4] "After the flood, in accordance with God's covenant and in pursuance of it, the Lord manifested his grace in making provision for the safeguarding and enhancement of life as the antithesis of death. These provisions are exemplified in three institutions—the propagation of life (Genesis 9:1, 7), the sustenance of life (Genesis 8:22; 9:2b, 3), and the protection of life (Genesis 9:2a, 5, 6)." But the Genesis 9 passage calls for a kind of capital punishment for the murderer: "Whoever sheds the blood of man, by man shall his blood be shed." Is this not in itself incongruous with the Sixth Commandment?

The Hebrew of the Old Testament uses several words which denote the taking of human life. The one used in the Commandment, refers to murder. Another word, translated "put to death" refers to capital punishment, and a third, translated "smite" is used of war. What is in view in the Sixth Commandment is willful, malicious assault upon the life of another. At the same time a distinction is made between premeditated murder and manslaughter;[5] for the latter case "cities of refuge" were provided to which the manslayer might flee. The populace was given explicit criteria for deciding whether a man was guilty of murder or manslaughter. Viewing the Decalogue in its biblical

---

[3] Josh. 7:1, I Sam. 15:9.
[4] John Murray, *Principles of Conduct* (London: Tyndale, 1957), p. 109.
[5] Ex. 21:13-14.

context, we discover that God prescribed the death penalty for a large number of offences. Executions were never viewed as murder but as just retribution for crime.

But is war not murder? Surely in war there is premeditation to destroy human life (if that is required to achieve the objective) whether the action is offensive or defensive. Regarding defensive action A. C. Knudson answers pointedly,[6] "Murder is, and justly so, a crime punishable with death if the public welfare requires it. This principle also applies to foreign foes who are seeking to destroy the state and the lives of its citizens. These foes, so long as they persist in their violent attacks, have in the eyes of the state the same status as that of murderers. They have forfeited their right to life, no matter how innocent of evil purpose they may be as individuals." Nevertheless, the extermination of the Canaanites was clearly an *offensive* action by Israel. Can it be justified? In particular, can God's command to commit genocide be justified?

THE CHEREM PRINCIPLE

The Hebrew word *cherem* comes from a root meaning "to separate" or "to shut off" and is generally translated "accursed" or "devoted" in the major English versions of the Bible. From the same root we get the word *harem* which refers to the women's quarters in an Arab dwelling, which is "separated" or "devoted." In the Bible it refers to that which is taken from men and surrendered to God in an irrevocable and irredeemable manner, viz. human beings by being put to death, cattle and inanimate objects by being either given up to the Temple forever or destroyed for the glory of the Lord. Such as were designated *cherem* were thus under the curse of God and marked for destruction.

Cherem was a most serious act. As Keil and Delitzsch observe,[7] ". . . the vow of banning could only be made in connection with persons who obstinately resisted that sanctification of life which was binding upon them; and that an individual was not at liberty to devote a human being to the ban simply at his own will and pleasure, otherwise the ban might have been abused to purposes of ungodliness. . . . There can be no doubt that the idea which lay at the foundation of the ban

---

[6] Albert C. Knudson, *The Principles of Christian Ethics* (New York: Abingdon, 1943), p. 228.

[7] C. F. Keil and F. Delitzsch, *Biblical Commentary on the Old Testament*, trans. J. A. Martin (2 vols; 6th rev. ed.; Grand Rapids, Mich.: Eerdmans, 1950), II, 484-85.

was that of a complusory dedication of something which resisted or impeded sanctification. . . . It was an act of the judicial holiness of God manifesting itself in righteousness and judgment." The designation is particularly employed by God in pronouncing judgment upon idolatry with its attendent evil practices. Such was the case with the Canaanites who were pronounced under the curse and thus "devoted" to God to be utterly destroyed.[8]

However, this "mark of destruction" was not merely pronounced upon the enemies of Israel. Warnings were given to Israel as well[9] and those threats were carried out. Jericho was pronounced accursed by God,[10] but when Achan took of these "devoted" things, Israel became accursed.[11] So also was the case of King Saul who refused to destroy the best of the things pronounced accursed by God and thus was rejected from being king.[12]

We conclude that the annihilation of the Canaanites was not the product of a war of aggression but the execution of God's judgment in obedience to Him. But can God's judgment upon Canaan be justified?[13] If we have vindicated Israel, what about God Himself?

THE INTRINSIC RIGHTFULNESS OF GOD'S POLICY OF EXTERMINATION

Because God is God He has the inherent right to destroy both nations and individuals. He gives life and He takes it away. Such is the analysis of Job, "The Lord gave, and the Lord has taken away; blessed be the name of the Lord. In all this Job did not sin or charge God with wrong."[14] However we may object to the fact, if God is God He has the inherent right to order the events of the universe as Greene observes, "The right to do involves the right to do deliberately and avowedly."[15]

---

[8] Deut. 7:1-2.
[9] Lev. 18:20-30.
[10] Josh. 6:17-19.
[11] Josh. 7:15, 24-26.
[12] I Sam. 15.
[13] For an excellent treatment of the subject see William Brenton Greene, Jr., "The Ethics of the Old Testament," *The Princeton Theological Review* (July, 1929), pp. 330-37..
[14] Job 1:21-22.
[15] Greene, *op. cit.*, p. 331.

Second, in the case of Canaan, the justice of God is revealed. It must be remembered that according to God's standards the Canaanite nations were a grossly immoral and wicked people. God declared to Israel that He was destroying those nations, not because of righteous merit on the part of Israel, but because of the gross wickedness of the Canaanites.[16] Recent archaeological discovery[17] has brought to light concrete testimony to this wickedness, consisting of unimaginably degenerate forms of polytheism and sexual perversity. Exaltation of public religious prostitution (male and female), public rites of beastiality, and infant sacrifice were common. In the graphic words of Scripture, "The land vomited out its inhabitants.[18]

The Canaanites had received ample warning. Thousands of years prior, Noah had pronounced Canaan, the ancestor of the Canaanites, accursed and the servant of Shem due to the immorality of his father, Ham.[19] Later, in the days of Abraham, judgment had fallen upon Sodom and Gomorrha[20] because of the gross wickedness of the inhabitants, a judgment which served as a warning to the neighboring peoples. God had already promised four generations (i.e., 400 years) for the Amorites to repent because their evil was "not yet complete." [21] Following the Exodus from Egypt forty years elapsed before the start of the conquest of Canaan, ample time for the idolatrous nations to repent (who certainly recognized God's impending judgment, see Joshua 2:8-11). Even the conquest was not a blitzkrieg but "little by little." [22] Still there was no repentance.

Third, it must be understood that God's policy was, in overall perspective, one of mercy and good. Sin is essentially self-centeredness as opposed to God-centeredness. It corrupts and does so gradually. Because of Adam, the first sinner, a curse was pronounced upon the ground;[23] to Cain, the first murderer, there was proclaimed a curse from the ground;[24] by the time of Noah the whole earth was declared "corrupt in

---

[16] Deut. 9:4-5.
[17] Gleason A. Archer, Jr., *A Survey of Old Testament Introduction* (Chicago: Moody, 1964), p. 261.
[18] Lev. 18:25.
[19] Gen. 9:25-26.
[20] Gen. 19.
[21] Gen. 15:13, 16.
[22] Deut. 7:22.
[23] Gen. 3:17.
[24] Gen. 4:11.

God's sight, and . . . filled with violence" [25] and was finally marked for destruction, except for Noah and his family. In order to remove the corrupting influence of gross immorality, lest it spread to all the people, it was necessary at this point to destroy many (who deserved it) to preserve the few through whom God's purposes were being accomplished.

This was particularly true in the case of Israel, the nation established by God as the avenue through which the Messiah would come. They must be kept a separated, distinct, and holy nation. T. B. Maston[26] states, "There was a separation from the peoples of the world, coupled with a separation unto God. The Lord's promise to make Israel 'a people holy to Himself' is conditioned upon their keeping His commandments and walking in His ways (Lev. 28:9). This condition underscores the ethical requirement of holiness. Walking in the ways of God meant the purging of evil from the midst of them.''

It may be objected that this then is a policy of "doing evil that good might come." We reply that the surgeon who amputates a gangrenous limb is not condemned for removing a limb but praised for having saved a body. It is necessary that the rotted flesh be cut off if the patient is to survive; it is unfortunate that the limb must be destroyed. God's course of action is therefore to do ultimate good.

It may still be objected that it is unfair to subject the innocent Canaanite children to such harsh punishment. We can answer such an appeal in two ways. First, God, who is the discerner of the thoughts and intentions of the heart,[27] is also revealed as the righteous Judge.[28] If our earthly life were the totality of our existence, then the death of the innocent would be an unthinkable act for a righteous judge. But if for the righteous, as the Bible claims there is life after death in an existence far superior to the earthly (as Paul claims in Philippians 1:21-23), then death for the innocent is righteous judgment indeed. If, on the other hand, one is irremedially guilty, the judgment is truly just. (Innocence may only be apparent. Modern recognition of the importance of the formative years of childhood seems to suggest that the sins of the parents may be latent very early in their children.)

Second, the death of the innocent in consequence of another's

---

[25] Gen. 6:11.

[26] T. B. Maston, *Biblical Ethics* (Cleveland: World, 1967), p. 30.

[27] Heb. 4:12.

[28] Gen. 18:25, Psalms 98:9.

sin is not without parallel. In the Old Testament economy it was required that an animal without blemish, often a lamb, be offered to God in token payment for sin.[29] The same principle is observed in human experience in that the wrong-doing of one often adversely effects the lives of innocent bystanders.

THE RIGHTFULNESS OF GOD'S METHOD

The annihilation of the vanquished Canaanites was not an unusual act for the period. Greene[30] notes that this was the common practice in war. Snaith[31] reports that the Moabite Stone inscribed by Mesha, king of Moab and contemporary of Ahab[32] states that the altar-hearth of the Lord was "devoted" (cherem) to the Moabite god Chemosh and 7000 captive Israelites slaughtered. Thus God did only what strict justice to them demanded according to the method of the times.

It might be argued that such direction by God could well corrupt the morals of Israel herself. But it need not be so. God is said to be the "discerner of the thoughts and the intentions of the heart" [33] and is thus able to protect his own from evil influences. That this was indeed God's intent is shown by several factors.

Israel was explicitly commanded to carry out this extermination, not from her personal passion or desire, but in obedience to God.[34] She was not left to her own discretion to decide which peoples and goods were to be utterly destroyed. Neither were these wars allowed to serve as precedents for the wanton destruction of foreign nations, for Israel was to treat the visiting stranger as an equal.[35] In no case was war for its own sake encouraged. Thus Israel was taught the extraordinary nature of her mission. And should Israel misunderstand, she was continually reminded of the teaching of God's Law concerning herself. Immediately after the battles of Jericho and Ai, for example, the people were read all the words of the Law, both blessing and curse.[36]

---

[29] Ex. 12:21-27, Lev. 1-7.
[30] Greene, op. cit., p. 334.
[31] Norman H. Snaith, *The Distinctive Ideas of the Old Testament* (London: Epworth, 1944), p. 33.
[32] II Kings 3:1-4.
[33] Heb. 4:12.
[34] Deut. 7:2.
[35] Lev. 19:33-34.
[36] Josh. 8:30-35.

In fact, the use of Israel as the instrument of God's judgment seems perfectly in accord with God's purpose. The command, insofar as obeyed, was just as effective as the forces of nature or disease in annihilating the Canaanites. Its real worth came in the singular impression it made upon Israel of the exceeding sinfulness of idolatry and its attendant vices. W. S. Bruce observes,[37] "Nothing was more fitted to develop in them a deep sense of the heinousness of the sin of a sensual idolatry, and to perpetuate the abhorrence of it among their descendants."

Finally, it is noteworthy that Israel was not the only nation used for such a purifying purpose. God declares that He has raised up one nation and put down another even among the Gentiles.[38]

THE ETHIC OF CHRIST

Space does not permit a full treatment of Jesus' view of war.[39] His view was no doubt in accord with Old Testament principles, however, for He fully accepted the Old Testament. That He accepted the entire list of the O.T. books is clear in His castigation of the Jewish rulers when He prophesied on them "all the righteous blood shed on the earth, from the blood of innocent Abel to the blood of Zechariah the son of Barachiah . . . ."[40] This is equivalent to saying "from Genesis to Chronicles" (the last book of the O.T. according to Hebrew arrangement). That He considered it authoritative and reliable is demonstrated by His frequent use of the Scripture, quoting at random from every representative part, even appealing to the finest detail.[41]

Some, however, have understood an absolute pacifism in Matt. 5:39-40 where Jesus urges "turning the other cheek." But Jesus declared that He came not to destroy the law, but to fulfill it.[42] His teaching emphasized the motive behind the act, illustrating the principle of sacrificial love as the one supreme and comprehensive law of social relationship. Should Jesus' teaching be held to demand absolute pacifism then several

---

[37] W. S. Bruce, *The Ethics of the Old Testament* (Edinburgh: T. & T. Clark, 1909), p. 287.

[38] Cf. Deut. 2, Amos 9:7.

[39] For a helpful discussion, see Murray, *op. cit.*, pp. 114-22, 174-80.

[40] Matt. 23:35.

[41] Matt. 5:17-19.

[42] Matt. 5:17-20.

serious consequences follow: (1) the right of self-defense is denied, (2) the right and duty of physical assistance to the weak who are being unjustly and violently attacked is excluded, and (3) the role of the state in defending itself and its citizens against attack from within or without is in serious doubt. That Jesus did not intend such an interpretation is further evidenced by His life; He did not condemn the state but rather declared its power to be derived from God,[43] and He obeyed its laws without quarrel. The apostles and the early church so interpreted His teaching.[44] Moreover Christ taught that there will be a final destruction by God of those who oppose Him and refuse to commit themselves to Him.[45] The New Testament teaches that God's final interaction with the present world system [46] will be as the God of war who is shown to be none other than Christ Himself! [47]

In reality God's purpose for the earth is peace.[48] Ultimately man will exist in eternal peace and purity with Him.[49]

A FINAL STATEMENT

Thus far we have endeavored to show on a factual, logical basis that there is no true inconsistency between God's command to destroy the Canaanite peoples and His own sovereign morality. The Old Testament writers voiced no such objection. The Sixth Commandment, "Thou shalt not kill," was shown to refer to murder, not capital punishment or war. The *cherem* principle demonstrates that God may pronounce the death sentence upon an individual or nation for gross immorality, the sentence being executed by His followers. Such judgment is proper not only because of His prerogatives as the creator and Governor of the Universe, but also because it is ultimately just and merciful. Furthermore, God's method of using Israel as the executor of His judgment served the double purpose of justice to Canaan and a severe reminder to Israel of the penalty for idolatry. All of this is in harmony with Jesus' own teaching and practice.

---

[43] John 19:11.
[44] Rom. 13:1-3, I Peter 2:13-14.
[45] Matt. 24:29-31, 25:31-46.
[46] Rev. 19:11-21.
[47] Cf. Rev. 19:13 and John 1:1 ff.
[48] Eccl. 9:16, 18, Isaiah 2:4.
[49] Rev. 21:7, 22:3.

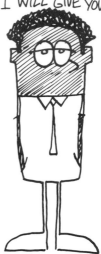

The Black Side of Christianity

Ronald Behm

The Black Man today has every reason to be suspicious of and hostile toward Christianity. The facts of history and of contemporary experience are ample ground for these emotions. In the following pages the attempt will be made to examine three factors contributing to this denigration of Christianity and to ask the truth question in their light.

THE EXPLOITATIVE ACTS OF
WESTERN CULTURE

The first reason for the Black Man's negative attitude toward Christianity, the dominant religious force in Western civilization, is the exploitative acts of Western culture. Both Black and White peoples know it. Richard Wright expresses this acidulously in his appeal, *White Man Listen!*

> Buttressed by their belief that their God had entrusted the earth into their keeping, drunk with power and possibility, waxing rich through trade in commodities, human and non-human, with awesome naval and merchant marines at their disposal, their countries filled with human debris anxious for any adventures, psychologically armed with new facts, White Western Christian civilization during the fourteenth, fifteenth, sixteenth, and seventeenth centuries, with a long, slow, and bloody explosion, hurled itself upon the sprawling masses of colored humanity in Asia and Africa.[1]

"White Western Christian civilization" committed deeds of inhumanity against "the colored humanity in Asia and Africa." The peoples of the non-Western world can produce damning evidence that Western civilization has subjugated, colonized,

---

[1] Richard Wright, *White Man Listen!*, Anchor Books (Garden City, New York: Doubleday, 1964), p. 1.

brutalized and robbed Asian and African peoples. These actions, falsely described as liberating and beneficent, are instead rightly attributed to self-interest. Obviously, the uneducated must be taught to understand whatever you tell them to do; hospitals are required because corpses cannot work for you.

Specifically, we do well to focus on the United States and its people, for in this country, the foremost "Christian" nation of our globe, the racial crisis is most crucial. What happens here affects the world. If this country fails to achieve racial justice and harmony, there is little hope that any other country can so succeed.

The experience of black people in America can be divided into three periods: slavery, segregation, and ghettoization. The slavery period, from 1619 to 1863, ended when Lincoln signed the Emancipation Proclamation; the segregation period, from 1863 to 1914, was for the most part manifested in the South by Jim Crowism; the onset of World War I in 1914 marked the beginning of the final period of ghettoization. From 1914 to the present, blacks from the South have migrated in large numbers to the northern and western cities and have been forced to live in restricted localities with members of their own race. We must now explore what each period of history taught the Black Man about white, "Christian," American society and its human values.

It was not "American ingenuity" which initiated and maintained slavery during the first era. Slavery itself is an ancient institution and the modern slave trade of western civilization finds its origins in the Portuguese who brought "ten Africans from the northern Guinea coast . . . to Portugal as a gift to Prince Henry the Navigator" in 1441.[2] Subsequently, all of the major European countries became involved in promoting the slave trade, each meeting with varying degrees of success. It was England however which came to dominate the slave trade and she was particularly responsible for its institution in her American colonies. To wrest the prime members of society from their culture and language, to separate them from their families, to transport them like animals under debilitating conditions, and to view and treat fellow human beings as unworthy of human respect and dignity was the crime of American slavery.

---

[2] James Pope-Hennessy, *Sins of the Fathers: A Study of the Atlantic Slave Traders, 1441-1807* (New York: Alfred A. Knopf, 1968), p. 8.

The institution of slavery which eventually developed was both tolerated and sanctioned in America; it was the most atrocious form of slavery which the world had ever known.[3] The slaves in America were not given legal rights to marry, to own property or to enter into contracts. There was no provision for the slave to assimilate into free society if he were liberated. The slave was not considered a person with definite human rights. He was a chattel and was so treated and recognized by the United States Supreme Court in 1857. This treatment had its effects on both the oppressors and the oppressed. The institution of slavery was a blatant contradiction of Christian and democratic ideals; only a bloody civil war could destroy it. Hangover conditions of hatred, fear, suspicion and the memories of the oppressed remain until this day.

After the Civil War, the Black man was legally considered a man and a citizen, but his economic, political, social, and educational standings were not greatly improved. It was not long before the progressive elements of the white society, tired of championing the Black man's cause, gave into reactionary discriminators. Because the abolition of slavery found both black and white communities unprepared for a flood of free men, the period following emancipation—a time in which full freedom should have been unreservedly extended to blackmen— was tumultuous. Idealistic reconstruction plans, "with malice toward none" and "charity for all," did not find fulfillment. Thus the period of segregation began "formally" when, in 1877, federal troops withdrew from the South.

The effect was disastrous: the black man was left a ward of the nation, the attempt to guarantee his civil and political equality was abandoned, and the country acquiesced to "the South's demand that the whole problem be left to the disposition of the dominant Southern white people." [4] C. Vann Woodward in his valuable work, *The Strange Career of Jim Crow*, summarizes the results of that surrender:

The segregation statues . . . lent the sanction of law to a racial ostracism that extended to churches and schools, to housing and jobs, to eating and drinking. Whether by law or by custom, that ostracism extended to virtually all forms of public transportation, to sports and recreations, to hospitals, orphanages, prisons and

---

[3] Frank Tannenbaum, *Slaves and Citizens*, Vintage Books (New York: Random House, 1946), pp. 82ff.

[4] C. Vann Woodward, *The Strange Career of Jim Crow*, Galaxy Books (New York: Oxford University Press, 1966), p. 6.

asylums, and ultimately to funeral homes, morgues and cemeteries.[5]

The result of this "separate but equal" code which the Supreme Court of the United States upheld in 1896, was a continuation of inequality of opportunity in all areas of life, a vicious circle which produced continued inequality of skills and abilities. Moreover, the bigoted inhumanity of segregation was enforced by threat and violence and, therefore, took its psychological toll. Blacks were led to believe that they were, in fact, inferior to their white neighbors and unworthy of being treated as human equals.

The third and final period of black history in America is the period of ghettoization. While it is true that some of the damnable features of the earlier period of segregation carry over into the present, the move to the northern and western cities by blacks signified an important change in the relations between blacks and whites. Charles Silberman documents this migration from the South and explains the discrimination and deprivation which resulted from it.[6] Black people who sought a better existence found that equal opportunities in housing, education and employment were also denied them in the North and West. Thus, the racism of white society was manifested in a subtle, institutional form which was necessarily based neither on active hatred nor on geographical location.[7]

THE WHITE INSTITUTIONAL CHURCH

The second factor which fuels the black fire of animosity toward Christianity is the reaction (inaction) of the institutional Christian Church to the crucial issues in each of the three periods of black subordination. During the first period many churches actively supported slavery. Others were simply silent on the issue while practicing discrimination and segregation themselves. The prophetic voice of condemnation, when raised at all, was raised neither consistently nor extensively. The voices of Christian abolitionists went mute as the institution of slavery became more profitable. The churches for the most

---

[5] *Ibid.*

[6] Charles Silberman, *Crisis in Black and White*, Vintage Books (New York: Random House, 1964), pp. 17ff.

[7] Stokely Carmichael and Charles V. Hamilton, *Black Power: The Politics of Liberation in America*, Vintage Books (New York: Random House, 1967), p. 5.

part merely reflected the evils in society and invoked God's approval of the status quo.[8] During the period of segregation the church was again silent. The Jim Crow laws received no forthright rebuke from the Christian community. The desire for peace and rest came before the desire for justice and equality. Until quite recently ghettoization has been unopposed by the Christian church. In fact white church members were primary participants in the great exodus to the suburbs. And then the white churches only supported the recent protest movement of the late Dr. Martin Luther King, Jr., when it became embarrassing for them to continue their traditionalistic non-involvement!

THE BLACK INSTITUTIONAL CHURCH

The third reason for hostility toward the Christian faith by blacks is the intrinsic nature of the Black churches. This is an indisputable fact. Here is a concise summary of the situation:

> As the result of the social forces to which the Negro population was subjected, a separate Negro world had been created in America; and the Negro church was partly the product of this segregated society with a distinctive life of its own. The worship was highly emotional, featuring a variety of liturgical innovations, designed to encourage group participation. The theology was characterized by a strong other worldly emphasis.[9]

Many black people therefore understand the emotional, other worldly emphasis, still prevalent today to be irrelevant and damaging to black people. The white slave owner used "Christianity" to focus the attention of his slaves on "the sweet by and by" and not the bitter here and now. An oft-repeated text was "servants, be obedient to your masters." Today Black Muslims ridicule Dr. King's non-violent, "Christian" approach because it asks the oppressed to love the oppressor and return kindness when he receives hatred, a practice which is said to be contrary to nature. A distinguished black sociologist, the late E. Franklin Frazier, scores the Black church in this

---

[8] H. Shelton Smith, Robert T. Handy, and Lefferts A. Loetscher, *American Christianity: An Historical Interpretation with Representative Documents* (2 vols.; New York: Charles Scribner's Sons, 1963), II, 168ff.

[9] Winthrop S. Hudson, *Religion in America* (New York: Charles Scribner's Sons, 1965), p. 351.

connection. It has, he believes, "cast a shadow over the entire intellectual life of Negroes and [has] been responsible for the so-called backwardness of American Negroes." [10] When the Black church is seen in this light, it is clear that blacks may dismiss the Christian faith with ease.

The exploitative acts of Western culture, the White institutional church and the Black institutional church have created a situation in which the Black Muslim cry has seemingly irresistible force:

> The Christian religion is incompatible with the Negro's aspirations for dignity and equality in America. It has hindered where it might have helped; it has been evasive when it was morally bound to be forthright; it has separated believers on the basis of color although it has declared its mission to be a universal brotherhood under Jesus Christ. Christian love is the white man's love for himself and for his race. For the man who is not white Islam is the hope for justice and equality in the world we must build tomorrow. [11]

Though many militant black spokesmen do not agree that Islam is the hope for justice and equality for blacks, they are nevertheless convinced that Christianity is not the answer. For them, Christianity is part of the problem. [12] But is this exactly true? Do the charges brought against Christianity warrant the conclusion that black Americans need not consider Jesus Christ and His teachings?

A CLOSER ANALYSIS

We have discussed three reasons which support the black case against Christianity. First, white Western Christian civilization in general and American society in particular perpetrated inhuman crimes against black people. Second, white churches themselves failed to take positive moral action in the three periods of black subordination in America. Third, the Christianity expressed by black America is repugnant to today's educated, militant Black.

These arguments are insufficient to prove Jesus Christ

---

[10] E. Franklin Fraizer, *The Negro Church in America* (New York: Schocken, 1964), p. 86.

[11] C. Eric Lincoln, *The Black Muslims* (Boston: Beacon, 1961), p. 111.

[12] *Ibid.*, pp. 68ff.

(who is the true center of Christian faith) unconcerned, irrelevant, meaningless, or damaging to black Americans today. There are additional historical facts which show that the previous analysis, while true, is incomplete. It does not present the total picture.

Not all Christians supported mistreatment of black people; some have consistently and forcefully opposed it. For example, early in America's history individuals within the Quaker movement opposed the institution of slavery.[13] In 1688, at the Monthly Meeting near Philadelphia, an anti-slavery resolution was presented. The Yearly Meeting did not accept the resolution but "the resolution expressed a position which would gradually attract more and more Quakers." Anti-slavery tracts and treatises appeared and an open drive against Quaker slaveholding began. "This crusade, led by Benjamin Lay, John Woolman, and Anthony Benezet, resulted in positive action by the Philadelphia Yearly Meeting in 1758 against both slavetrading and slaveholding by Quakers."[14] Through these efforts, many southern Quakers left the South and migrated into the Northwest Territory to avoid collusion with the sin of slavery.[15] By 1800 American Quakers had virtually ceased to be slaveholders.[16] Some of the Methodists too have a record of anti-slavery action. In 1780, the Baltimore Conference required its travelling preachers to set free the slaves which some held. They also acclaimed that "slave-keeping is contrary to the laws of God, man and nature, and hurtful to society, contrary to the dictates of conscience and pure religion. . . ."[17] Finally it must be noted that many Christians were involved in the abolitionist movement prior to the Civil War. Albert Barnes, an outstanding example, argued on biblical grounds that slavery was wrong and that abolition was the proper goal towards which all Christians should work.[18]

---

[13] Smith, op. cit., pp. 180ff.

[14] Ibid.

[15] William Warren Sweet, Religion in the Development of American Culture: 1765-1840 (New York: Charles Scribner's Sons, 1952), p. 279.

[16] Smith, op. cit., p. 293.

[17] Ibid., p. 465.

[18] Ralph L. Moellering, Christian Conscience and Negro Emancipation (Philadelphia: Fortress, 1965), p. 76ff. Cf. J. Oliver Buswell, III, Slavery, Segregation and Scripture (Grand Rapids, Mich.: Eerdmans, 1964), p. 32ff.

Of course several instances of an anti-slavery attitude manifested by organized churches and individual Christians do not establish that Christians everywhere were opposed to slavery. But they do indicate that at least *some* Christians opposed slavery. It is however impossible today to poll the past to ask what percentage of persons who called themselves Christians were pro-slavery. Furthermore, if we were to analyze other forms of injustice against blacks, such as discrimination in employment, housing, education, or social relations, we would find the same principle to be true: some who call themselves Christians support discrimination, some oppose it and some try to be neutral. It is therefore impossible to say that "Christianity" *corporately* endorsed the crime of slavery or *corporately* endorsed the crimes of discrimination.

This discussion brings us to the key issue: Can the truth of Christianity be determined by the conduct of those who call themselves Christians? Or as C. S. Lewis puts the question, "If Christianity is true, why are not all Christians obviously nicer [or less racist, etc.] than all non-Christians?" [19] There is something which is reasonable and right about that question and there is something which is unreasonable and wrong. Lewis goes on to explain:

> If conversion to Christianity makes no improvement in a man's outward actions—if he continues to be just as snobbish or spiteful or envious or ambitious as he was before—then I think we must suspect that his "conversion" was largely imaginary. . . . In that sense the outer world is quite right to judge Christianity by its results.[20]

This practical test of the reality of Christian conversion is implicit in Christ's words: "Every tree is known by the fruit it bears. . ." (Luke 6:44).

But the question of Christian behavior also has an unreasonable part to it. Not only does the critic demand that there should be improvement in the life of each man who becomes a Christian, but he also demands that the whole world should be neatly divided into two camps—the good Christians and the bad non-Christians. Several considerations make this demand unreasonable. To begin with, the world is not that simple. Each person in our society, in terms of his ethical

---

[19] C. S. Lewis, *Mere Christianity* (New York: Macmillan, 1958), p. 161.
[20] *Ibid.*

behavior, has both Christian and non-Christian influences brought to bear upon him, and he behaves in a way which evidences that fact. When one does become a Christian, Jesus taught that there is a new moral power which produces a change in his life, but that change does not produce immediate perfection. The exhortation to "give yourselves to God, as men *who have been* brought from death to life, and [to] surrender your whole being to him to be used for righteous purposes" (Romans 6:13) can be understood only in this light. Then there are doubtless a great many people who are not Christians in the biblical sense but who still call themselves by the name "Christian"; some perhaps are even clergymen. Finally "there are other people who are slowly becoming Christians though they do not yet call themselves so." [21] The world is therefore too complex and our information too limited to insist upon a neat two-camp division.

When we evaluate individuals, one a Christian and the other not, we must be exceedingly careful. If Christianity is true two things follow: any Christian will be morally better than the same person if he were not a Christian and any person who becomes a Christian will be morally better on the average than he was before. Thus,

> Christian Miss Bates may have an unkinder tongue than unbelieving Dick Firkin. That, by itself, does not tell us whether Christianity works. The question is what Miss Bates' tongue would be like if she weren't a Christian and what Dick's would be like if he became one.[22]

All men, for countless reasons apart from religion, have unique temperaments. The question is not whether Miss Bates is as good as (or better than) Dick Firkin but whether Jesus Christ has made a moral improvement *in her life.* Therefore, we conclude that the failures of Christian churches and individual Christians in their relations with black Americans does not *in itself* prove that the Christian faith is untrue. The failures simply indicate that some "Christians" aren't Christians and some Christians aren't perfect.

Recent studies in prejudice support this conclusion. In summarizing the recent analyses of the relation of religion to prejudice, Simpson and Yinger conclude that religious beliefs, as a variable that makes one more or less prejudice,

---

[21] *Ibid.*
[22] *Ibid.*

are primarily dependent upon factors of personality and temperament and, therefore, taken alone, do not determine a person's level of prejudice.[23] They also conclude that the quality of one's religion is "partly a cultural phenomenon"; the culture itself teaches prejudice, often relating it to religious ideology. A Christian, instead of being controlled by Jesus Christ, may be irresistibly influenced by his personal psychological development and by his culture. These primary factors then, direct him to act against his underlying religious belief and, in this case, to discriminate against black people.

Hence the truth of Christianity cannot be determined by its sociological expression in history or at present. Though ample ground for suspicion and hostility has been mapped, non-Christian black men and white men must ask the elemental question: What is true Christianity and how do I know it is true? For centuries Christians have maintained that the basis of their faith is found in the documents of the New Testament; it is clear that we must now turn our attention to the sources of the Christian faith to discover its true and original form. In so doing it is reasonable and proper to ask if "the Book" of Jesus Christ has anything relevant to say to blacks today?

The New Testament teaches that the central figure of the Christian faith was an individual who lived above the prejudices and hatreds of his society. Jesus Christ, the self-confessed God-Man, was a Jew—a member of a nation which was persecuted and sub-ordinated by Roman society. Many of the Jewish people transferred this "racial" hatred by discriminating against the half-Jewish Samaritans and all other non-Jews. The fourth chapter of the Gospel of John shows that Jesus respected an immoral Samaritan woman as a person who deserved human dignity. One of his famous parables, a damning criticism of Jewish bigotry, was the story of the Good Samaritan recorded in the tenth chapter of Luke. Jesus healed even Gentiles who were in need and commended those who had faith in Him regardless of their race or nationality.[24]

The New Testament as the source of Christian doctrine also teaches that Jesus' purpose in becoming man was to die

---

[23] George Eaton Simpson and J. Milton Yinger, *Racial and Cultural Minorities* (3rd ed.; New York: Harper & Row, 1965), p. 399.

[24] Mark 5, Matthew 8, et al.

for the selfishness, bigotry, discrimination, inhumanity and rebellion of *all* men who would put their trust in Him, regardless of their economic, political, social, or racial status. He said, "he came to serve and to give his life to redeem many people" (Mark 10:45). And that those people were to be from all nations of the world is clear from His command to His apostles to "Go, then, to all peoples everywhere and make them my disciples. . ." (Matthew 28:19). The entire New Testament is in harmony with this theme when it describes the people who have come to believe in Jesus as a fellowship in which racial and social differences are of no importance: "So there is no difference between Jews and Gentiles, between slaves and free men, between men and women: You are all one in union with Christ Jesus" (Galatians 3:28). The warring Jews and Gentiles were reconciled under God through their common faith in Jesus Christ as Lord and Savior (Ephesians 2). In fact, the group of those who believed in Jesus are at the last judgment represented as coming from "every nation, tribe, people, and language" (Revelation 7:9). Therefore the original form of Christian faith—the true Christianity of Jesus and his disciples—shows God's concern for all people and races. The meek and mild, white, Nordic Jesus is a phony! Jesus is not the God of white people; He is the God of the universe and He died a death for men of all races.

The Bible also teaches that God is the Creator of all men in that all men derive from an original pair created by God. All men are equally made in His image. Humanity is thus a unity: the external differences God has allowed to exist between men do not mean that He treats dissimilars unequally. Peter realized the truth that "God treats all men alike. Whoever fears him and does what is right is acceptable to him, no matter what race he belongs to" (Acts 10:34, 35). But only in a personal connection with God does man find full dignity; we may be eternally grateful that God fully accepts *any* man who comes to Him in trust and in obedience to His will.

Finally the Bible does *not* teach that there is a curse upon black people which relegates them to an inferior biological or social status. This fact must be underscored because in both black and white communities the question still occasionally arises. Such a doctrine of racial discrimination is the product of racist thinking which perverts the Bible, twisting it to say what the racist wants to read. Charles Silberman in *Crisis in Black and White*, conclusively refutes this gross misinterpretation.[25]

The relevance of these Biblical teachings to the needs of black and white people in racial tension has been evidenced in the lives of many people. John Newton, a white, lived in England during the slavetrading days. Born in 1725, his early life was one of rebellion and debauchery. At the age of twenty-three while sailing back from Africa to England, he was converted from free-thinking to Christianity. Two laters later, when captain of a slavetrading ship, he wrote that "the slave trade was not only respectable, but seemed indispensable to English prosperity. Slavery was accepted generally without question." [26] Yet it was not long before God brought him to see that his occupation was incompatible with his Christian faith. Later in life he wrote, "I think I should have quitted it [the slavetrade] sooner had I considered it as I now do to be unlawful and wrong." [27] This Christian man was influential in convincing William Wilberforce of the morality of abolition. Newton testified "against the trade to the Privy Council in 1784 and in 1790 to a Committee of the House of Commons." In an anti-slavery tract, he wrote, "I hope it will always be a subject of humiliating reflection to me, that I was once an active instrument in a business at which my heart now shudders." [28] Today, Tom Skinner, a black man, has, like John Newton, experienced the power of God in his life through trust in Jesus Christ. Skinner writes that

> for the first time in my life ... I have dignity. For the first time I have a sense of being. I have a sense of being someone. I don't have to struggle for human dignity ... I *am*, present tense, a son of God.[29]

He preaches the good news of Jesus Christ within the context of the Black Power Movement. He believes the black man's struggle for social, political, and economic equality in our republic is just and valid. He recognizes the need for black pride and black solidarity and believes that this can only come through a genuine acceptance of Jesus Christ. This relationship with

---

[25] Silberman, *op. cit.*, pp. 172ff.

[26] Bernard Martin and Spurrell Mark, ed., *The Journal of a Slave Trader: (John Newton) 1725-1807* (London: Epworth Press, 1962), p. xi.

[27] *Ibid.*, p. xii.

[28] *Ibid.*, p. 98.

[29] Tom Skinner, *Black and Free* (Grand Rapids, Mich.: Zondervan, 1968), p. 150.

Jesus Christ which he has also affects his attitude toward whites. To them Tom Skinner says, "All I know is that Jesus Christ is alive and in me, and because He is living in me, the love of God is actually springing up within my soul. All I ask for is the privilege to love you." [30]

Far from being irrelevant to racial hatred, damaging to self-pride, and meaningless to our society of discrimination, mistrust, and misunderstanding, the person of Jesus Christ, the center of Christian faith and the touchstone of Christian teaching is the sole answer to these problems. There is a "black side" of Christianity as practiced, but in Jesus Christ the Black side of Christianity—the aspect uniquely relevant to the situation of the Black man—is clearly revealed.

---

[30] *Ibid.*, p. 151.

From the Great Refusal to the Great Affirmation:
A Christian Comment on Herbert Marcuse

Gregory Best

Herbert Marcuse—a pleasant old professor castigated by conservatives, denounced by *Pravda*, feared by liberals, and revered by the New Left—is often criticized by serious philosophers for his irrationality and unfounded assertions. Many books and articles are devoted to showing that Marcuse-the-philosopher is second-rate.

There is, however, another Marcuse. Robert Marks observes, "Marcuse is in essence a poet, rebelling against a world unsatisfactory for the spirit..." [1]; as poet he speaks that which is written on the hearts of university students in Tokyo, Prague, Paris, and Palo Alto. My paper concerns this latter Marcuse, Marcuse-the-poet. It is not my intention to demolish his arguments so that snug and secure Christians may ignore his conclusions; "from the fact that Marcuse tends to substitute assertion for argument and to offer no reason for believing what he says is true, it does not follow that what he says is false." [2] Instead, I address my fellow students who sense what Marcuse senses and recognize value in his (perhaps undemonstrated) conclusions, and attempt to show that the Christian faith offers the most complete analysis of and the best alternatives to a one-dimensional society.

MARCUSE'S THESES

Marcuse's view of man and society is based on Marx and Freud. With Marx he holds that the causes of man's history

---

[1] Robert W. Marks, *The Meaning of Marcuse* (New York: Ballantine Books, 1970), p. 58.

[2] Alasdair MacIntyre, *Herbert Marcuse: An Exposition and a Polemic* (New York: Viking Press, 1970), p. 14.

of domination are economic-political,[3] but that this domination functions through the mechanics of surplus repression. A certain amount of repression of the pleasure principle (immediate gratification) is necessary for man's very survival, but today society is overloaded with surplus repression—restrictions on behavior beyond those necessary for the perpetuation of the race.[4] Repression paid off well in allowing the development of civilization, but culture has its negative aspects: concentration camps and atom bombs are the outgrowth of civilization at its highest;[5] "the most effective subjugation and destruction of man by man takes place at the height of civilization, when the material and intellectual attainments of mankind seem to allow the creation of a truly free world."[6]

While resting on these Marxist and Freudian positions, Marcuse's thought operates entirely through the Hegelian dialectic. Thus, "reality" is a cognitive construct, a creation of Reason rather than that which is,[7] and a *thing* (rather than a proposition) is *true* only if it fulfills the potentialities inherent in its reality.[8] In the two-dimensional world of thesis and antithesis (or negation), change comes as a synthesis of the contradictions. "Dialectical logic . . . denies the concreteness of immediate experience. To the extent to which this experience comes to rest with the things as they appear and happen to be, it is a limited and even false experience."[9] The duty of the dialectic is to recognize the disparity between what is and what should be, and then to guide the thinking subject to the goal it understands.[10] *One-Dimensional Man* comes as a critique of a society that has lost the dialectic (in both thought and action) by eliminating its negation.

In *One-Dimensional Man*, Marcuse agrees with Marx that the negation inherent in society normally would be the proletariat. However, the Marxist predictions never came to fruition, and in the advanced capitalistic nations of the West, the workers ally *with* the status quo *against* turbulent change. Mar-

---

[3] Herbert Marcuse, *An Essay on Liberation* (Boston: Beacon Press, 1969), p. 25.

[4] Marks, *op. cit.*, p. 45.

[5] *Ibid.*, p. 42.

[6] Herbert Marcuse, *Eros and Civilization* (Boston: Beacon Press, 1955), p. 4.

[7] Marks, *op. cit.*, p. 23.

[8] *Ibid.*, pp. 27-28.

[9] Herbert Marcuse, *One-Dimensional Man* (Boston: Beacon Press, 1964), p. 141.

[10] Marks, *op. cit.*, p. 20.

cuse attributes this proletarian passivity to society's ability to control men's needs and aspirations.[11]

For man to be free, Marcuse asserts, his true needs must be met. Primary among these are the needs for food, shelter, and basic goods, and traditionally the struggle to obtain these has left man without the time to meet other needs. "Non-repressive order becomes possible only at the highest maturity of civilization, when all basic needs can be satisifed with a minimum expenditure of physical and mental energy in a minimum of time. . . . Freedom is not within but outside 'the struggle for existence.' " [12]

But the advance of technology does not by itself bring freedom.[13] Though basic needs have been met, one-dimensional society burdens a man with a plethora of *false needs*—needs for material goods "gratified at the expense of his and others' needs for liberty and other such goods," [14] needs for massive consumption of soon obsolete commodities. Marcuse assumes that these false needs are instilled in a man totally through socialization (throughout his life), that the mass media and advertising methods completely dictate a man's wants. Once society has told a man what he wants, it achieves domination by filling these false needs; the mass media and the narrowing of the consumption gap have brought the workers under control.[15] "The result is euphoria in unhappiness. Most of the prevailing needs to relax, to have fun, to behave and consume in accordance with the advertisements, to love and hate what others love and hate, belong to this category of false needs." [16]

Hence, the society achieves the domination of man by its unprecedented power to produce that which it can make him want. This power is so great that man can safely be allowed a large measure of (supposed) civil liberties (in the Western nations); the media and the very structure of our journalistic language preclude his thinking in certain categories and train him not to ask certain questions.[17] Thus, the free societies are in reality unfree, and we live under domination in the guise of wealth and liberty.

[11] Marcuse, *One-Dimensional Man*, p. xv.
[12] Marcuse, *Eros and Civilization*, pp. 177-78.
[13] Marcuse, *One-Dimensional Man*, p. 230.
[14] MacIntyre, *op. cit.*, p. 72.
[15] Marcuse, *Essay on Liberation*, pp. 15-16.
[16] Marcuse, *One-Dimensional Man*, p. 5.
[17] *Ibid.*, p. 95.

As *One Dimensional Man* went to press in 1964, Marcuse was pessimistic about the emergence of alternatives to our advanced capitalist society. The power of domination was strong, society precluded its negation, and forces of opposition were nearly mute. But with the publication of *An Essay on Liberation* in 1969, Marcuse's poetry turned bright, for though the chances for liberation were still slim, there now was at least some hope. The intervening half-decade had seen the struggle of the National Liberation Front, Mao's Cultural Revolution, the student-worker strike in France, and uprisings on university campuses throughout the world. Rising to eloquence, Marcuse writes, "the revolt against the old societies is truly international: the emergence of a new, spontaneous solidarity. This struggle is a far cry from the ideal of humanism and humanitas; it is the struggle for life—life not as masters and not as slaves, but as men and women." [18]

In *Essay on Liberation*, Marcuse turns to the biological needs of man. Alasdair MacIntyre accusingly notes, "His biology is in fact as speculative as his metaphysics, and Marcuse explicitly disavows any scientific basis for his speculations. This does not, however, lead him to be less dogmatic in his mode of assertion." [19] This is unfair, for Marcuse has simply engaged in his old practice of giving common words esoteric meanings. When he speaks of needs that are "biological," he really means needs that have been socialized into the "instincts" and reactions of a man.

To be liberated, man will have to eliminate the false needs from his biological makeup, for the domination goes deep.[20] The "voluntary servitude" men have accepted "can be broken only through a political practice which reaches the roots of containment and contentment in the *infrastructure of man* . . . aiming at a radical transvaluation of values" [21] (italics mine). In the new society of true needs, the cult of beauty will be the essence of freedom and the aesthetic dimension the standard of life;[22] no longer will the demands of a class society repress the free play of imagination.

To usher in this new society there must be a revolution that ruptures "the self-propelling continuum of needs" based in the

---

[18] MacIntyre, *op. cit.*, p. 70.
[19] *Ibid.*, p. 100.
[20] Marcuse, *Essay on Liberation*, p. 17.
[21] *Ibid.*, p. 6.
[22] *Ibid.*, p. 27.

present economic-political system.[23] However, economic-political changes will succeed only "if carried through by men who are physiologically and psychologically able to experience things, and each other, outside the context of violence and exploitation." [24] The vanguard of the new society must already have attained the new sensibility. "Understanding, tenderness toward each other, the instinctual consciousness of that which is evil, false, the heritage of oppression, would then testify to the authenticity of the rebellion." [25] The needs of the new society must be the needs of those who fight for it, the needs of a new kind of man. This change in consciousness must precede the change in action.[26]

"Political radicalism thus implies moral radicalism: the emergence of a morality which might pre-condition man for freedom," [27] and the new sensibility will break the chain of guilt that linked generations. The past will not be redeemed, but neither will it be repeated,[28] once the men of new sensibility are in control.

The practical import of Marcuse's theses is that before there can be liberation, there must be men with new values, men without false needs. Though Marcuse would prefer not to put it in quite these terms, the search is on for a vanguard of philosopher-kings.

THE CHRISTIAN VIEW

"All liberation depends on the consciousness of servitude," [29] says Marcuse, and the Christian must agree; but according to the Christian position, Marcuse has failed to note the most pervasive servitude, the strongest bondage. He states that guilt feelings constitute another order of domination,[30] but fails to note that true, objective guilt, not just guilt feelings, is the real source of this domination.

Marcuse's assumption is that a man is born a *tabula rasa* and his needs and instincts are shaped by socialization and economic-political demands;[31] from this milieu he acquires

---

[23] *Ibid.*, pp. 18-19.
[24] *Ibid.*, p. 25.
[25] *Ibid.*, pp. 88-89.
[26] *Ibid.*, p. 53.
[27] *Ibid.*, p. 10.
[28] *Ibid.*, pp. 24-25.
[29] Marcuse, *One-Dimensional Man*, p. 7.
[30] Marks, *op. cit.*, pp. 44-45.
[31] Marcuse, *One-Dimensional Man*, p. 5.

false needs. The Christian doctrine of sin, in contrast, asserts that most false needs are already inherent within the man at his birth. What Marcuse calls the "second nature of man"—the false needs in his biological makeup—the Christian identifies as the genuine, sinful nature of man. When Marcuse states that the innate drive to counter aggressiveness is "an instinctual foundation for solidarity among human beings," [32] the Christian counters that the innate drive toward pride, jealousy, and greed is the instinctual foundation for strife among human beings.

The Christian will certainly not disagree *a priori* with Marcuse's analysis of a one-dimensional language structure, of surplus repression, or of advertising that promotes wasteful over-consumption, but will go beyond Marcuse by identifying the root cause as man's sin; false needs (marked by greed and selfishness) predate advanced capitalistic society! Though the economic-political system desperately needs changing, to change a man's needs and sensibility you must ultimately change his relationship to God.

Marcuse recognized the political implications of morality. "In the face of an amoral society, it becomes a political weapon, an effective force which drives people to burn their draft cards . . . to unfold signs saying, 'Thou shalt not kill,' in the nation's churches." [33] However, Marcuse never identifies the *content* of the requisite new morality, never says on what it is to be based. We need a new sensibility somehow connected with aesthetics, he asserts, but he tells us no more. The principles of Christian morality, in contrast, are explicitly stated in Scripture; those with political implications include the injunctions to love one's neighbor as oneself,[34] to feed the hungry, clothe the naked, and care for the sick,[35] to obey God before men, to seek the righteousness of the Kingdom of God and not be concerned with the overconsumption of food and clothes,[36] to be peacemakers,[37] to defend the poor and fatherless and do justice to the afflicted and needy,[38] etc.

The Christian position contrasts with Marcuse's not only by giving a deeper analysis of the problem and a content to

---

[32] Marcuse, *Essay on Liberation*. p. 10.
[33] *Ibid.*, p. 8.
[34] Matthew 22:39.
[35] Matthew 25:34-46.
[36] Matthew 6:31-34.
[37] Matthew 5:9.
[38] Psalm 82:3.

morality (with its political repercussions), but by offering the *ability* to realize the new sensibility. Marcuse rightly states that understanding, tenderness, and an instinctual revulsion to evil and oppression are to be the marks of the new men,[39] but never says how this can be achieved; even a cursory look at the New Left finds this new sensibility often sadly lacking there. In contrast, the Christian faith promises that as a man defers to the dynamic influence of God in his life, he will begin to exhibit the qualities of love, joy, peace, patience, kindness, goodness, faithfulness, gentleness, and self-control.[40] The "Christian sensibility" is not an undefined Marcusean mindset, but an explicit standard that is in practice approached asymptotically through the action of God in eliminating false needs.

To recapitulate briefly, Marcuse concludes that the only hope of rescuing a one-dimensional society lies in a vanguard of men with new values, with a new sensibility; however, he gives no guidelines for the development of this new sensibility. The Christian faith goes beyond Marcuse in identifying man's sinful nature as the ultimate cause preventing the emergence of a new sensibility, and claims to be able to set men free, to give them the *ability* to live by new values.

THE TRUTH OF THE ALTERNATIVES

The question then arises: which (if either) view is *true*? Marcuse writes that all propositions claiming truth must be verifiable,[41] yet he fails his own test by leaving many assertions unfounded, and grounding many others in dubious arguments. Most important are his Marxist-Freudian presuppositions concerning man. He ignores all religious aspects of human nature, and assumes that man's instincts are formed almost entirely by environment and socialization—false needs are learned. In contrast, the Christian view says that man's sinful nature is "congenital," and that man's relationship to God is the overriding factor in his well-being.

How do we choose? Many will consider it a self-evident truth that man is sinful, but some do not. Social science cannot be the arbiter, for social scientists disagree among themselves on issues of heredity vs. environment, and much (if not most) work done in the social sciences includes unrecognized presuppositions concerning the nature of man. Since Marcuse de-

---

[39] Marcuse, *Essay on Liberation*, pp. 88-89.
[40] Galatians 5:22-23.
[41] Marcuse, *One-Dimensional Man*, p. 230.

faults in offering evidence for his assumptions, we turn to the evidence for the truth of the Christian system.

The veracity of the Christian faith rests squarely on the deity and authority of Jesus of Nazareth; and His claims to divinity may be verified by his death and return to life. There is solid evidence for the Resurrection. Though some make dubious attempts to assail the record of the events connected with it, the New Testament documents remain among the most reliable historical literature of the ancient world. Hence, our knowledge of the death and resurrection of Christ is extremely reliable, and our confidence in his authority to pronounce on man's needs and their solution is well-founded.

The Christian can go *beyond* Marcuse in a critique of advanced technological society because (1) the Christian message is grounded in history and objective reality; (2) its analysis of man's nature rests on the word of the God-man Jesus Christ and thus penetrates deeper than Marcuse's Marxist-Freudian presuppositions; (3) while Marcuse writes poetically about a new sensibility, the Christian faith offers a means for its realization— a personal relationship with Jesus the Christ and the reworking of one's values and false needs under the influence of God.

In *Essay on Liberation*, Marcuse writes that the men of the new sensibility will usually be defeated in challenging the Establishment—in fighting the brave new world—but that they must challenge it nonetheless, to weaken and expose it.[42] This is true for the Christians as well. It is doubtful that men of the Christian consciousness will prevail against the established order of sin and false needs, but they must constantly expose and subvert the false order—they must be leaders in the Great Refusal. And first of all they must be men of personal liberation, men who live the new sensibility and the new values, men who go beyond the Great Refusal to the Great Affirmation of Jesus as Leader and Liberator.

> And do not be conformed to this world, but be transformed by the renewing of your mind.[43]
>
> —Paul

---

[42] Marcuse, *Essay on Liberation*, p. 68.

[43] Romans 12:2a (New American Standard Bible).

Part Three

RELIGION AND TRUTH

The Inadequacies of the Structural-Functionalist Approach to Religion

Bruce Bonecutter

Since its birth as a distinct social science, anthropology has been interested in the study of religion from both the descriptive, ethnographic and the theoretical, explanatory points of view. Early theoretical anthropological writers such as Edward B. Taylor and Wilhelm Schmidt [1] sought the explanation for this human phenomenon by trying to discover its origins. Their approach was partly historical and partly ethnographic, assuming "primitive religions" to be historically primary. More recent anthropologists have, however, given up on this approach and have turned to the structural-functional approach, investigating religion not in a time perspective but in a social-psychological perspective. It is on this approach that this essay centers.

The structural-functional approach is most often encountered in popularist writings: Eric Hoffer's *True Believer*—a working man's philosophical approach, Desmond Morris's *Naked Ape* and *Human Zoo*—an evolutionary biological approach, Konrad Lorenz's *On Aggression*—a blend of biological, sociological and psychological approaches, and the various writings of Sigmund Freud and other psychoanalysts on the subject of religion. The central thesis of these writings is that Christianity or any other religion is best explained naturalistically as offering various functional and structural values to man and society. However, we shall turn to the more scientifically rigorous proponents of this view.

It should be pointed out that the structural-functional approach is not really new; in fact Radcliffe-Brown, a professor

---

[1] Edward B. Taylor, "Animism," and Wilhelm Schmidt, "The Nature, Attributes and Worship of the Primitive High God," in *Reader in Comparative Religion*, ed. by William Lessa and Evon Z. Vogt (New York: Harper & Row, 1965), pp. 10-21 (hereafter referred to as *Comparative Religion*, ed. by Lessa & Vogt.)

emeritus at Oxford, claims that Confucius and Hsun Tzü had adopted it.[2] Yet, its historical roots properly derive from the writings of Fustel De Coulenges, Charles Darwin, Karl Marx, Emile Durkheim and Max Weber.[3] Though structural-functionalism is indeed a mixed bag of various theories its theoretical explanations pertaining to religion may be divided into three main categories: psychological, sociological and logical.

The psychological argument asserts that ". . . the religious urge appears to be a primitive tendency, possessing biological survival value, to unify our environment so that we can cope with it."[4] This explanation says that for a religion to flourish it must bring reward to the lives of participating individuals. If you buy the evolutionary argument, Lorenz asserts that this urge may even have its roots in man's very biological-animal inheritance.[5] The explanation is most alluring intuitively for we are all, if honest, willing to admit to many superstitious rituals which help settle us psychologically. Even the religion of "scientism" is clearly related to the obsessive-compulsive neurosis which underlies all organized thought.

Talcott Parsons delineates two kinds of events in man's life to which he cannot remain emotionally indifferent, events which he cannot control through the normal behavior of everyday life. These events are the sources of frustration that give rise to religion. (1) Men are "hit" by mortal circumstances they cannot foresee, such as a premature death; (2) Men are also frustrated in a situation where there is a strong emotional investment, such as in war, agriculture or a business venture.[6] Primary among the "hit" type events is the fact that all men know

---

[2] A. R. Radcliffe-Brown, *Structure and Function in Primitive Society* (Glencoe, Illinois: The Free Press, 1952), p. 157.

[3] Particularly Max Weber's *The Sociology of Religion* (Boston: Beacon Press, 1963), recently resurrected and reverenced as one of the seminal works leading to the birth of the scientific study of religion.

[4] Hoagland (no reference given) as quoted by Clyde Kluckhohn "Myths and Rituals: A General Theory," in *Comparative Religion*, ed. by Lessa & Vogt, p. 158.

[5] Konrad Lorenz gives examples of animal rituals and even his pet goose's idiosyncratic superstitions in the early part of his chapter, "Habit, Ritual and Magic," in *On Aggression*, trans. by Majorie Kerr Wilson (London: 1966), pp. 54-81.

[6] Talcott Parsons, "Religious Perspectives in Sociology and Social Psychology," in *Comparative Religion*, ed. by Lessa & Vogt, pp. 128-133.

that they have to die but do not know *when* they must die. Radcliffe-Brown asserts that funeral rites and mythology[7] are more for the living than for the dead in that they promise some form of immortality thus consoling the bereaved and urging the community involved to bear their burdens courageously in this life in hope of that which is beyond.[8] The unsettling problem of evil is also explained. Why do the good die young and the wicked flourish like green trees? Religion provides the answer, i.e. the book of Job. These "hit" events needn't be bad or evil experiences but may be unexpected good fortune which requires psychological adjustment for the individuals involved as in the American mythology and ritual surrounding "Thanksgiving."

As to the longer term "emotional investment" events, Malinowski points out that men never rely on religion exclusively but do all that they know to do scientifically and use religion to assure the desired result.[9] Man plants the seed, fertilizes, irrigates and cultivates as best he can and then relies on religion to secure the harvest. Religion relieves man's strain of uncertainty. It enables him to face life with its difficulties and insecurities in the confidence that there are powers, forces and events on which he can rely even though he must submit to their supernatural regulation. Myth gives something to hold on to. Thus a Christian can better face the reverses of his plans when he hears the words, "Lift up your hearts."

Konrad Lorenz finds two other psychological functions of religion: (1) channeling aggression and other emotions, and (2) forming a bond between two or more individuals.[10] The first of these functions may readily be observed not only in primitive dances but also in Christian liturgy. The second shades off into the sociological function which will be taken up next. Lorenz sums up a general law of structural-functionalism when he states that:

> it is in their character of independent motivating factors that rituals transcend their original function of communication and become also able to perform their equally important secondary tasks of controlling aggression and

---

[7] I use the term "mythology" in the modern sense referring to any religious teachings.

[8] Radcliffe-Brown, *op. cit.*, pp. 153-178.

[9] Bronislaw Malinowski, "The Role of Magic and Religion" in *Comparative Religion*, ed. by Lessa & Vogt, pp. 102-112.

of forming a bond between certain individuals.[11]

This stress on the secondary tasks is common to the structural-functional approaches.

The structural-functionalists also assert that as religion has a psychological function it also has an important sociological one. Radcliffe-Brown's theory of the social function of rites, which he developed from his field work with the Andumen Islanders, goes as follows:

> an orderly social life amongst human beings depends on the presence in the minds of the members of a society of certain sentiments, which control the behavior of the individual in his relation to others. Rites can be seen to be the regulated symbolic expressions of certain sentiments.[12]

Ritual and myth teach the good and the bad early in life. That is, belief in God and country goes right along with toilet training. Religion, then, is most functional to a society. Most often listed functions include: (1) its use to restore equilibrium in a society after a crisis or disturbance, (2) marking "les rites de passage" as important events as well as reducing some of the anxiety surrounding them,[13] (3) creating a cosmic police force for enforcing societal rules, and (4) stirring up moral courage and national unity in a time of war.[14] The list of functions could go on and on since the general function is the same but the specific function depends on particular needs of individuals and societies. For example, the difference in Hebrew and Mesopotamian religions can be partly explained in terms of differing geographic-ecological settings.[15]

---

[10] Lorenz, *op. cit.*, p. 74.

[11] *Ibid.*

[12] Radcliffe-Brown, *op. cit.*, p. 157.

[13] To what extent does it create anxiety by making a great "to do" and what extent does it alleviate anxiety? See Bronislaw Malinowski, "The Role of Magic and Religion," A. R. Radcliffe-Brown, "Taboo," and George C. Homans, "Anxiety and Ritual: The Theories of Malinowski and Radcliffe-Brown," in *Comparative Religion*, ed. by Lessa & Vogt, pp. 102-128.

[14] This is an accusation thrown out at all "true believers." Note, for example, ex-Beatle John Lennon's recent hit, "Imagine," in which one of the requirements for his imagined peaceful world is *no religion*.

[15] H. and H. A. Frankfort, "Interrelations Between Religion and Nature in the Ancient Near East," in *Comparative Religion*, ed. by Lessa & Vogt, pp. 488-494.

The structural-functionalists do not make the mistake of Fustel De Coulanges in his work *La Cité Antiqué* by positing a causal relation between a religion and the society espousing it. Radcliffe-Brown and his followers hold to the view that these factors change together and are mutually influential but not strictly causal.

Structional-functional theory seeks to test its theories against ethnographic research. Radcliffe-Brown tests his basic theory against ethnographic data dealing with ancestor worship and totemism and finds that both serve to strengthen the sentiments on which the social order depends. However, he urges further research while holding that his views are in the "most likely" category.

In addition to religion's function of answering ultimate questions, institutionalizing moral values and regulating moral conduct it also has the function of symbolic expression. On this subject the leading theoreticians are Claude Lévi-Strauss and Edmund Leach. For Lévi-Strauss the basic function of religious myth is to furnish a culture with a "logical" model by means of which the human mind can evade unwelcome contradictions. Lévi-Strauss and Leach demonstrate this by applying their method to several myths, such as the Greek Oedipus myth, the Zuni emergence myth and the Judeo-Christian genesis myth.[16] They divide the myth into the shortest possible sentences. These units are then arranged and plotted into a pattern as in an orchestra score. Their meaning, Lévi-Strauss asserts, comes from the context of the myth itself but must be pulled out by this process of isolating elements and determining their relations. This analysis may even be done by computers. Lévi-Strauss and his disciple, Leach, find that myth almost universally displays the dialectic process of explaining contradictions (Marxian term) and contraries (Hegelian term). This is not surprising in light of Lévi-Strauss' own admission:

> I am a transcendental materialist because I do not regard dialectical reason as *something other than* analytical reason, upon which the absolute originality of a human order would be based, but as *something additional* in analytical reason: the necessary condition for it to

---

[16] Claude Lévi-Strauss, "The Structural Study of Myth" and Edmund Leach, "Lévi-Strauss in the Garden of Eden: An Examination of Some Recent Developments in the Analysis of Myth," in *Comparative Religion*, ed. by Lessa & Vogt, pp. 561-581.

venture to undertake the resolution of the human into the non-human.[17]

Of the three structural-functionalist explanations of religious phenomena this latter "logical" method seems to be the poorest. K.O.L. Burridge gives a more than adequate critique of Lévi-Strauss in his article "Lévi-Strauss and Myth." [18] Burridge's first criticism, and one which must strike any thoughtful reader of Lévi-Strauss with great force, is the fact that he has a neat system but a very closed one. There is no attempt to anchor his theory in what might be called empirical reality as in the social and psychological regions of structural functionalism. Lévi-Strauss deals at the level of linguistic analysis which is indeed rigorous but admits to studying a closed system. If one accepts Lévi-Strauss's theory that the purpose of myth is to provide a logical model capable of overcoming a contradiction then, since he offers no outside evidence, and since all myth tellings in fact present an audience with quasi-concrete situations it is just as valid to assert that myths provide concrete situations capable of overcoming logical contradictions. Lévi-Strauss's position is of the kind which asks whether "the purpose of the skull is to keep the ears apart, or whether the ears are separated in order to allow for the skull." [19] Lévi-Strauss thus explains everything and really nothing. Field work, the raw data of anthropology, can neither validate nor invalidate his theory. It is perfectly self-explanatory. "Like the children who followed the pied piper, once caught by the jigging beat of binary oppositions, enthusiasts jump for joy, not caring whether their next meal is raw or cooked." [20] Burridge also criticizes Lévi-Strauss for trying to mix or equate Hegel's "contraries" and Marx's "contradictions."

Lévi-Strauss tries to view myth as a "thing in itself" with no relation to its historical validity or its cultural explanation. His theory has value in the linguistic or literary sense but is not, as has already been pointed out, verifiable in the real world. One also suspects that Lévi-Strauss and Leach could

---

[17] Claude Lévi-Strauss, *The Savage Mind*, trans. by George Weidenfeld and Nicolson Ltd. (Chicago: University of Chicago Press, 1966), p. 246.

[18] K. O. L. Burridge, "Lévi-Strauss and Myth," in *The Structural Study of Myth and Totemism*, ed by Edmund Leach (London: Travistock Publications—ASA series, 1967), pp. 91-115.

[19] *Ibid.*, p. 112.

[20] *Ibid.*, p. 113.

pull many more sorts of contradictions from the myths they analyze, in fact almost an infinite number. "If the purpose of myth is to overcome a real contradiction, and one has particular kinds of contradictions in mind, then it will no doubt be possible to find these contradictions and there are few purposes a myth will not adequately serve." [21] Like run-away Freudians who sexually symbolize everything, Lévi-Strauss and Leach "dialecticalize" everything by choosing subjectively determined "elements" from a myth and viewing them in various dialectical schemata. The fact that computers may be used does not authenticate the technique. If one were to apply Lévi-Strauss' method to his own writings breaking his sentences into small unit sentences and then asking a computer to compute all possible relations along a dialectical formula there would be quite a few interpretations of Lévi-Strauss's mythology-mythology.

The interpretations which these "logical" structural-functionalists generate are most interesting, especially Leach's genesis analysis,[22] but they violate a cardinal principle of textual criticism and anthropology by ignoring the myth's own manifest interpretation and the interpretation of the primary group or the group espousing the myth.[23] When interpreting the Biblical "myth of genesis" one should therefore consider the immediate text's own interpretation, the author's own views on his subject and the views of later writers and "believers" who followed in the same cultural tradition.

As for the psychological and sociological categories of the structural-functionalist position there is, in one sense, no real conflict between Christianity and their findings. In fact, some of their findings can be viewed as supportive. Such findings would include Dr. Lowie's assertion that since religion has a universal manifestation it must have some crucial value to mankind and his other assertion that science and religion really

---

[21] *Ibid.*, p. 107.

[22] Leach, *op. cit., Comparative Religion,* ed. by Lessa & Vogt, pp. 574-582.

[23] The text is the primary interpreter of its own meaning. The primary interpreter is not dialectical philosophy or Freudian Symbolism or anything else. Any interpretation of a cultural phenomenon must take into consideration the culture's interpretation(s) of that phenomenon. A good anthropologist questions a few of the "natives" if he wishes to determine just what they believe they're doing. He may have his own ideas and interpretations but he must not exclude or ignore the indigenous views.

conflict on very few points[24] or Frankfort and Frankfort's assertion, cited earlier, that geography is important in a people's view of "God." The Bible flatly states that God "chose" the Hebrew tribes and it could possibly be in part because of their ecological setting. The Christian's real argument with the structural-functionalist point of view comes not in the realm of their findings but in the realm of their assumptions.

Investigating "secondary functions" as the real issue in the phenomenon of religion is questionable, especially when it becomes exclusive. Searching for its real meaning in the unconscious or psychological "needs" of man may indeed reveal one function of religion but one can never be certain of this. Positing reasons beyond reasons, i.e., "Ah-ha, but deep in your unconscious you really do this because . . . ," leads to an infinite regress and really says nothing. The good doctor Sigmund Freud himself warns of this in dealing with clients by stressing the principle that one should draw the interpretations of symbols from the client rather than from some grandiose scheme of interpretation which has no real base even within the subjective reality of the client.[25] Thus we are left with religion filling many fuctions for many people. This is a legitimate psychosociological observation but it says nothing as to the validity or invalidity of religion or of a particular religion.

Structural-functionalism urges that no validity judgments be made. Radcliffe-Brown says, "The usual way of looking at religions is to regard all of them, or all except one as bodies of erroneous beliefs and illusory practices." [26] Most logicians and scientific thinkers would admit that this is wrongheaded; even Christian apologists stress that this is a wrong starting point. Radcliffe-Brown then adds,

When we regard the religions of other peoples, or at least those of which are called primitive peoples as systems of erroneous and illusory beliefs we are confronted with the problems of *how these came to be accepted.* It is to this problem anthropology addresses mostly.[27]

---

[24] Robert H. Lowie, "Religion in Human Life," in *Comparative Religion*, ed. by Lessa & Vogt, p. 141.

[25] Sigmund Freud, *The Complete Introductory Lectures on Psychoanalysis*, trans. and ed. by James Strachey (New York: W. W. Norton & Company, 1966).

[26] Radcliffe-Brown, *op. cit.*, p. 158.

[27] Radcliffe-Brown, *op. cit.*, p. 158 (italics mine).

In less dogmatic moments Radcliffe-Brown admits that his theory's value really is not established but seems to be the most profitable. His method is indeed the most profitable if all we have is subjective experience to study objectively. All subjective experience is equal. So we can be good humanitarians and not push one religion over another. Religion fits similar needs and patterns of functions in all societies and we can build testible, verifiable theories to explain these functions. Dr. Lowie states, "I will study as many religions as I can but I will judge none of them. I doubt if any other attitude is scientifically defensible." [28]

But it could also be said, "I will study as many theories of science as I can but judge none of them. I doubt if any other attitude is scientifically defensible." And that doesn't sound quite right. Scientific theories and religions both claim to embody truth, that is in their manifest content, their assertions. Refusing to investigate primary claims is really refusing to investigate the most important facet of science or religion.

Even more important than this failure of structural-functionalism is what the social anthropologist S. Cook of Michigan State University calls "historic myopia." [29] Doctors Cook, Kasdan and others at Michigan State as well as a few other social anthropologists are awakening to this error under impact of historical studies such as those made by Oscar Lewis.[30] What is being asserted by these gentlemen is that one cannot fully understand religious, or any other human practice, without knowing a bit of its actual historical origination. This, in fact, brings anthropology back to the early ideas of Taylor and Schmidt who were trying to uncover historic origins. Not only the history just previous to a specific ritual or myth's recounting but the origination itself is important. But, as Schmidt and Taylor's work bears out, there are many problems in searching for this data by assuming that "primitive" peoples are closer to original man than peoples in "major" traditions. Modern anthropology disputes this claim and labels it as racist. Lévi-Strauss and others claim, from their studies of so-called "primitive" thought, that whatever his cultural niche, man has been

---

[28] Lowie, op. cit., p. 134.

[29] S. Cook, Department of Anthropology—Michigan State University, course titled "Social Anthropology 463," lecture delivered on December 1, 1969.

[30] Oscar Lewis, *Five Families* (New York: New American Library, Mentor series, 1959), and *Tepoztlan* (New York: Holt, Rhinehart and Winston, 1960).

thinking equally well. "Primitives" have just as much history behind them as do peoples of the "major" traditions.

Since religions claim some root in history, "mythological history" or the "real history" of the major religions, this aspect of their claims needs to be researched. Also as a few structural-functionalists are having to admit, from a purely scientific point of view, the historicity of an event has a good deal to do with the meanings and functions of any system generated by it—be it ever so perverted and diverted from the original event or teachings (i.e., the institutionalized church).

History is also a confusing discipline; however, history plus anthropological analysis is better than either separately. In fact, together they make for more scientific anthropology. Without history it is impossible to study religion or any other aspect of life. Consider the following quote:

> the man who doubts the possibility of correct historical evidence and tradition cannot then accept his own evidence, judgment, combination and interpretation. He cannot limit his doubt to his historical criticism, but is required to let it operate on his own life. He discovers at once that he not only lacks conclusive evidence in all sorts of aspects of his own life that he had taken for granted but also that there is no evidence whatever. In short, he finds himself forced to accept a general philosophical scepticism along with his historical scepticism. Any general philosophical scepticism is a nice intellectual game but one cannot live by it.[31]

The historic myopia of anthropology has fostered the wrong-headed notion that religious practices have little to do with a historic heritage. In fact everyone, even the structural-functionalist theoretician, is dependent on history for the very tools with which to build a theory. The present is understood on the basis of past knowledge. This is especially true of religious tradition which tends to be, if anything, a bit more tenacious in its hold on the past than other traditions. Radcliffe-Brown and his associates recognize this in its stabilizing function on society but fail to investigate the content of historical claims and thus have an incomplete and insufficiently scientific approach.

A historically verifiable event with a high probability of

---

[31] Johan Huizinga, "De Historische Idee," in his *Verzamelde Werken,* VII (Haarlem, 1950), as quoted in translation in Fritz Stern (ed.), *The Varieties of History* (New York: Meridian Books, 1956).

having occurred could cause a reasonable anthropologist to admit that the claims of one religion have a greater claim to validity than those of another. This would be especially true in the case of incarnational (god on earth) religions such as Christianity. Merely claiming primacy for Christian events would not require that one become a Christian; but if Christianity has as much or more historical veracity behind its central claim that "God was in Christ reconciling the world unto himself" than other alleged historical events, then one must take a non-logical view of reality if he is to avoid Christian commitment. And this retreat into unreality is exactly what the social scientist, structural-functionalist or not, is trying to avoid.

Some Weaknesses in Fundamental Buddhism

James R. Moore

The critical discussion between religions has fallen on hard times. Due in large measure to what Francis Schaeffer calls "escape from reason," men are coming to view religion as an exclusively non-cognitive activity, the doing of one's "thing" which somehow infuses human life with transcendental significance. Thus Alan Watts makes this telling observation with reference to his influential book, *The Spirit of Zen:* "a book . . . is something of a hoax in the respect that the more it succeeds in giving the reader an impression of intelligibility, the more it has failed to give understanding." [1]

But what results when men purchase religious understanding at the price of intelligibility? No less than outright and irremediable chaos. The list of those "teased out of thought" (to use Watts' words) reads like a veritable cultic "Who's Who": Madame Blavatsky and the Theosophical Society, Mr. and Mrs. Ballard and their I AM mumbo-jumbo, Timothy Leary and the Neo-American church, Baha'ism, Soka Gakkai, and Zen Buddhism.[2]

Moreover, current theological fads—equally the product of doing one's own irrational religious thing—are manifesting this trend no less decisively: Thomas J. J. Altizer identifies Nirvana with the Kingdom of God; Paul Tillich says that "Eastern wisdom . . . must be included in the interpretation of Jesus as

---

[1] *The Spirit of Zen* (New York: Grove Press, 1958), p. 14.

[2] On Soka Gakkai, see the startling report in *Life*, January 9, 1970. For a general summary of the religious impact of the orient on America consult William Braden's remarkable *The Private Sea: LSD and the Search for God* ([New York: Bantam Books, 1967], esp. pp. 66-79, 91-92), a book which shows that Eastern mysticism, especially the brand sold at the "psychedelicatessan," is currently offering a major challenge to orthodox theology (pp. 37-40).

the Christ;"[3] and Pierre Teilhard de Chardin advocates a Christic pantheism culminating in a universal "Omega," a kind of cosmic Nirvana.

What has all this to do with Buddhism? Simply that the attractive doctrinal credentials of fundamental (Theravada, Hinayana) Buddhism must ultimately have the greatest appeal to the irrational mind-set conditioned by the theologies and theosophies of our day. In an atmosphere of scientific empiricism, where a university student can attend a physics lecture immediately after engorging a psychotomimetic drug, it is a short step from the prevalent and facile monism of neo-western thought to the individualism, mysticism, and atheism offered in original Buddhist teaching.

In view of this eventuality the Christian cannot remain silent. Reason alone cannot overcome an unbending disposition to nonreason, let alone the hardness of a sinful heart. But "rational Christianity" administered by one who "has access to both the reasons of the heart and the reasons of the head" will always prove remedial because it sets forth the inescapable fact of Jesus Christ.[4] In this article we shall explore both kinds of reasons as they bear on showing the inadequacies of fundamental Buddhism.[5]

HISTORICITY AND THE BUDDHA

"A history of Buddhist thought might be expected to begin with an account of the teachings of the Buddha himself, or at least of the beliefs current in the most ancient community. The nature of our literary documents makes such an attempt fruitless and impossible." This is not the statement of some axe-grinding Occidental, but rather the learned judgment of

---

[3] Tillich, in Harold E. Fey, ed., *How My Mind Has Changed*, Meridian Living Age Books (New York: World, 1961), p. 164.

[4] Elton Trueblood, *A Place to Stand* (New York: Harper & Row, 1969), p. 31.

[5] Not only by reason of incipient popularity, but "in fairness to Buddhism we ought probably to judge it, not primarily by its wilder perversions and developments, but on the merits of such views as can be clearly traced back to the founder himself" (David Bentley-Taylor, "Buddhism," in *The World's Religions*, ed. by J. N. D. Anderson [3d. ed.; Grand Rapids, Mich.: Wm. B. Eerdmans, 1955], p. 135). On "the problems of 'Original Buddhism' " see Edward Conze, *Buddhist Thought in India*, Ann Arbor Paperbacks (Ann Arbor, Mich.: University of Michigan Press, 1962), pp. 31-33.

Edward Conze, a sympathetic Buddhist scholar and author of several books on Buddhist thought.[6] In the end, it leads to crucial questions that a follower of the Buddha must honestly face. For example, how is it possible to assess the character of a religion's founder whose biographies "are centuries later than the period of which they speak" and were "composed after the time when the movement had broken into separate schools?" [7] Or, can the original form of a religion be reconstructed whose primary documents, as we have them, "date back no farther than the Christian era," nearly 500 years after its founder's death? [8]

Edward J. Thomas has set forth the essential answer in his definitive *Life of Buddha:* [9] namely, that "in the present state of our knowledge we cannot in any instance declare that Buddha said so and so. The fact that we start from is that we have a collection of documents, which were held some two centuries after Buddha to contain his utterances." [10] We read on to discover that a comparison between the New Testament and the Buddhist scriptures is "extremely misleading." While recognizing that "the composition of the Gospels and the Epistles is not without problems," Thomas declares that "the questions concerning the origination and growth of the Buddhist Canon are far more complex." [11] For example, "all of them [the legends] belong to a period far removed from the stage which might be considered to be the record, or to be based on the record, of an eyewitness." [12] (On the other hand, we know that *all* of the New Testament records belong to the lifetime of both hostile and friendly eyewitnesses to the life of Jesus!) Thus Thomas concludes: "the only firm ground from which we can start is not history, but the fact that a legend in definite form existed in the first and second centuries after Buddha's death." [13]

---

[6] Conze, *op. cit.*, p. 31.

[7] Edward J. Thomas, *The History of Buddhist Thought* (2d ed.; London: Routledge & Kegan Paul, 1951), p. 1.

[8] Conze, *op. cit.*, p. 31.

[9] Edward J. Thomas, *The Life of Buddha as Legend and History* (New York: Barnes & Noble, 1956), pp. 1, 252.

[10] *Ibid.*, p. 251, Cf. p. 2.

[11] *Ibid.*, p. xviii.

[12] *Ibid.*, p. 1.

[13] *Ibid.*, p. 2.

LANGUAGE, TRUTH, AND LOGIC

Nietzsche called Buddhism the only positivistic religion in history because of its unswerving commitment to the Four Noble Truths: (1) All life involves suffering; (2) suffering is the product of attachment to this world, and ultimately the product of ignorance; (3) eliminating the cause (attachment and ignorance) will eradicate the effect (suffering); (4) The discipline of the Eightfold Path will lead to this end. However, unlike contemporary philosophical positivism, Buddhism is forced to operate in a "closed circle" of confusion through neglect of the basic questions of truth, logic, and language.

It is clear from the Four Noble Truths that "the supreme concern of the Buddha was not truth but salvation." The Buddha began with a definite existential world view which subordinated the concern for discovering truth to the metaphysics of experiencing *a priori* truth, the achieving of freedom (*moksha*) in Nirvana. For in fact the two concerns are mutually exclusive: "Any hunger for truth that would keep a man awake at night and set his soul on fire would be a disease"—suffering —something to be overcome through the discipline of the Eightfold Path.[14]

Where philosophically does fundamental Buddhism begin? Parting ways with Hinduism and monistic philosophies, Buddhism holds that there is no Brahman, no Absolute, and no persisting substance whatsoever in the universe. Instead "the most important of the conceptions which underlie the Buddhist religion" is that everything is momentary *(kshanika)*.[15] What appears to persist is no more than the momentary occurrence of things in certain patterns:

> There is no other ultimate reality than separate, instantaneous bits of existence. Not only eternal entities, be it God or be it Matter, are denied reality, because they are assumed to be enduring and eternal, but even the simple stability of empirical objects is something constructed by our imagination. Ultimate reality is instantaneous.[16]

---

[14] Walter Kaufmann, *Critique of Religion and Philosophy*, Anchor Books (Garden City, N.Y.: Doubleday & Co., 1958), p. 262-53. Cf. Floyd H. Ross, *The Meaning of Life in Hinduism and Buddhism* (Boston: Beacon Press, 1953), p. 95, 105, n. 2.

[15] T. W. Rhys Davids, *Buddhism* (3d rev. ed.; New Rochelle, N.Y.: Knickerbocker Press, 1896), p. 123.

[16] F. Th. Stcherbatsky, *Buddhist Logic* (reprinted.; 2 Vols.; New York: Dover Publications, 1962), 1, 204.

In the face of this total flux the Buddha had to account for his premise that all life involves suffering. How did this predicament come about? The Buddha solved this problem (and avoided the pitfalls of the cosmological argument) by his theory of dependent origination. Causality in human life works in ·a circle. The chain begins in ignorance (that all is impermanent) and continues through the phenomena and epiphenomena of life, birth, old age, and death. The latter are once again the causes of ignorance. Hence A causes B causes C causes A. If A causes B causes C causes D, *ad infinitum* then of course one might ask the cause of A. This would require the admission of an uncaused cause, a persisting something that the Buddha felt must be avoided at all costs.[17] Thus because of circular causality the Buddha could account for suffering by showing simply that it had always existed.[18]

Yet the Buddha taught that *moksha* or freedom from this vicious circle was possible. Therefore his causal chain consisted of at least some links which are necessary but not sufficient conditions for following links. For if they were not (i.e., if the links were necessary *and* sufficient conditions), then the chain could never be broken. The absence of one link (e.g., desire) is a necessary condition for the absence of the preceding link, *et cetera*, until one reaches total freedom in Nirvana.

What can we say about this intriguing system? Is it logical? We might ask, to begin with, how one can guarantee that freedom is possible in a world where nothing lasts long enough to have anything happen to it. How can a person persist long enough to reverse the causal chain in order to gain freedom? But the real problem lies far deeper. Suppose that we are able to attempt to eliminate desire, for example. "To produce sufficient conditions for the absence of . . . desire, however, and to be sure that our efforts will succeed, we must be able to avoid a necessary condition for . . . desire."[19] And in order to avoid a necessary condition for desire we would have to achieve the absence of the sufficient condition

---

[17] Cf. Thomas, *The History of Buddhist Thought*, p. 59, explained in greater detail in Ram Chandra Pandeya, *A Panorama of Indian Philosophy* (New Delhi: Motilal Banarsidass, 1966), pp. 18-20.

[18] See Karl H. Potter's helpful discussion in *Presuppositions of India's Philosophies* (Englewood Cliffs, N.J.: Prentice-Hall, 1963), pp. 102-104, 129-37.

[19] *Ibid.*, p. 130.

for the absence of that necessary condition, and so on, around the circle, *ad infinitum.*

> We are in effect facing the question . . . how can the stream of events known as "I" enter into a chain of causation and produce, not another link in the chain, but just the opposite, the non-occurrence of that link? For that is what it will take to gain freedom . . . . the question . . . remains at the end . . . how can that which is by law [karma] supposed to produce A in fact be made to produce non-A? [20]

As if this were not a sufficiently large problem, the statement "suppose we attempt to eliminate desire" camouflages the final, inescapable contradiction. The contradiction appears full force if we say, "suppose we desire to eliminate desire"!

This entire discussion is enough to make one suspect a mistake somewhere. Buddhist religious philosophy does not "make a sharp distinction between *a priori* and *a posteriori*" and it simply does not believe "that philosophical problems can be resolved merely by closer attention to common language or thought." [21] Within Buddhism terms "which concern the particularly sacred core of the doctrine [e.g., *moksha, kshanika*] disclose their meaning in a state of religious exaltation. To give them a precise logical definition would seem a task too trivial to bother about." [22] However, if truth is one's concern (which it seems not to be, *ex hypothesi,* in Buddhism), he simply must distinguish between the views and feelings he brings to an inquiry and the data arising from the inquiry itself. A religion which confuses *a priori* and *a posteriori* and requires mystic exaltation to define its crucial concepts, an understanding of which is prerequisite to committing oneself to mystic exaltation, is condemned to misapprehend the cosmos.

HUMANISTIC PRINCIPLES

We will now do well to examine Buddhist views on man, society, and salvation, fully expecting to find them as unusual

---

[20] *Ibid.,* pp. 130-31.

[21] Potter, *op. cit.,* p. 52.

[22] Conze, *op. cit.,* p. 28. It should be noted in passing that "Eastern logics" offer no problems at all, for they are merely varieties of that universal system of inference based on the Law of Non-Contradiction which Westerners designate as "classical" or "symbolic" logic. I. M. Bochenski says of Indian logic, "that in quite different circumstances and without being influenced by the west, it developed in many respects

and as inhospitable to Christianity as the ideas we have been examining in the historical and philosophical realms. R. E. Hume, translator of the thirteen principle Upanishads and late professor of the history of religions at Union Theological Seminary, has listed fourteen elements of weakness in Buddhism, half of which concern human values: a low estimate of human life and the human body; a low estimate of woman and the family; checking of individual initiative; refusal of social responsibilities; an excessive emphasis on self-saving; a generally negative method of salvation; and an empty idea of a blissful Nirvana.[23] Though careful examination of each of these baleful weaknesses is clearly beyond the scope of this article, it should be clear by now that the metaphysic of *karma* and *kshanika* underlies them. When the so-called ego is really only an agglomeration of point-in-time existences, ever changing through the cycle of causality according to the inexorable law of *karma*, then the foundation has been laid for the demise of man and his society. Buddhism, however, stops short of absolute pessimism by inconsistently embracing doctrines of self-salvation and Nirvana.

On the surface Buddhist teaching appears laudably self-effacing. The devout are instructed to "banish every ground of · self" which "shades every lofty good aim" and to "cut out the love of self." But the notion is summarily destroyed in the Buddha's pessimistic analysis of the universe which offers as rationale for self-effacement the "fact and the fixed and necessary constitution of being, that all its constituents are transitory, . . . misery, . . . lacking in Ego."

Such a view has vast individual and social implications. Whereas a Christian is commanded to love others as he loves himself, the Buddhist is instructed to "cut out the love of self."

> The essential thing, the thing that puts a gulf between Buddhist charity and Christian charity, is that in Christianity the neighbor is loved for himself. In Buddhism this is impossible. It is true that in both religions charity consists, at least in its early stages, in loving the other for himself; but since in Buddhism the ego is entirely

---

the *same problems* and reached the *same solutions*" (*A History of Formal Logic*, trans. by Ivo Thomas [Notre Dame, Ind.: University of Notre Dame Press, 1961], p. 447).

[23] *The World's Living Religions* (rev. ed.; New York: Charles Scribner's Sons, 1955), p. 82. See the chapter on Buddhism for specific supporting references.

illusory, or exists only to be destroyed, it can hardly be loved for itself. How then can anyone really be loved? Since it is not taken seriously, another's personality can never be the object of any serious love. "The insignificance of the individual is for the Buddhist a fundamental axiom, like the infinite value of the human soul for the Christian." [24]

Women, for example, are neither respected nor honored as they should be. The Buddha on one occasion asserted that women are easily angered, full of passion, envious, and stupid, and that they therefore have no place in public assemblies or in the professional world.[25] Ananda K. Coomaraswamy concedes that "Buddhist thought gives honor [sic] to woman to this extent, that it never doubts the possibility of her putting off her woman's nature, and even in this life becoming, as it were, a man." [26] At the societal level, Arthur F. Wright has observed that in modern China, Buddhism "seemed to many to teach a lesson of passivity or tolerant resignation at a time when the mood of the intellectuals and the political leaders called for a program of positive action." He cites the dissatisfaction expressed by Ch'en Tu-hsiu, a founder of the Chinese Communist party, with the abominable political and social state of Oriental peoples, and maintains that Tu-hsiu's dubious cliches should not obscure the fact that he and others like him "were passionately seeking a solution for China's ills, and that the Buddhist ethos as they understood it was anathema to them." [27]

Could the Buddha have understood that "in Christ . . . there is neither male nor female" and had Ch'en Tu-hsiu fully comprehended the positive connection between the Christian doctrine of man and the struggles of Western democracies for freedom and individual rights, then one might find today a more liberated Orient, free from the impersonal shackles of Buddhist doctrine. Instead one finds war, slavery, poverty, and the starvation of anonymous millions.[28]

---

[24] Henri de Lubac, S. J., *Aspects of Buddhism*, trans. by George Lamb (London: Sheed and Ward, 1953), p. 37.

[25] *Buddha and the Gospel of Buddhism*, rev. by Dona Luisa Coomaraswamy, Harper Torchbooks (New York: Harper & Row, 1964), p. 162.

[26] *Ibid.*, p. 164.

[27] *Buddhism in Chinese History* (New York: Atheneum, 1965), pp. 116-17.

[28] Men inevitably reap the results of departure from religious reality. Thus Ernst Benz notes that Buddhism "has not produced a

Buddhism escapes the pit of pessimism through a rigorous system of self-salvation and an empty hope of Nirvana. How close it comes to the brink can be measured by comparing Rhys Davids' summation that men are "the mere temporary and passing result of causes that have been at work during immeasurable ages in the past, and that will continue to act for ages yet to come," [29] with Bertrand Russell's infamous credo in his essay, "A Free Man's Worship." On the surface Nirvana seems to mean the highest conceivable freedom from all disturbances, a passionless peace. However, "an utter extinction of personality and consciousness would seem to be implied by the fundamental principles of Buddhism and also by explicit statements of Buddha." [30] On one occasion he allegedly said: "Those whose minds are disgusted with a future existence, the wise who have destroyed the seeds of existence, and whose desires do not increase, go out like this lamp." In other words, it seems that Nirvana is reached when somehow (the word carries a great ambiguity) the reborn pattern of events called an individual dissolves into the universal chaos of momentary occurrences. A body may appear to the eyes, but in reality, "within" the individual, total dissolution has occurred. Beyond this even the Buddha was silent.[31] And could he have been otherwise? With Samuel Beckett he might have asked,

> How am I, an a-temporal being imprisoned in time and space, to escape from my imprisonment, when I know that outside space and time lies Nothing, and that I, in the ultimate depths of my reality, am Nothing also? [32]

How is the chimerical hope of Nirvana realized? As indicated earlier, the Eightfold Path prescribed by the Buddha leads to this salvation. It is the way of high ethical conduct and

technological culture but has a distinctly anti-technological attitude in many of its schools" because "the fundamental religious premise of technological activity is the Christian concept of God as the Creator" (*Evolution and Christian Hope*, trans. by Heinz G. Frank, Anchor Books [Garden City, N.Y.: Doubleday & Co., 1968], p. 122). Hume encapsulates the issue with this observation: "Buddhism teaches the salvation of the individual apart from society. Christianity teaches the salvation of the individual and of society" (*op. cit.*, p. 80).

[29] Rhys Davids, *op. cit.*, p. 127.

[30] Hume, *op. cit.*, p. 72.

[31] Pandeya, *op. cit.*, pp. 22-23.

[32] Richard Coe, *Samuel Beckett* (New York: Grove Press, 1964), p. 18.

stringent mental discipline.[33] Indeed, we might have expected a doctrine in the sharpest possible contrast with Christianity, for Buddhism is a religion "which without starting with a God leads man to a stage where God's help is not necessary." [34] That is, in the absence of the Eternal and Immutable Personal, the conceptions of sin, alienation, and immorality have practically no significance. Thus the Buddha's "salvation" needs only be a finite prescription for liberation from human discomfort.

No way of salvation could be more thoroughly opposed to the salvation purchased by Jesus Christ. In contrasting the (Mahayana but representative) Buddhist *Saddharma-Punderika* (*The Lotus of the True Law*) with the Epistle to the Colossians, one very perceptive writer puts it this way:

> Buddha delivers ignorant men, not by some direct action on their behalf, but by triggering a mechanism of salvation within them. Their release from sorrow and ignorance emerges from within them. By means of artful deception, Buddha simply precipitates their inner resolves to escape. Obviously this understanding of deliverance is contrary to that of the Colossian letter. There the predicament needing divine remedy is both interior and exterior to men. They are helpless in two ways. Not only does the letter describe them as "alienated and enemies in your mind in evil works (1.21);" but it also suggests that they are hindered outwardly by the demonic influence of hostile "principalities" and "powers." Christ functions as their deliverer, not merely through a reconciliation wrought inwardly in his followers, but also through a "cosmic" reconciliation wrought throughout the whole creation. *Whereas the Buddha introduces a new and saving truth, by means of which men find release, the Christ introduces a new and saving situa-*

---

[33] " '(I) First, you must see clearly what is wrong. (II) Next decide to be cured. (III) You must act and (IV) speak so as to aim at being cured. (V) Your livelihood must not conflict with your therapy. (VI) That therapy must go forward at the 'staying speed,' the critical velocity that can be sustained. (VII) You must think about it incessantly, and (VIII) learn how to contemplate *with the deep mind.*' " Quoted by Nancy Wilson Ross, *Three Ways of Asian Wisdom*, Clarion Books (New York: Simon and Schuster, 1968), pp. 91-92.

[34] D. T. Niles, *Buddhism and the Claims of Christ* (Richmond, Va.: John Knox, 1967), p. 27.

[35] Irving Alan Sparks, "Buddha and Christ: A Functional Analysis," *Numen*, XIII (October, 1966), 199 (emphasis mine).

tion, under whose conditions men are reconciled and redeemed.[35]

We began this essay by considering the historical foundations of Buddhism. Again we have reached the historical level. Ninian Smart reminds us in his essay, "The Work of the Buddha and the Work of Christ," that "Christian soteriology has always been conceived as closely tied to history. God's saving work is thought of as manifested in history (i.e., in the flow of human events) and as grounded in history (i.e., in historical evidences). On both counts, and in both senses of 'history,' " adds Smart, "Buddhism has a different attitude . . . . historical evidences are not vital where the truth is seen in inner experience." [36] Furthermore, as we saw in the second section, this inner experience "precludes discursive knowledge." [37] A religious philosophy which grounds its truth in non-historical legend and non-cognitive inner experience is thus bound to produce a way of salvation and a salvation itself far removed from "the Way, the Truth, and the Life" of Christianity.

Though many moderns may plunge into a morass of mysticism and irrationality, justifying themselves to a "Christian" society on the basis that Buddhist and Christian doctrines are "about the same," we must remember that a gulf yawns at once when we consider the roots and aspirations behind them. In one system Buddha's sovereignty has practically no connection to history, whereas in the other, Christ's eternal Lordship can be verified in history. In Buddhism the ultimate reality is found in an intuition of emptiness, while in the other it is in a personal God. In Buddhism a man's liberating work is to bring men to an impersonal *gnosis*; Christ's work is the reconciliation of men with men and with their loving Father.

---

[36] In *The Saviour God*, ed. by S. G. F. Brandon (New York: Barnes & Noble, 1963), p. 171. Sparks makes the exact distinction: "The difference in their relating history and eternity, then, is that whereas Buddha 'enters' history to exhibit compassion and to reveal a saving truth which is independent of history, Christ 'enters' history in order to accomplish and confirm by his death and resurrection a salvation which is incomplete without such historical involvement" (*op. cit.*, p. 195).

[37] Smart, *ibid.*, p. 162.

Eric Hoffer and the True Believer

Mel Loucks

He has been called "the philosopher of the misfits," "Dockside Montaigne," "Blue-Collar Plato." A San Francisco longshoreman with no formal education beyond the age of seven, Eric Hoffer today travels freely in intellectual circles, has authored four books, lectures at the University of California at Berkeley, and is considered to be one of the most significant social thinkers of our day. His work in the area of social studies has received significant recognition in academic circles and there is barely a sophomore sociologist who has not read his best known work, *The True Believer*. Hoffer's feeling for a good clear sentence, his penchant for bold generalizations, his telling use of the wry epigram and icy aphorism, and his capacity for making the obvious obvious has made him one of the most popular writers among college students in the past decade.

Eric Hoffer, the only son of Alsatian parents, was born in Bronx, New York in 1902. Raised in poverty, he was required to face tragedy for the first time at the tender age of seven. The death of his mother was followed shortly by the mysterious loss of his eyesight. Eight years later, however, his vision returned as suddenly as it had been lost and the joy of seeing again gave Hoffer what he called, "a terrific hunger for the printed word." It was then that his long process of self-education began. Jobless at eighteen, Hoffer migrated to California where he ended up on "skid row" in Los Angeles. It was there that Hoffer claims he learned to live without hope. The next twenty years were spent with laborers and migratory workers throughout California. He worked just enough to keep his stomach full while spending every free moment gorging his mind with material from every library between Oregon and Mexico. In 1941 Hoffer began working on the docks in San Francisco where he has been ever since.

Hoffer still works three days a week on the docks—he hopes to die working—and spends one day a week as "Senior Research

157

Political Scientist" at the University of California. He has never married, has few friends, and still lives simply in a San Francisco flat doing what he loves most—studying that fascinating species called man.

After having spent most of his life among the undesirables of America Hoffer has come to champion their cause. From them he has gained insights into the nature of mass movements. What he has seen among the masses he has employed to substantiate theories he gained from his wide reading. The writers of France have perhaps molded Hoffer's thinking more than any other group or tradition. From Montaigne he learned the art of writing aphorisms. Pascal gave him the feeling for a good clear sentence while at the same time telling him something about the nature of man. And Renan helped mold his somewhat skeptical outlook. "Without Renan," he says, "I probably wouldn't have written *The True Believer*." [1] Bergson and de Tocqueville were also instrumental in his intellectual development. Outside France, Hoffer is especially fond of Francis Bacon, Jacob Burckhardt, and Lostoevsky. The Germans were of no help to him however. "They know nothing of what lucidity is." [2]

Hoffer's writing style has qualities reminiscent of the oldline lay preachers. "By placing himself among the undesirables [he] has come to be one of the most desirable lay preachers in secular America." [3] His strength is "his capacity for bold generalizations. He cuts straight to the heart of whatever subject he is discussing, with a minimum of diversions." [4] Some of his generalizations are brilliant, while others are only partially self-sufficient. The danger in reading Hoffer comes when one becomes enthralled with his strengths to the point of accepting his false generalizations as well.

The True Believer is the first of four works by Hoffer. However only *The True Believer* will concern us here for two reasons: the book is by far Hoffer's most influential work and Hoffer himself regards it to be the essence of his thought. To use his words:

---

[1] "Profiles: The Creative Situation," *New Yorker*, January 7, 1967, p. 56.

[2] *Ibid.*

[3] "Eric Hoffer: Secular Preacher," *Christian Century*, May 29, 1963, p. 727.

[4] *Ibid.*

I've only written one book in my life—*The True Believer.* . . . Not until I finished writing *The Ordeal of
Change* did I realize that I had been dealing all the
time with the "true believer!" [5]

THE MAN AND THE MOVEMENT

Who is the true believer to whom Hoffer devotes a whole
volume? He is the insecure non-thinker who is desperately grop-
ing for identity with something that will make his life seem
worthwhile. He is, "a permanent misfit, a person who feels
for one reason or another that his own life is inseparably spoiled
and who therefore seeks a new, collective self in blind allegiance
to a holy cause . . . (He) is ripe for any effective movement
that satisfies his craving for self-renunciation." [6] He is the
man with a guilty conscience, who hates things as they are,
and therefore feels he must support some cause.

The content of *The True Believer* is perhaps better understood
by its subtitle: *Thoughts on the Nature of Mass Movements.*
Hoffer divides the book into four sections, the first two dealing
with the type of people who make up mass movements and
the last two with the movements themselves.

Because people cannot accept themselves or things as they
are, and because they tend to locate the shaping forces of
existence outside themselves, they desire change. This disen-
chantment with oneself leads also to a desire for self-renunciation. From a feeling that self-interest is evil there is derived
an urge to find acceptable substitutes for self-interest. "Faith
in a holy cause is to a considerable extent a substitute for
a lost faith in ourselves." [7] The potential converts to mass
movements are these "true believers." Interestingly enough,
however, almost anyone could be placed on the list, including
the modern "organization man." The college student—the acti-
vist, the hippie, the rebel—find especially prominent places.

More is needed to make a successful mass movement than
just the right kind of people, claims Hoffer. There must be
a vigor that arises out of their propensity for united action
and sacrifice. This can best be brought about when the people
come into a fanatical identity with their movement. Fantasy

---

[5] "Profiles: The Creative Situation," *op. cit.*, p. 68.

[6] *Ibid.*, p. 35.

[7] Eric Hoffer, *The True Believer* (New York: Harper and Row,
1966), p. 23.

which forgets the present and looks forward to a future utopia is the best means of producing such unity. And what are the results? Man is stripped of his individuality and deprived of free choice and of independent judgment. One is incomplete and insecure unless he can cling to the ideals of the collective body.

Hoffer sees a definite process involved in a successful mass movement. Before a movement can arise in a society the present order must first be discredited. This discrediting is done by the intellectuals or "men of words" who are often not part of the actual movement. These individuals discredit the prevailing creeds and institutions and indirectly create a hunger for faith within those who cannot live without faith. They then furnish the doctrine and slogans for this new faith. Finally they undermine the convictions of the "better people" so they will not want to struggle for the preservation of their convictions, but rather yield to the new order. After the way is prepared by the men of words the "better people" are swept aside by the fanatics who hatch the movement and give it its momentum. The last step in the movement comes when "practical men of action" consolidate the ideals of the movement and make it possible for the people to live in the world they have just possessed. This necessarily calls for the compromise of many of these ideals and therefore for a split between the idealists and the pragmatists.

Hoffer attempts to discuss mass movements with objective detachment, avoiding value judgments concerning any particular mass movement. But though he believes that there is evil in all movements, he feels that mass movements are basically good because they are often a factor in awakening a stagnant society. They are the instruments of resurrection, raising societies and nations from the social, political, or economic dead.

In *The True Believer* Hoffer's view of man is pessimistic and his observations on human nature are bleak. He devotes great space in his writings to the ills of society that afflict modern man. His view of man parallels that of the novelist, John Steinbeck, who like Hoffer has associated himself with the educated as well as the common man. After viewing all facets of society they cry in unison, "Everybody's a tramp some time or other. Everybody. And the worse tramps of all are the ones that call it something else." [8] Even the more

---

[8] John Steinbeck, *The Wayward Bus*, Bantam Books (New York: Viking, 1964), p. 205.

sophisticated men of words are motivated by a "craving for recognition; a craving for a clearly marked status above the common run of humanity." [9] In his book, *The Temper of Our Time*, Hoffer champions the misfits, vicious and selfish though they be, because he finds the intellectuals to be the greatest powergrabbers and tyrannizers of all. His view of man should be known by all those who care to take an objective look at themselves. It seems that the only way one could conclude that man is basically good is either to close his eyes to the facts of history or to redefine what one means by "virtue" as does Ayn Rand in *The Virtue of Selfishness*. Perhaps this is one reason for the wide appeal of *The True Believer*. We read Hoffer's verdict on the nature of man and exclaim, "Yes, that is just the way people are!" Hoffer's pessimism lies not in the belief that man is evil and greedy, but in the idea that man strives for a utopian goal he will never reach. He sees man hoping for something that does not exist, a quest that can lead only to despair. It seems that if there is a deliverance from this pessimism, it will be a hope that truly exists, a viable hope that is objectively obtainable.

CHRIST AND CHRISTIANITY

If Christianity is considered to be just another mass movement Hoffer can fit it into his scheme with ease. Christ would be a man of words, the apostles would be the fanatics who give momentum to the movement, and the Church Fathers would be the practical men of action who consolidated the movement into the accepted religion of the day. But what about that utopian goal—that holy cause—which gave rise and rationale to the movement? Is the Christian seeking goals which are beyond the possibility of realization? Is Christianity but a movement based upon the false teaching of a man seeking no more than personal recognition? If there is no objective basis to Christianity the answer to these questions would very likely be yes. Hoffer seems to reach this conclusion by understanding Christianity, like any other movement, to be no more than the wish fulfillment of a mass of insecure persons. He accomplishes this by ignoring the possibility of an *objective* basis for the Christian faith which constitutes rational, persuasive evidence for the true believer *and* non-believer.

If Christ was an ordinary mortal He might well fit into

---

[9] Eric Hoffer, *op. cit.*, p. 121.

Hoffer's category of the man of words, but if He is truly divine as He claimed, it is likely that what He said is true, and what he founded is legitimate. According to C. S. Lewis, if the Bible accurately records what Jesus taught, we must arrive at one of two conclusions concerning him:[10]

> He would either be a lunatic—on a level with a man who says he's a poached egg—or else He would be the devil of hell. You must make your choice. Either this man was, and is, the son of God: or else a madman or something worse.

It goes, almost without saying that there are some movements within Christianity which may support Hoffer's theory, and there are undoubtedly some men who, in the name of Christianity, seek to gain recognition as men of words. But it would be an obvious fallacy to judge the truth of a religion on the basis of its adherents. Similarly it is superficial to conclude that all Christians are "true believers." Hoffer suffers from what Anthony Standen calls the "common factor fallacy." He tells of a man who got drunk one day on whiskey and soda water, the next day on brandy and soda water, and the third day on gin and soda water. This led to the conclusion that the common factor, soda water, was obviously what made the man drunk.[11] For Hoffer the factor Christianity has in common with other movements is the true believer's need to have a cause to support. But the truth claims of Christianity are bound up in the life, death, and resurrection of Jesus Christ, not merely in the lives or the minds of the adherents. C. S. Lewis, whose unusual journey from atheism to Christianity removes him entirely from the "true believer" category, has a better appraisal of Christ's movement:[12]

> It is a religion you could not have guessed. If it offered us just the kind of universe we had always expected, I would feel we were making it up.

---

[10] C. S. Lewis, *Mere Christianity* (New York: Macmillan, 1958), p. 41.

[11] *Science is a Sacred Cow* (New York: Dutton, 1950), p. 25.

[12] *Op. cit.*, p. 33.

Part Four

PSYCHOLOGY
AND RELIGIOUS EXPERIENCE

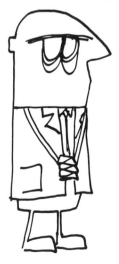

Existential Psychology and Christian Faith

Clark Eugene Barshinger

Existentialism focuses on the "existing" person where he is, presently, in his process of becoming his mature self. The word "existence" comes from the Latin "ex-sistere," which means "to stand out, emerge." The significance of the word "existence" is seen when compared with traditional Western emphasis in psychology and philosophy upon "essence," the concept of immutable principles, truth and logical laws which come before existence. According to Rollo May, in *Existential Psychology*: "There is no such thing as truth or reality for a living human being except as he participates in it, is conscious of it, has some relationship to it." The only truth with the power to change a human being, or to fulfill him, is truth genuinely experienced on all levels of the person's experience.[1]

In the same volume Abraham Maslow describes several of the concepts fundamental to existential psychology. One such concept is the total collapse of all sources of values outside the individual. With all value-systems around mankind failing to touch the meaning of his existence, man supposedly has no other place to look for values and meaning than in himself. This, however, is not to say that all value-systems fail to touch the meaning of an individual's experience. An external value-system may agree with the values from within the individual. However, all external value-systems are ultimately tested by the individual through his experience of their trustworthiness.

For example, in his book *Man's Search For Himself*, May discusses the validity of the religious experience as a source of strength or weakness. The criterion of whether or not a religion is valuable is the inward use of the religion and not the objective claims. If a religion is used to make the person

---

[1] Rollo May, (ed.), *Existential Psychology* (New York: Random House, 1966), p. 17.

more dependent and allows him to escape from himself and life, it is harmful. If, on the other hand, the religious faith helps the person toward greater independence and courage to face life, it is helpful and valid.

Furthermore existential psychology holds that both human aspirations and human limitations—what the human being is and what he would like to be—are equally part of man's existence. Along with integrative techniques to bring these two poles together exists the realization that some problems must remain forever beyond solution. A third concept is that as the human being moves toward his real, "authentic" existence, he will not only fulfill more of his human potentialities, but will also become more detached from the need to fulfill the expectations of his culture and become less involved in the structure of his society.

This emphasis upon individuality as opposed to group structure, along with the emphasis upon subjective experience as opposed to theoretical reason, is reflected in the fact that existentialism has never produced any noteworthy social ethic or social philosophy.[2] The uniqueness and individuality of the human being is stressed seemingly at the expense of his social environment. Each person must face his responsibility to himself and to life alone. Existential psychology stresses this ultimate aloneness of the individual. Since subjective experience is the only meaningful criterion of truth, one must stand ultimately alone. According to Maslow, this aloneness causes us to work out the concepts of decision, responsibility, choice, self-creation, autonomy and identity. It also adds to the mystery of communication between 'alonenesses." This alonenesses, according to Maslow, also leads to a significant emphasis, upon thinking. A person is supposedly better able to face the seriousness and profundity of living rather than retreating into a shallow and superficial existence which serves as a defense against the ultimate problems of life.

Existential psychology is also mapping the limits of verbal, analytic, and conceptual rationality. This is part of what Maslow sees as a current emphasis upon experience that is more important than concepts or abstractions. Here philosophy of science is understood to be undergoing a revolution. The Cartesian split between subject and object, so much a part of traditional

---

[2] John Wild, *The Challenge of Existentialism* (Bloomington, Indiana: Indiana University Press, 1959), p. 184.

Western thought, is now being abandoned for existentialism, the testing of reality by the psyche and raw experience.

Finally comes the proposition that existential thought in general is more willing to look at the future. Whether good or evil, the future must be faced with courage. Self-actualization is meaningless without dealing with the future, and only a flexible, creative person can manage an unexpected, unpredictable future. In pointing out some basic differences between European and American existentialism, Gordon Allport observes that European existential psychology seems to emphasize resignation, acceptance, and even the "courage to be" more than American existential thought. American existentialism strikes Allport as being more optimistic about life.[3] However, there seems to be no justification for this optimism. Why should existentialism offer more courage to face the future than any other philosophy of life? It would appear—and Sartre for one readily admits it—that the optimistic courage of existentialism to face life is simply imposed upon existence.

Herman Feifel, in *Existential Psychology*, discusses the real significance of existential psychology in helping human beings face the future inevitability of death. In Western culture, death has been a subject to avoid at all costs. With the weakening of Christian beliefs in the certainty of the afterlife, there has developed an inability to contemplate the idea seriously. However one's concept of death has a definite bearing upon his philosophy of life. Allport expresses his belief that, in regard to religion, the person with "intrinsic" religious values (comprehensive and integrative in their lives) will be less afraid of death, while the person with "extrinsic" religious values (defensive, escapist, ethnocentric) will be more afraid to face death.[4]

AN EVALUATION OF
EXISTENTIAL PSYCHOLOGY

Upon reading the works of leading existential psychologists, one cannot help but be impressed with their keen insights into the emptiness and meaninglessness of intellectualism used as an escape from serious evaluation of oneself. They speak to us about the real stuff of life, problems, fears, disappointments,

---

[3] May, *op. cit.*, p. 97.

[4] *Ibid.*, p. 96.

and joys. They speak with the sympathy and understanding of the world of personal relationships. This is a refreshing philosophy in our modern world, which has over-emphasized things and produced dehumanized mass-existence. Existential psychologists are teaching us to recognize the reality of the personal realm and intimate individuality. We thus owe a great deal to existentialism.

Yet one finds a troublesome over-reaction in existential thought to the use of reason. There seems to be an exaggeration of the validity of subjective experience in the intense reaction against a detached intellectualism. The result is the indefensible opposite extreme of antiobjectivism. Brute facts are allowed but causes and reasons are avoided. The principle of sufficient reason is denied. John Wild, a distinguished American philosopher, states in his book, *The Challenge of Existentialism*:

> The denial of any causal principle is an extremely dubious metaphysical assumption lacking empirical support, and implying the ultimate unintelligibility of the universe.... In a world entirely lacking in structure, we could not distinguish chaos from order, knowing would be impossible.[5]

To reject rationality and objectivity is to throw out the baby with the bath. The perils of abstract intellectualism are disposed of at the expense of human reason. John Macquarrie cautions against this temptation to reject the rational aspect of choice and to deny sufficient reason:

> It is justifiable to criticize an abstract intellectualism, to remind us that man is more than a cognitive being, and even to hold that some things which are veiled from the intellect may be disclosed in feeling or in striving. But it is going far beyond this when one begins to decry reason, or to claim that when reason contradicts our personal desires, it is a liar. Reason is admittedly not the whole of man and its pretensions need sometimes to be held in check, but on the other hand it is an integral element in personal life which would be less than personal without a rational element to sift, guide and criticize our feelings and desires. A philosophy of personal being need not and ought not to fly in the face of reason, ... In the concrete, life undoubtedly has its contradictions, its paradoxes and its discontinuities, and we can appreciate the fear that these features may be

[5] Wild, *op. cit.*, pp. 179, 80.

glossed over in an abstract rationalism; but the fear of a misuse of reason becomes a phobia when it attacks reason itself.[6]

Francis Schaeffer, in *The God Who Is There*, analyzes this loss of a rational approach in dealing with the meaning of life. Here, as in his book, *Escape From Reason*, Schaeffer speaks of the "Line of Despair," the point at which one abandons the hope for a unified answer to the problems of knowledge and life. According to Schaeffer, there are three principles involved in coming to knowlege; rationalistic ability of man, including his inward experience of truth; rationality of the universe; and a unified knowledge.

Modern science has tended to obtain a unified field of knowledge by ruling out freedom, and to this the existentialists justifiably reacted. Existential man, however, clings to his irrationalism and autonomous revolt without hope of rational truth or a unified field of knowledge. Schaeffer therefore says that man has made the leap from a lower level of rationality and limited, isolated, knowledge to an upper level of non-rational subjectivism where some kind of order and truth are purchased at the expense of verification of ideas in the real world. This leap became necessary when man's effort to reach meaningful truth through the lower level of rationality apparently failed. Schaeffer sees personality and experience as either having a source and meaning or else being an impersonal chance-occurrence of matter, time, and motion. To suggest that personality and experience come by chance and time from an impersonal, is, according to Schaeffer, simply an illusion.

There is an undue separation of essence and existence in existential psychology; yet, in reality, one is never given without the other. When we are told to authenticate ourselves and that the decision is unimportant just as long as we choose and act, the command presupposes an unrealistic estimation of the nature of free choice. There must be structure in order for freedom to exist at all. Freedom is impossible without some structure to define just what it is and where it lies. Freedom must have a rational element to give direction and purpose. One does not simply make free choices in a vacuum; choices are always based on some sort of criteria.

The problem of stressing experience while neglecting reason leads us to question the assumptions of existential psychology

---

[6] John Macquarrie, *Twentieth-Century Religious Thought* (New York: Harper & Row, 1963), pp. 208-209.

itself. Reality cannot be tested by the psyche and raw experience alone without a solipsistic result. Ultimately all choices must take into account our own egocentric perceptions, but the validity or morality of the various choices cannot be determined by ego alone. To ignore objective reality is therefore to operate on the assumption that subjective experience is superior in determining matters of truth to a combination of objective evidence and an inward response to it.

This appears totally inadequate. To hold to the superiority of subjective experience over objective, empirical evidence is to fly in the face of common sense. Consider for example the man who "feels" that blacks are inferior to whites in every way and holds to this subjective truth in the face of all evidence to the contrary. His subjective experience may make his claim more meaningful to him but it obviously cannot establish its validity. Because this approach to truth is basically intuitive, it is susceptible to error due to personal aprioris involved in an individual's experience. Hence all intuitive principles and systems must be screened for truth from without by empirical evidences for every truth-claim.

EXISTENCE AND CHRISTIANITY

Arthur Holmes addresses himself to the relationship of the objective and subjective sides of Christian truth-claims in his small book, *Christianity and Philosophy*. He points out that the revelation which brings men to a knowledge of the Christian God is not exclusively objective.

> Scripture insists that spiritual truths only become personally relevant when impressed upon the mind by God's Spirit. The seed must germinate and take root if it is to produce fruit. But the necessity of a subjective work of God denies neither the objectivity of the truth nor the demand for a careful, rational study of Scripture.[7]

Faith is neither blind, nor purely emotive or mystical. Faith must have a known object, involve clear ideas and have a rationale. It does not involve a blind leap in the philosophical dark, but, on the contrary, attempts to give "a reason for the hope" it embraces.

> Faith is a function of the entire personality. . . . It is impossible to mistake the intent of the early Christians.

---

[7] Arthur F. Holmes, *Christianity and Philosophy* (Chicago: Inter-Varsity, 1963), pp. 14-15.

Fact and value, objective truth and subjective experience were wholly inseparable within their one total commitment of faith in Jesus Christ. Vital faith and rational contemplation are not the antithetical states supposed by Kierkegaard. It is not a case of either/or. To regard the crisis of faith as simply a confrontation by the Inscrutable or an attainment to authentic existence is as fallacious as to regard it as simply a mental assent to historical facts or objective truths. Faith integrates both subjective and objective factors.[8]

To assume that all religious values, based on external, objective evidence, are always incongruent with personal experience and therefore a sign of psychological weakness and dependency is highly questionable. Even if religious experiences were fully searched and accurately described, existential psychology could not establish either the validity or the invalidity of such experience. Modern religious existentialism attempts to place the mystical experience of religious belief prior to objective truth-content. Yet, the final claims of historic Christianity upon the individual rest ultimately on the sufficiency of the objective evidences. John Warwick Montgomery, in dealing with William James' *Varieties of Religious Experience*, points out that James tends to make sharper distinctions than the facts warrant when he refers to the "overbelief" (myths, superstitions, dogmas, creeds, and metaphysical theologies) as always secondary to the original, primary religious experience.

To assume that all propositional assertions of faith are secondary and distinguishable from religious experience itself is surely to fly in the face of empirical fact . . . the experience and the theological assertion are blended into an inseparable unity.[9]

Christian believers have never been able to separate their religious experience from the positive assertions of Scripture regarding the nature and authority of Jesus Christ. Doubting Thomas is the prime example. He refused belief until he saw

---

[8] *Ibid.*, p. 19. For a helpful discussion of the validity of Christian experience in its relation to objective criteria, see Paul E. Little, *Know Why You Believe* (Wheaton, Illinois: Scripture Press Publications, 1968), pp. 88-96; Clark H. Pinnock, *Set Forth Your Case: Studies in Christian Apologetics* (Nutley, New Jersey: Craig, 1968), pp. 46-51; and D. Martyn Lloyd-Jones, *Conversions: Psychological or Spiritual?* (Chicago: Inter-Varsity, 1959).

[9] John Warwick Montgomery, *The Shape of the Past* (Ann Arbor, Michigan: Edwards Brothers, Inc., 1962), pp. 316-17.

the evidence of the resurrection. When this evidence was provided, the religious experience became existential truth and he responded, "My Lord and my God." [10] The existential Christian experience rests in the revealed truth of God embodied in the resurrected Christ and the authoritative Scripture.[11]

Existential psychology has well warned us against scientistic objectivism and dehumanization in Western culture. It has acquainted us with the stuff of which human existence is made. It also causes us to give a more sensitive ear to our experience as regards the ultimate meaning of our lives. It cannot, however, speak to the validity of a philosophy of life. That must be determined on the combined basis of objective evidence and existential commitment. The Christianity of the Bible has always taught that faith is a cordial trust, a concerned, inward response, to the person and work of Jesus Christ. This existential faith—grounded objectively in the person and work of the historic Christ—gives meaning to life and death. It opens the door to freedom and individuality, and answers with courage the problems of shallowness, purposelessness, and meaninglessness in life. It offers personal value and acceptance to each person who will put his trust in Christ.

---

[10] John 20:28.

[11] Although this essay seeks to demonstrate that Christian experience is ultimately grounded in the objectivity of the Biblical claims, it is not the purpose of this essay to validate these claims in detail. The reader is referred to the following works for such evidence: F. F. Bruce, *The New Testament Documents: Are They Reliable?* (Grand Rapids, Michigan: Eerdmans, 1967), and Frank Morison, *Who Moved the Stone?* (London: Faber and Faber, 1967).

RUN, RUN, RUN
RUN, RUN !

WHAT A LIFE,
WHAT A WILD LIFE..

AND I DON'T EVEN
KNOW WHERE
I'M GOING !

Man Apart from God:

Martin Luther as a Case Study

Douglas W. Frank

Seldom has one man evoked such a variety of emotional and intellectual responses as that towering spokesman of the Protestant Reformation, Martin Luther. His partisans have exhausted their vocabulary in search of adulatory terms nearly as completely as have his opponents in search of ever more pungent denunciations. Naturally, in a man of Luther's stature, the controversy has not been confined to theology; personality and moral character have been debated with as much vigor and vitriol as any other issue.

It would be a simple matter, in an essay of this sort, to enumerate the charges against Luther; and it would be quite possible, if not as simple, to defend Luther on each of the charges. But this process would make little contribution to the defense of the Christian faith. For proving Luther morally faultless would not insure the ultimate truth of his beliefs, just as demonstrating his culpability would not negate his theological insights. A promising alternative to this approach, I believe, is to seek in Luther some confirmation of the Biblical view of man's predicament apart from God, and to follow through Luther's discovery of a Biblical cure for this condition which will hopefully be applicable to men today.

THE HUMAN PREDICAMENT

What is the Biblical view of man's predicament? Scripture plainly teaches that all men violate God's will and that the result of this trespass is separation from God: man can no longer enjoy intimate association with his God apart from a radical healing.[1] The repercussions of man's revolt are felt

---

[1] Genesis 3; James 4:1-4; Romans 3:23; 5:12; Ephesians 4:17-19.

175

universally, issuing in his alienation from nature, from other men, and from the self. Thus man's fear of the forces of nature, and the sticky sociological and psychological problems he faces in the modern world all stem from man's chosen enmity with God.[2]

This in broad outline is man's dilemma. And this was Martin Luther's dilemma: in particular it was a devastating awareness of moral imperfection, a knowledge of the gulf between man and God, and a total frustration at the impossibility of placating the divine wrath. One author has attempted a full-scale analysis of Luther's anxiety. Erik H. Erikson's *Young Man Luther*, though offering a controversial analysis (as we shall see), provides a helpful vantage point from which to consider the Biblical notion of man's predicament.[3]

Erikson's method is that of the psychoanalyst, and his frame of reference is strongly Freudian, well-spiced with original insights. This means that, while Erikson excludes any overt naturalistic bias from his work, he does seek natural causes both for Luther's inner turmoil and for his theological conclusions. His central thesis describes the predominant influence in young Luther's life as an identity crisis, the major crisis of any individual's adolescence. In this crisis

> each youth must forge for himself some central purpose and direction, some working unity, out of the effective remnants of his childhood and the hopes of his anticipated adulthood; he must detect some meaningful resemblance between what he has come to see in himself and what his sharpened awareness tells him others judge and expect him to be.[4]

To this crisis, as Erikson analyzes him, Luther brought boyhood experiences involving an authoritarian father, frequent harsh disciplinary beatings, and great family pressure to excel in the rising legal profession in the nascent German middle class. These pressures, together with his father's plans for his son's early marriage, left Luther in a state of *tristitia*, or excessive sadness. In deep anxiety on the occasion of a severe thunderstorm, he grasped the only way out: abandonment of his father's plans for his life, and dedication to a new life in the monastery.

---

[2] Francis A. Schaeffer, *The God Who Is There* (Chicago: Inter-Varsity, 1968), p. 152.

[3] *Young Man Luther: A Study in Psychoanalysis and History* (New York: Norton, 1958).

[4] Ibid., p. 14.

This decision, according to Erikson, embodied Luther's rejection of his father's authority under the auspices of God's authority. There followed a "moratorium," the period in the monastery during which Luther could reconsider his chosen identity, to "find that immutable bedrock on which the struggle for a new existence can safely begin and be assured of a future." [5]

By this action, Luther achieved peace of mind for one year. But following his crisis in paternal obedience, and upon the occasion of his first Mass, Luther's *Anfechtung* returned to haunt his soul. During this "identity diffusion" he experienced a deep regression, marked by a "totalism, a to be or not to be which makes every matter of differences a matter of mutually exclusive essences; every question mark a matter of forfeited existence; every error or oversight, eternal treason." [6] Foremost in this regression was a search for mutual recognition, normally the experience of a child in the first year of life, but here involving Luther in a quest to meet God, face to face. Knowing himself to be inadequate for this encounter, and thus feeling rejected by a wrathful God, Luther rebelled against monkhood by too-scrupulous obedience to its rules, a hyper-sensitivity of conscience, and a compulsive use of the confessional. Finally Luther's rebellion against his father, who would not justify his entry into the monastery, became rebellion against the God under whose banner he had hoped to escape his father's authority. God became increasingly wrathful, arbitrary, and contemptible in Luther's eyes.

> Martin was further away than ever from meeting God face to face, from recognizing Him as He would be recognized, and from learning to speak to Him directly.
> This point was the rock bottom on which Martin either would find the oblivion of fragmentation or on which he would build a new wholeness, fusing his own true identity and that of his time. [7]

Several observations can be made on the validity of Erikson's provocative analysis to this point. First, it shares some of the rigidity of a doctrinaire Freudianism, but certainly we must agree with C. S. Lewis that, despite his naturalistic bent, Freud has shown us a great deal about the human organism. [8]

---

[5] *Ibid.*, p. 103.

[6] *Ibid.*

[7] *Ibid.*, p. 165.

[8] C. S. Lewis, *Mere Christianity* (New York: Macmillan, 1960), pp. 69-70.

Second, Erikson's account rests evidentially upon a relatively small base of source material, much of it the product of Luther's later years. But assuming Luther's general honesty, this is all we really have to aid us in plumbing the depths of his personality. Third, Erikson's interpretation can on occasion be modified by a simpler, less devious interpretation. For instance, in developing Luther's idea of God, Erikson relies heavily on Luther's negative father-image. While this had an influence, it underestimates the strength in Luther's mind of the Biblical image of God and of elements of Luther's scholastic heritage. Yet it is neither unreasonable to believe that Luther's father-image gave substance and poignancy to his image of God, nor that this is in any way unique; for has not God, in the Judeo-Christian tradition, been known as Father? In His Person, according to Scripture, He combines the love and authority, the mercy and discipline of the ideal earthly parent.

More positively, Erikson's insights provide a realistic view of Luther's melancholy search for truth while affording us a picture of the human predicament after man's fall into disobedience of God. Of course Erikson himself would not trace man's problems to a prehistoric event; this would give the human predicament a mark of inevitability which Erikson clearly disputes. Still his analysis of Luther is a paradigm of our earlier description of the Fall as separation from those with whom we should rightly be in harmony: God, nature, other men, and self.

Erikson's work abounds with examples, a few of which will suffice to illustrate each of these Biblical separations. Luther's separation from God was predominant in his melancholy and in his later theology. His alienation was manifest in a sense of futility in placating a just God by any religious deed, and involved "a state of conscious and outright hatefulness, invidiousness, and contrariness toward God Himself." [9] Then, somewhere between Luther's separation from God and his separation from nature was his fear of sudden death, involving dread of non-existence or of appearance before God's judgment. This fear, we might add, seems even more realistic today than in Luther's time. Sudden death in an automobile and in the event of a nuclear holocaust are factors which Luther never dreamed of. And is not evidence of Luther's separation from nature his horror at the thunderstorm through which he thought

---

[9] Erikson, *op. cit.*, p. 163.

God to be speaking? [10] Luther's alienation from fellow-humans consists mainly, in Erikson's work, of examples of educational and family experiences: the mistreatment of young Luther in school for minor offenses, and the alleged vindictiveness of his father. Perhaps all of these elements enter into a fourth separation, Luther's separation from himself. No student of Luther can deny his deeply troubled spirit, his pessimistic introspection, his feelings of inadequacy before God, and his inability to control his basic drives.

THE UNIVERSAL LUTHER

In the presence of these symptom's of man's separateness in the universe, was there something abnormal or morbid about Martin Luther's melancholy? We must agree with Albert C. Outler, who states that "if the naturalist denial of God be allowed, then obviously the notion of sin as estrangement from God *is* morbid. But if God is, and is man's Creator, then man's relation to Him is the very crux of existence." [11] A deep despair must certainly be expected in a man of Luther's sensitivity, a man who realized the utter uncontrollability of his passions, his strong bent for sinning, and his overt rebellion against God.

At this point Luther becomes more than a single alienated individual. Erikson himself makes the broader application: "Born leaders seem to fear only more consciously what in some form everybody fears in the depths of his inner life. . . ." [12] Erikson's work is replete with statements recognizing the universality of Luther's inner turmoil, both in his own time and in the whole of human history.[13] The Christian endorses this conclusion without reservation and accepts the claim of Scripture, bolstered by his own observation, that all men sin. Luther is what we are, in our most contemplative moments.

Despite the scientific and cultural advances of the past four centuries, man's nature is still the same as in Luther's day. Man is still at odds with other men, perhaps more so because the revolution in communication has placed him in intimate contact with all races and cultures. The modern university might be regarded as a model, a cross-section of interacting

---

[10] *Ibid.*, pp. 163, 111, 59, 91-92, 59-61.
[11] Albert C. Outler, *Psychotherapy and the Christian Message* (New York: Harper & Row, 1954), p. 137.
[12] Erikson, *op. cit.*, p. 110.
[13] *Ibid.*, pp. 15, 39, 74, 128, 149, 177, 195, 261.

mankind whose relationships are often poisoned by the same jealousies, petty prejudices, and senseless antipathies which cause nations to declare war. Man's separation from nature can be seen in the ironic ability of man to destroy his fellow-man with the same scientific knowledge that he might have used for preserving human life. Man's separation from God has never before been quite so terrifying to him as in this day when he fails to find God at the end of his radio telescope, his electron microscope, or in the subjective processes of the human psyche. Taken as a whole, this alienation weighs upon the individual, harrowing him with feelings of guilt, demonstrating to him his inability to meet the ideals dictated even by the weakest of consciences, revealing a life and universe void of ultimate meaning. Though modern technologies have devised more means of escaping this anxiety than ever before, outside of suicide, escapes are temporary, and in their wake the anxious gloom of modern life returns to haunt twentieth century man.

These, then, are the consequences of sin. Erikson ties them together according to his understanding of the human psyche, and the result seems to the Christian to eliminate the "spiritual" causes of man's condition. But, until more is known, it is doubtful whether we can sharply distinguish spiritual from psychological in man's experience before he turns to God. Is it not therefore possible that, given this separation from God, the psychologist can define and analyze its symptoms without knowledge of ultimate causes? However the *cure* for the human patient's sickness is a different matter. Here Erikson stands in need of Christian re-interpretation, or at least a shift in emphasis.

THE UNIVERSAL CURE

It seems obvious that the Luther who, as Erikson describes him, after much struggling came to recognize the intricacies of introspection and the problems involved in combining "intellectual meaning with an inner sense of meaning it," would demand something objective, some unchanging principle outside himself by which to solve the human dilemma.[14] Thus Erikson's analysis makes God's objective truth necessary. The Christian finds this truth in the Bible. But when Erikson gives the impression that Luther had to mold the Bible to fit his psychological needs, the Christian protests that, since Luther's anxieties represented those of mankind, and since the Bible claims to speak to mankind's anxieties, it is just as sensible to believe that the Bible was *already* molded by God to meet the needs

---

[14] *Ibid.*, p. 176.

of mankind in general and Martin Luther in particular. Scripture met Luther's needs because it was written to meet the common needs of the human race. Erikson describes Luther's theology as "ideology," thus excusing himself from the necessity to pass upon the objective truth of that theology.[15] But, *pace* Erikson, it should be noted that Luther discovered not *an* ideology, but *the* Ideology. Protestant orthodoxy, accepting the Bible's authority on Christ's testimony, sees no need for Luther to have placed a subjective interpretation upon the Bible in order to find a cure for his spiritual illness. He needed only to recover authentic biblical teaching, obscured as it was by the institutional machinery and doctrinal accretions of the Roman Church.

The details of this cure, as outlined by Erikson, bear the marks of his preoccupation with the developing psyche; to criticize them would necessitate another complete essay. What matters here is the relation of this cure to the ongoing human condition, and here Erikson's view is quite acceptable.

> Luther saw that God's justice is not consigned to a future day of judgment based on our record on earth when He will have the "last word." Instead, this justice is in us, in the here and now; for, if we will only perceive it, God has given us faith to live by, and we can perceive it by understanding the Word which is Christ.[16]

That is, man cannot achieve justice in God's eyes by doing just works; he does just works if he has already achieved justice. The human condition is overcome by God's gift of forgiveness in Christ. God is thereby shown to be full of compassion even as He is of wrath. For modern man, attempting to re-make himself and his world, the Biblical answer holds the same refreshing promise: when you cannot overcome your condition, God can. He alone can remove the stifling guilt, the anxieties, and the inadequacies which are consequences of man's sinful predicament. Justice in God's eyes and intimacy with God are not earned by man: they are a free gift. The man whom God thus heals is truly able to worship God, love his neighbor in all sincerity, and begin to understand and control himself.

This analysis, then, helps us understand the anxieties of the young Martin Luther. But it seems that the older Luther, who had already accepted God's offer of healing, was still plagued by depression. Most criticisms of Luther's conduct

---

[15] *Ibid.*, pp. 22, 41.
[16] *Ibid.*, p. 201.

find their basis in Luther's later years, criticisms centering on his violent and obscene language, his alleged proclivity to hate, and his political and social prejudices which are said to have laid the foundation for Hitlerism.

Now most of these charges either totally misrepresent Luther's writings (for example, in neglecting the extent to which his conservatism was based on a distaste for violence), or they forget how his theology proved a firm antidote for his later depressions, or, most frequently, they betray shoddy historical method by removing him from his social, political, and intellectual context and demanding sixteenth-century answers for twentieth-century problems. Luther has been ably defended in this regard by Roland Bainton, whose *Here I Stand* is but a short synthesis of a lifetime of scholarly work on Luther's life and thought.[17] More recently, John Warwick Montgomery has replied to charges of political authoritarianism and anti-Semitism levelled by Peter F. Wiener in his *Martin Luther: Hitler's Spiritual Ancestor* and repeated by William L. Shirer in his otherwise admirable *The Rise and Fall of the Third Reich*.[18] In fact it is possible for Luther's advocates not only to defend him from such attacks, but to point to overwhelmingly positive aspects of his personality, his willingness to forgive, his acts of love and self-sacrifice.

On the other hand it is impossible to "whitewash" Luther, as one critic has charged Luther's apologists are doing.[19] Luther never claimed perfection; indeed, he admitted his faults whenever he saw them.[20] His Biblical theology recognized that the results of man's separations linger on after these separations have been eternally overcome.[21] Luther preached

---

[17] *Here I Stand: A Life of Martin Luther* (New York: New American Library, n.d.).

[18] John Warwick Montgomery, "Shirer's Re-Hitlerizing of Luther," *The Christian Century*, LXXIX (December 12, 1962), 1510-12.

[19] See Warren Kliewer, "Anti-Semitism and the Reformation: Charging John W. Montgomery with a Whitewash," *Christian Century*, LXXX (February 6, 1963), 179-80.

[20] In a brief note in 1537, Luther wrote: "At the beginning of the cause which I espoused (*meiner Sache*) I wrote many things with heat.

"May Jesus Christ bear with us, be patient with us, and finally free us also from ourselves. Amen." (cited in Ewald M. Plass [comp.], *What Luther Says: An Anthology* [Saint Louis: Concordia Publishing House, 1959], III, 1321.

[21] "So all sins are indeed removed through Baptism, but in such a way that God does not impute them. However, they are not gone;

freedom, and freedom involves risk, including the risk of misuse of that freedom. Interesting in this context is Luther's statement, *"Pecca fortiter, sed fortius fide et gaude in Christo."* In interpreting this, Bonhoeffer highlights Luther's realistic view of the continuing human dilemma: "Take courage and confess your sins, says Luther, do not try to run away from it, but believe more boldly still. You are a sinner, so be a sinner, and don't try to become what you are not." That is, you cannot reach perfection in yourself. Trust God's grace, and daily follow Christ in a genuine discipleship.[22] Likewise, the Apostle John commended sinlessness but pointed to Jesus Christ as our intercessor with the Father, available to all those Christians who do commit sin. Francis A. Schaeffer's comments on this passage are directly applicable to our understanding of Luther and ourselves:

> On the one hand, we must stand against all standards lower than perfection.... Yet on the other hand we must stand against all the romantic concepts of perfection in this life, except in the area of justification. It does not promise us in this life perfection morally, physically, psychologically or sociologically.[23]

Finally, does the presence of imperfection in Luther preclude or compromise his ability to arrive at truth? Obviously not, for Biblical writers themselves admitted imperfection, and yet are accepted as bearers of God's truth, on Christ's testimony.[24] Kenneth S. Latourette, in *A History of the Expansion of Christianity*, supplies numerous examples of men whose imperfections did not eliminate their capacity to proclaim truth in word or deed. But most important, Luther's solution was true because its foundation lay outside himself. Luther went directly to Scripture for an understanding and cure of his dilemma. We must do the same, for in so doing we will better understand both Luther and ourselves, and find escape from the alienation which characterizes man apart from God.

---

one must continue to heal them constantly as one has begun to do. When we die, all will be completely healed." (*Ibid.*, III, 1298-99).

[22] Dietrich Bonhoeffer, *The Cost of Discipleship* (rev. ed.; New York: Macmillan, 1963), pp. 55-57.

[23] Schaeffer, *op. cit.*, p. 155.

[24] Philippians 3:12-14; I John 1:8—2:2. Schaeffer stresses the Apostle John's use of the word "we" in the latter passage, indicating that he too was still imperfect and in need of an advocate (*Ibid.*).

ONCE UPON a CAMPUS THERE WAS A REAL SWINGER!

HE HAD GRADES (A SCHOLARSHIP, EVEN!)

A A A TOP! COOL! A+ GO! GO! BRIGHT! GO MAN! DIG A TOPS! SWING! HEAVY MAN! COOL IT! A CRAZY MAN!

MAN, HE HAD Girls...

HE HAD LOOT A ROD PAD A WILD AND PLACES TO GO...

ROBIN

HIS ONLY PROBLEM! WHAT NEXT, MAN? SO HE PLANNED...

1. GRAD SCHOOL
2. DIG LIFE MORE, YET!
   ☑ MORE GIRLS
   ☑ MORE LOOT
   ☑ NEW CAR
3. SECURITY
   ☑ KEEP UP THE GRADES
   ☑ INSURANCE
   ☑ SAVINGS
4. LIVE, MAN!

BUT...

HE DIDN'T.. HE LEFT THE SCENE..

READ HIS LIFE STORY IN THE BIBLE LUKE 12:16

YES, JESUS CALLED THAT MAN A FOOL

HE ALSO SAID...

" SO IS HE WHO LAYS UP TREASURE FOR HIMSELF AND IS NOT RICH TOWARD GOD. "

The Problem of Pleasure

Loren Wilkinson

Here is a man with a glass of wine, and the pleasure of it—the smell, the sweetness on the tongue and the warmth in the throat—is so unquestionably *good* that the memory of it glows in his veins and his brain for the rest of the evening.

Here is a man swimming in the ocean, and the waves are giant and smooth around him. When he wades out of the surf the retreating foam pulls the tickling sand from beneath his feet, but further up the beach it is packed, black, and cool.

Here is a man in bed with his wife, and the smoothness of her, the weight and warmth of her body, is good. And the union of their loins, spreading like a sacrament through all their nerves, is also good, and a symbol of the greater union that makes her his wife.

Indeed no man lives without pleasure. He can no more escape it than he can escape breathing. But it is curious that despite the ubiquity of pleasure—or perhaps because of it—we seldom philosophize about it; we are far more exercised by the problem of pain. Pain is a great enigma. It grates our philosophical nerves. The overwhelming and apparently unanswerable question following the effects of a collision, a bullet, or a cancer, is "Why?" And to that grief-filled question no complete, humanly satisfactory answer has been given.[1]

But whatever we do with the problem of pain, the problem of pleasure remains. The question "Why?" ought to hover as perplexingly over the pleasures of sex and music as it does over the pains of cancer and starvation. That the question is seldom asked in contexts of pleasure is understandable; a person in pleasure seems less inclined to philosophy than

---

[1] One of the best contemporary discussions of the problem of pain may be found in C. S. Lewis, *The Problem of Pain* (New York: Macmillan, 1966).

a person in pain. But explaining our neglect of the question does not answer it. *Why* indeed do we enjoy? What (if anything) lies behind the whole human capacity for pleasure?

Ultimate answers to the "Why" of pleasure (like ultimate answers to the "Why" of pain), are usually given in evolutionary terms.[2] The pleasure-pain continuum is present in men (and animals) because of its survival-value. Organisms with little sensitivity to helpful stimuli are eliminated before they can reproduce; organisms with progressively higher sensitivities to pleasure and pain are perpetuated. According to this theory, pain has negative survival-value: it is life's way of keeping an organism from blundering into its own destruction.

Likewise many pleasures are connected with activities which have positive survival-value. Sexual intercourse yields intense pleasure, and also provides for the survival of the species. Eating and drinking also provide certain pleasures and are physically vital. So it is with a number of pleasures: they seem to be enticements, built into our bodies, which keep us doing the things we must do in order to stay alive—as individuals and as a species.

The explanation of pleasure as positive survival-value is inadequate, and for at least three reasons. In the first place, it does not explain many—perhaps most—of our intense pleasures. Music, for example, seems to have little survival-value, yet it brings great pleasure to many people. The same could be said of numerous activities: chess, tennis, mountain-climbing, poetry, going to the theater, walking in the woods—everyone has his own list. It is significant that such activities seem to be impractical, for survival or, in some cases, anything else. They are simply good. We just enjoy them.

Not only is the survival-value theory inadequate to explain the breadth of our pleasures; it is also inadequate to explain their *depth*. Many pleasures which obviously have survival-value—eating, drinking, procreating—seem *over*loaded with capabilities for pleasure. We do not merely eat; we enjoy thousands of combinations of flavors, textures, and temperatures in food. Food becomes a thing good in itself, and appetite a drive capable of countless complex fulfillments. The same observation can be made of sex. Far from being a simple physical need, it is a complex yearning which is fulfilled, if

---

[2] Charles Darwin, *The Origin of the Species* (New York: Mentor, 1963), pp. 87 ff.

at all, only in the unique and hard-to-define relationship we call love. Some "simple" physical pleasures which man supposedly shares with the animals turn out to be parts of intricate patterns of pleasure which include everything that makes man human. Indeed, his unparalleled capacity for pleasure is one attribute which seems to distinguish men from animals. Animals eat; humans have meals. Animals copulate; humans make love.

A third inadequacy of the survival-value theory of pleasure becomes evident when we examine the nature of pleasure itself. No pleasure is ever quite perfect. Every activity seems to lose its luster a short time as our desires lead us on to something else. Our pleasures, no matter how intense, are never quite what we thought we wanted.

A quick look at advertising illustrates this persistent dissatisfaction. Cigarette advertisements, for example, abound with phrases like "it really satisfies," "a *real* cigarette," and "the filter you've been looking for." These slogans contain an implicit admission that no smoke yet has *really* satisfied. The problem is summed up nicely in the question (which, with slight changes in the wording, could be applied to nearly every human activity): "Are you smoking more now but enjoying it less?"

That question is more than just an advertising slogan. It points to one of the main difficulties in life: everything gets boring. Pleasures tend to start at the almost-perfect and go downhill toward the humdrum. Perhaps this suggests one reason why the suicide rate is higher among countries with high standards of living. A high standard of living permits greater exploration of the gamut of pleasures while also permitting more disillusionment when pleasure wears out. Man's longings for pleasure are never quite satisfied. On the one hand we cannot explain the staggering depth and breadth of a man's capacity for pleasure; on the other, we cannot explain why lasting pleasure always eludes him.

The collapse of the survival-value theory of pleasure leads to a greater understanding of the problem of human pleasure and to a new realization of the nature of man. Man's inordinately high capacity for pleasure seems to indicate a qualitative difference between himself and the lower animals, and his failure to completely fill that capacity seems to point to something unattainable in his present experience. For though we do indeed find ourselves in the chaos of mere existence, our unfilled longings seem to indicate vaguely that there is—or ought to be—a solution to the problems of pleasure and beyond the empty non-solution of courageously facing the apparent absurdity of it—like Camus' Sisyphus, who found his happiness in rolling a boulder (eternally, futilely, and without illusion) to the top of a mountain. But the details of a more satisfactory answer lead either into the sort of oversimplified, inadequate explanation of ultimate problems attempted in theories like the survival-value explanation of pleasure, or they lead in the opposite direction to the labyrinth of the world's religions.

A variety of religious answers have been presented to the problem of pleasure. The eastern religions answer the problem by saying that both pleasure and pain are illusory, based on change, and are to be transcended by a union of the individual with the universal Nothing which is beyond change.[3] The difficulty with this sort of solution (and it has its counterpart in some of the mystical and ascetic eddies of Christianity) is that in denying pleasure, it practically denies man, since pleasure is an inextricable part of human experience. The logical terminus of such a solution is a kind of total solipsism which is tantamount to suicide.

Another religious answer to the problem of pleasure is provided by the Judeo-Christian religions, which see man as the creation of a personal God whose destiny is fulfilled within a personal relationship to that God.

Such an explanation is aesthetically and metaphysically pleasing, but it appears to invite the same criticism that all metaphysical answers to ultimate questions invite: metaphysics is purely speculative and goes beyond the data of human experience. Ludwig Wittgenstein's dictum bears directly on this point: "the sense of the world must lie outside the world." [4] By "world" Wittgenstein means all the possible data of sense experience. Any human experience must be explained in terms of other human experience, but our desire for ultimate answers demands that we go outside human experience—"the world"— entirely. But by definition, such escape to a world outside our experience is impossible. Our religious and philosophical problems—including the problem of pleasure—seem to indicate that solutions lie beyond the limits of human experience. And if

---

[3] Arthur Koestler, *The Lotus and the Robot* (New York, Harper and Row, 1960): an excellent critical summary of the claims of Indian mysticism (Yoga) and Japanese Mysticism (Zen).

[4] Ludwig Wittgenstein, *Tractatus Logico-Philosophicus*, trans. D. D. Pears and B. F. McGuiness (London: Routledge and Kegan Paul, 1961), p. 145.

that is the case, the solution itself cannot be had—even by speculation.

So the Judeo-Christian answers to the problems posed by
pleasure—that man is made in the image of God (God-like)
and that his ultimate fulfillment is found in relationship to
God himself—are as useless as other metaphysical answers—
yes, *if indeed they have the same sort of speculative base
as other answers.*

But the Christian solution to the pleasure-problem differs
in one all-important respect from other metaphysical answers.
If Wittgenstein is correct, the only way we can obtain a final
answer to the problem of pleasure and the variegated problems
of man's existence is for us to receive information from outside
the world of human experience. Since, however, we cannot
get outside our world, the alternative is for a message—or
messenger—to come from outside the world and speak an answer
to men.

The claim to be such a messenger would be an enormous
one. But Christianity is founded on just such a claim, that
someone—in fact, the One who made the world—entered the
world and confirmed in His own person and revealed in His
words the answers to the problems posed by pleasure, by pain,
and by the whole human condition. Here Christ differs from
other religious figures. Not only is He the only major religious
figure to make such a claim, but He was able to attest the
truth of His claim. The documents which present his life and
deeds are accurate, first-hand accounts.[5] They describe a man
who claimed to be God, and who supported his claim with
miracles, and with the ultimate miracle of resurrection which
demonstrated his power over and solution for that eternal dilemma, death. Such a claim, supported by such events, points
to a staggering possibility: a first-century Palestinian Jew,
Jesus of Nazareth, was and is the very one Christians address
as God.

If Christianity, the religion based on this man, is true, how,
specifically, does it provide an answer to the problems raised
by pleasure? Before looking at the answers which it does
provide, it must be understood that not all Christians have lived
according to the answer which Christianity provides. Some
Christians have "solved" the problems by denying pleasure

---

[5] F. F. Bruce, *The New Testament Documents: Are They Reliable?* (Grand Rapids, Mich.: Eerdmans, 1963), an excellent study
of the historical reliability of the New Testament.

much as the Eastern religions have done. But the picture of a Christian as one who abstains from all things pleasurable is a caricature of a genuine Christianity which provides highly satisfactory answers to the problem of pleasure.[6]

First, the problem of man's inexplicably high capacity for pleasures of non-functional kinds—from reading poetry to drinking Chianti—is suddenly explicable in the light of the concept of Divine creation. The Christian view of man is that God made him "in His own image," and part of that image is the capacity for pleasure. The God of Christian revelation, often caricatured as a God of wrath, is also a God who delights and rejoices.[7] In fact the rest of his creation, the stars, seas and mountains, are poetically pictured as breaking forth in an ecstasy of delight. The Old Testament contains many references like "The Lord reigns, let the earth rejoice," "Let the floods clap their hands, let the hills be joyful together," and "Sing, O heavens, and be joyful, O earth, and break forth into singing, O mountains."[8]

Man's capacity for pleasure is God-given. The very way in which his first home is described points to man's preparation for pleasure. His place, described as a garden, is a sensuous delight, yet in it were put creatures made in the image of the infinite Spirit who made the universe. Man is the only creature in the universe whose nerve-endings are connected in a God-like soul.

The Divine pleasure principle is confirmed in the words and actions of incarnate Deity Himself. Jesus was no ascetic, but joined in the pleasures of food and work and wine to the extent that his critics called him "a wine-drinker and a glutton."[9] Indeed, His first miracle seems to sanctify the principle of pleasure: He heightened the delight of a long wedding party by changing water into wine. And among His last words to

---

[6] Knowledge of "genuine Christianity" is easily accessible in the original documents, the Bible, which draw their authority from the words of Jesus. If the picture of Jesus which the Gospels present is even roughly correct, we must acknowledge that this he was God. Being God, he would thus speak authoritatively about the Old Testament writings—and he regarded them as without error. He gave to his immediate disciples a promise to guide them in the writing of equally authoritative books. From those disciples came the New Testament.

[7] I Kings 10:9: "Blessed be the Lord thy God, which delighteth in thee." Micah 7:18: "He delighteth in mercy."

[8] Psalm 97:1; Psalm 98:1; Isaiah 49:13.

[9] Matt. 11:19.

His followers, just before the long pain of the cross, were promises of joy.

Thus Christianity answers the first question of man's high capacity for pleasure by showing that he was made for pleasure by the Being who invented pleasure. Pleasure presents another major question in man's insatiable desire for it. Men seem to be built for something they cannot experience, but have a dim knowledge of. This longing is expressed in many of his works and words.

Much of the literature of the world, from primitive folklore to modern fiction, deals with the image of the lost paradise: the walled garden (from *Paradise Lost* to *Alice in Wonderland*), the forgotten island, the sunlit glade in the center of the forest. Every Utopian vision, from Thomas More to the hippie, has something of this lost paradise about it. These images, which have a particular strength and poignancy, are bound together by two ideas: pleasure and inaccessibility. The perfect place is lost. We feel that loss even in music, whose keenest pleasure often comes with a pang because that instant of pleasure cannot be recovered. Every pleasure we seek is perhaps a quest for that ultimate pleasure hinted at in our moments of deepest longing. It is this sense of something lost —of a numinous homeland, vastly distant in time and space— which gives J. R. R. Tolkien's *Lord of the Rings* such force. We are all like the three hobbits, standing in tears at the Grey Havens watching the last tall ship sail—without us— into the True West. C. S. Lewis, late Professor of Medieval and Renaissance English at Cambridge University, and a brilliant writer in fields as diverse as philosophy and children's fiction, has described this longing as well, perhaps, as anyone. He calls it Joy. Joy is a painfully clear glimpse of the unattainable pleasure and perfection which we desire. Those flashes of Joy (which come most often in childhood) point to the reason why no pleasure is ever perfectly satisfying. It is as though this one pleasure were beyond all pleasures. It is the thing that could, if we found it, restore the lost center to man, and open at last the door in the wall that surrounds his own lost paradise. It is the object of this pleasure that we seek through and beyond all other pleasures. Wine is good, and music is good, and so are the million other pleasures around us. But none of these things is quite what we want. And so we keep searching for the object of that ultimate longing.

C. S. Lewis describes in his autobiography, *Surprised by*

Joy, his long search for the object of Joy. He concluded (reluctantly, for he was not attracted to either theism or Christianity) that the source and object of Joy was God. More significantly, he concluded that the only way to communicate with that source of all true desire was through the way established in the life, death, and Resurrection of the man Jesus, who also was God.

Lewis arrived by hard experience at the sort of answer to the problem of pleasure that the Bible also presents: that God is the source of all that is good; that man has cut himself off from that God and that goodness; and that the only way back to God and His promised "abundant life" [10] is the way He provided when He became a man. In *A Philosophy of the Christian Religion* E. J. Carnell has beautifully developed the idea that none of man's life, from his pleasure to his reason, is in perfect focus until man has established a personal acquaintance with the God who is at the apex of the pyramid of all man's aspirations.[11]

Christians are offered no immediate guarantee of pleasure, just as they are offered no immediate exemption from pain. What they are offered is a knowledge of who they are: immortal creatures containing the image of their Creator—and a knowledge of their destiny: eternal, increasing pleasure, of the sort they were made for, and of which their present pleasures are only—at best—a glimpse and a beginning. But the way back into this pleasure is not one we enter by simply seeking pleasure—that way lies only pain. The way is opened for us by the historical participation of God in man. It is only through obedience to that one Man that we may enter the state where pleasure will not fail and become pain, but will remain pleasure, full and increasing, forever.

It was this sort of understanding of man and God which the Psalmist grasped when he shouted to a yet unseen God, "At Your right hand are pleasures forever." [12]

---

[10] John 10:10.
[11] E. J. Carnell, *A Philosophy of the Christian Religion* (Grand Rapids, Mich.: Eerdmans, 1952), pp. 179 ff.
[12] Psalm 16:11.

LSD and Religious Truth

Robert A. Sabath

Many today are desperately seeking to experience some reality that will give their lives meaning. In 1938 a new ingredient was tossed into the pot of alternatives for those pursuing the quest with the accidental discovery and synthesis of "D-lysergic acid diethlamide tartrate-25" by the Swiss biochemist Albert Hofmann—an event hailed by at least one in religious circles as a spiritual Copernican revolution that gives ready access to "the most captivating and transforming experience known to man." [1]

That the psychedelic drugs can trigger a mystical experience which has far-reaching personality effects is attested to by the statements of many who have ingested the drugs, by controlled experimentation, and by a comparison of drug-induced with non-drug-induced religious experience. Aldous Huxley, one of the first to make the public aware of the relationship of psychedelic drugs to subjective religious phenomena by recounting his experiences under the influence of mescaline, advocated drugs as a safe road to a mystical perception that alone had power to change man's personality at a deep level.[2] Before Timothy Leary was dismissed from Harvard University in 1963 for experimentation with the drugs, over 75 per cent of the sixty-nine religious professionals who took psychedelic drugs under his supervision reported intense mystical experiences, more than half asserting that they had had the deepest religious experience of their life.[3] Walter H. Clark, professor emeritus of Psychology of Religion at Andover Newton The-

---

[1] Walter Houston Clark, *Chemical Ecstasy* (New York: Sheed & Ward, 1969), p. vi.

[2] Aldous Huxley, *The Doors of Perception* (New York: Harper & Row, 1963).

[3] Timothy Leary, "Religion: Its Production and Interpretation," *Dialogue*, III (Summer, 1964), 215.

ological Seminary and one of those sixty-nine religious professionals in Leary's experiments, subsequently argued strongly that "in proper circumstances, in certain people properly prepared, the psychedelic drugs have a strong tendency to release mystical experience." [4] So convinced is Leary of the religious potential of the drugs that he calls them "the instruments of systematic religion" and "the religion of the twenty-first century." He writes: "If you are really serious about your religion, if you really wish to commit yourself to the spiritual quest, you must learn how to use psychochemicals." [5]

One of the most convincing pieces of evidence supporting the claim that psychedelics do in certain circumstances release profound religious experience is Walter N. Pahnke's 1963 Harvard doctoral dissertation, known as The Good Friday Experiment. [6] In a double blind design in which neither subjects nor experimenters knew in advance who would receive the drug and who would receive the placebo, ten first-year protestant theological students were given thirty milligrams of psilocybin in pill form and ten an indistinguishable nondrug substitute. After attending a two and one half hour Good Friday service, three judges rated the data collected from the subjects for evidences of mysticism, using nine different criteria. Nine out of ten in the experimental group which had received psilocybin reported unmistakable evidence of mystical consciousness, the majority to a marked degree, while only one of the control group experienced even minor mystical consciousness. The results of the experiment were significant to the .001 level, meaning that the probability the results could be duplicated in subsequent experiments was .999.

A third line of evidence indicating the value of certain drugs in triggering mystical experience comes from comparing drug-

----

[4] Clark, *op. cit.*, p. 77.

[5] Timothy Leary, *The Politics of Ecstasy* (New York: World Publishing Co., 1968), p. 44.

[6] Walter N. Pahnke, "Drugs and Mysticism: An Analysis of the Relationship Between Psychedelic Drugs and Mystical Consciousness" (unpublished Ph.D. dissertation, Harvard University, 1964). The full account of the Good Friday Experiment is summarized in Walter N. Pahnke and William A. Richards "Implications of LSD and Experimental Mysticism," *Journal of Religion and Health* (July 1966), 175-208.

induced with non-drug-induced religious experience. Clark undertakes such a comparison in the first chapters of his book, reaching the conclusions that, though there is not a one-to-one relationship between religious experiences which are characteristically individualistic, nevertheless: (1) all religious experience, drug-induced or not, has the power "to mediate wholesome personality change," and (2) the drug experience bears "a family resemblance" to religious experience of the more traditional variety; that is, "the fruits of the drug-induced religion parallel what are considered the more normal variety." [7]

Much of the distrust of LSD's ability to produce wholesome mystical experience stems from the fact that the religious experience is not the only type of experience produced by the drug. Current evidence suggests that the type of experience triggered depends on several factors: (1) the intrinsic properties of the drug itself and, to some extent, the dosage level; (2) the "set" or expectations and general state of the subject before the session, including the mood of the subject and, in part, certain hereditary conditions; and (3) the "setting" or external conditions at the time of the administration. [8] The mystical experience is a delicate combination of psychological set and setting in which the drug itself is only the triggering agent. It is currently theorized that the experiences triggered by the drug are due to a slowing of the rate of synaptic transmission of nerve impulses coming in as input to the brain decoding and processing centers. [9] This perplexes the brain and allows the brain to focus on itself and its incoming signals, which is not normally possible. Walter Pahnke pinpoints five

---

[7] Clark, op. cit., pp. 38, 84. Objections at this point have been raised by Zaehner, an Oxford scholar, who tried mescaline and claimed that the drugs don't induce truly religious mysticims. It was a blend of natural and monistic mysticism which was on a lower plane than the more orthodox, theistic variety. (See R. C. Zaehner, Mysticism, Sacred and Profane [Oxford: Clarendon Press, 1957].) Walter N. Pahnke contends that as a devout Roman Catholic Zaehner was too eager to disprove the potential of drugs in producing mystical experience. In his eagerness and tenseness he did not experience mystical consciousness with the drugs, but rather a shallow aesthetic experience typical of subjects with considerable anxiety and resistance (Pahnke and Richards, op. cit., p. 194).

[8] A. E. Wilder Smith, The Drug Users (Wheaton, Illinois: Harold Shaw Publishers, 1969), p. 14.

[9] Ibid., p. 27f.

main types of psychological experiences generally recognized as belonging to the total LSD experience:[10] (1) the aesthetic experience—distorted spacial perception, intensified color and form, geometric patterns; (2) psychoanalytic experience—regression to infancy or childhood, confrontation with guilt and hostility, unconscious thrust into consciousness; (3) psychotic experience—fear, paranoia, panic, detachment from the world, unreality; (4) cognitive experience—meaning of words, lucidity of thought, new insights; and (5) mystical experience. Pahnke in turn classifies the mystical experience under nine headings:[11] (1) unity—sense of oneness with the cosmos; (2) objectivity and reality—experience known to be true; (3) transcendence of time and space—subject feels himself to be outside the three dimensions and time; (4) sense of sacredness of the experience—awe, wonder, humility, reverence; (5) paradoxicality of experience—identity of opposites recognized; (6) deeply felt positive mood—joy, peace, love, deepest emotion; (7) alleged ineffibility—not possible to be communicated by means of words; (8) transiency of the experience; and (9) positive persistent changes in attitude and/or behavior— new insights into the meaning of life and a new sense of values. Pahnke also noted that following the mystical experience his subjects reported increased "personality-integration, increased sensitivity to authentic problems of other persons, responsible independence of social pressures, deeper purpose in life, loss of anxiety about death, guilt, and meaninglessness."[12]

This ability of the psychedelic drugs to release a mystical experience which produces profound shifts in personality ac-

---

[10] Walter N. Pahnke and William A. Richards, *loc., cit.* Other non-mystical experiences include photic (white light), electrical flow in body, psychosomatic (nausea, clamminess, stomach contractions), evolutionary (foetal) experiences, somatic change, parapsychological, consciousness of bodily processes, etc.

[11] Walter N. Pahnke, "LSD and Religious Experience," in *LSD, Man and Society*, ed. by Richard C. Debold and Russell C. Leaf (New York: Grove Press, 1967), pp. 61-64. Walter H. Clark used the following twenty criteria in his experiments with mysticism: "timelessness, spacelessness, unity and loss of self, unity with objects and growing things, unity with people, ultimate reality, blessedness and peace, the holy and divine, paradoxicality, ineffability, fear and terror, mystery, joy, sense of dying, rebirth, presence of God, esthetic experience, color intensity, music moving, significance of experience (Clark, *op. cit.*, p. 81f.).

[12] Pahnke, "Implications of LSD and Experimental Mysticism," p. 193.

counts for their therapeutic effectiveness.[13] Hoffer and Os-
mond, doing important pioneer work in the use of LSD in the
treatment of alcoholics, discovered that the key to its effectiveness seemed to reside in its religious properties.[14] With
sixty alcoholics for whom neither psychiatry, medicine, nor
AA had availed, a five year follow-up showed that one large
dose of LSD was effective in maintaining abstenence when
the drug experience had been transcendental. LSD has also
been used successfully as an adjunct to psychotherapy.[15]
Grof's research in Czechoslovakia with the mentally ill found
that LSD was clinically effective in helping the neurotic and
psychotic achieve normal adjustment when the drug con-
tributed to the attainment of the mystical vision through "ego
death" and the sense of rebirth which followed.[16] Some
evidence also exists that LSD is useful in the treatment of
chronic psychopaths and sociopaths,[17] as well as in the
treatment of terminal illness to alleviate pain and to help the
patient achieve a healthy attitude towards death.[18]

The evidence supporting the therapeutic value of the
psychedelic drugs has been dulled by current misconceptions
concerning physiological and psychological complications produced by them.[19] Though the actual dangers of ingesting

---

[13] Arthur H. Becker, "What the Minister Ought to Know About
LSD," *Pastoral Psychology*, XVI (October, 1965), 42. See also Clark,
op. cit., p. 96.

[14] H. A. Abramson, ed., *The Use of LSD in Psychotherapy and
Alcoholism* (Indianapolis: Bobbs-Merrill, 1967), pp. 18-19, 114-15. See
also Clark, *op. cit.*, p. 45 and Becker, *op. cit.*, p. 40ff.

[15] Becker, *op. cit.*, p. 42 and Abramson, *loc. cit.*

[16] Abramson, *op. cit.*, pp. 154-90.

[17] Timothy Leary and Walter H. Clark, "The Religious Implica-
tions of Consciousness Expanding Drugs," *Religious Education*, LVIII
(May-June, 1963), 251-56; Timothy Leary, *High Priest* (New York:
World Publishing Co., 1968), pp. 173-211. G. Castayne, "The Crime
Game," in *The Ecstatic Adventure*, ed. by R. Metzner (New York:
Macmillan, 1968), pp. 168-75; R. Crockett, *et al.*, eds., *Hallucinogenic
Drugs and Their Psychotherapeutic Use* (Springfield, Ill.: C. C. Thomas,
1963), pp. 101-106.

[18] E. Kast, "Pain and LSD-25," in *LSD: The Consciousness-
Expanding Drug*, ed. by D. Solomon (New York: G. P. Putnam's Sons,
1964).

[19] "Playboy Interview: Timothy Leary." Reprinted from the September, 1966 issue of *Playboy* magazine, which can be obtained free
by writing Playboy Magazine, 919 N. Michigan, Chicago, Illinois. Scare
tactics include warnings that those who ingest the drug take a dangerous
risk in precipitating an acute psychotic reaction, playing up only the

LSD have been trumped up all out of proportion to the facts, the results of present medical research are so ambiguous as not to preclude cautious use of the drug.[20] Sidney Cohen, in one of the most comprehensive studies of the undesirable side-effects of LSD, indicates that incidence of serious reaction to LSD among normals is as low as 0.08 per cent.[21] Current increase in dangerous after-effects is caused by indiscriminate use of LSD among untrained persons and the ingestion of the drug by psychologically unstable persons.[22] Because the incidence of adverse reaction is so rare, and because of the increasing possibility of synthesizing a psychedelic that will be as harmless as caffeine, objections to the religious experience released by the drugs should not be based on medical findings.

It cannot be emphasized too strongly that every psychological bi-product of Christianity can be reproduced by LSD and by almost every other religion,[23] including a sense of meaning in life, integration of personality, increased sensitivity to others, greater self-acceptance, psychological relief from anxiety and guilt feelings, tranquility and inner harmony. The religious experience with all its emotional and behavior concommitants is not unique to Christianity. The most one can infer from it is that man is so constituted that he can have this experience.[24] What is the difference, then, between Christianity

---

bad trips, and predicting the loss of inhibitions and possibly suicide, etc.

[20] Clark, *op. cit.*, p. 131. For references dealing with the possibility of chromosomal breakage see J. H. Tjio, W. N. Pahnke, and A. A. Kurland in *Advances in Psychopharmacology*, ed. by E. Costa and P. Greengard (New York: Raven Press, 1969), pp. 191-204.

[21] Sidney Cohen, "LSD: Side Effects and Complications," *Journal of Nervous and Mental Disease*, CXXX (1960), pp. 30-40. Surveying 44 experimenters who gave 25,000 doses of LSD to 5,000 individuals, both normal and psychiatric, no suicides were reported among the normals and fewer than one administration in 1,000 resulted in psychotic reactions lasting longer than 48 hours.

[22] Pahnke, "Implications of LSD and Experimental Mysticism," pp. 201-202. Jerome Levine and Arnold M. Ludwig, "The LSD Controversy," *Comprehensive Psychiatry*, V (1964), 314-21. W. A. Frosch, Edwin S. Robbins, and Marvin Stern, "Untoward Reactions to Lysergic Acid Diethylamide Resulting in Hospitalization," *New England Journal of Medicine*, CCLXXIII (1965), 1235-39.

[23] James R. Dolby, *I, Too, Am Man* (Waco, Texas: Word Books, 1969), pp. 127-36.

[24] Dolby, *op. cit.*, p. 130. Cf. Acts 17:26-27: "God made . . . every nation of men . . . that they should seek God, in the hope that they might feel after him and find him." (RSV)

and LSD if their subjective experience and psychological bi-products turn out to be essentially the same?

Both Christian experience and the LSD experience are alike in their inability to move from psychological language to God-language. The mere fact that a psychological event has taken place in one's brain cannot establish the truthfulness of any metaphysical assertions. No psychological datum necessarily leads to a metaphysical discovery. The assertion "God exists" does not follow from the assertion "I had an experience of God" simply because experiences admit to radically different interpretations. If God exists—the kind of personal creator God most Christians and theists talk about—he must exist independent of my subjective experience of Him; his existence must therefore be validated by a criterion other than my own private experience. The uniqueness of Christianity is that there is such a criterion in the personal invasion of God Himself into the public world of our objective experience. Christian existential experience is rooted in objective, external works of God Himself, fleshing out His life in space and time in the person of Jesus Christ and showing Himself to be God by his resurrection from the dead.[25]

Those who have had the LSD experience are able to give some credibility to their truth claims by redefining religion in psychological terms and by operating on the epistemological premise that "subjectivity is truth." The LSD cult has defined the essence of religion as psychological rather than metaphysical, in terms of subjective experience rather than objective content. When asked in what way the LSD experience is religious and in what way one discovers divinity through LSD, Leary remarked: "I consider my work basically religious, because it has as its goal the systematic expansion of consciousness and the discovery of energies within, which men call divine. . . . All religions are attempts to discover the inner potential. . . . The aim of LSD is basically to get high: that is, to expand your consciousness and find ecstasy and revelation within."[26] Only in this way can Leary move from psychological language to God language. However, great dangers arise when one gives a spiritual interpretation to psychological phenomenon.[27] Again it must be emphasized that

---

[25] See John 1:9-18 and I Corinthians 15:1-19.

[26] Leary, "Playboy Interview," p. 8.

[27] Ernest White, *The Christian Life and the Unconscious* (New York: Harper & Row, 1955). White distinguishes between conversion,

experience in itself has no necessary relationship to truth. Viktor Frankl "gutted out" his existence in a concentration camp by contemplating reunion with his wife who, unknown to him, was not even alive.[28] His experience was his own; it did not establish that his wife was, in fact, alive. To be more pointed, and to hint at the psychotic consequences of imbedding religion solely in the psyche: if a man comes into a room with a fried egg dangling over his left ear and glows, "this egg gives me existential satisfaction, joy, peace, purpose in life," the experience has no necessary connection to a "divine rooster in the sky."

Modern man's inability to capture meaning by a rational-istic net has forced him into a delicate dichotomy between reason and meaning. If he remains rational, he must live without meaning, in hopelessness and despair. Only by blindly escaping from reason into a subjective experience can his life be infused with any meaning. Truth has been shifted from the logical and rational in which no meaning is found to the non-rational, non-cognitive of subjective experience. Timothy Leary's own statements seem to indicate that he has found no meaning outside himself: [29]

> Where are the laughing Christians . . . Mystics, prophets, holy men, are all laughers because the religious revela-tion is a rib-tickling amazement—insight that all human purposes, including your own, are solemn self-decep-tions. You see through the game and laugh with God at the cosmic joke.

Such flailings of the mind are little different from those of existentialists whose only claim to meaning is the ironic insight that no meaning is to be found.

Francis Schaeffer claims that the "overwhelming desire for some non-rational experience is responsible for most of the serious use of the drugs LSD and STP at this time." [30] It is man's desperate attempt to experience the reality of some-thing that will make some sense of his life, to locate within

---

which he describes as basically a natural psychological experience, and the new birth. Cf. Dolby, op. cit., p. 128.

[28] Viktor E. Frankl, Man's Search for Meaning (New York: Wash-ington Square Press, 1963).

[29] Leary, The Politicis of Ecstacy, p. 321.

[30] Francis A. Schaeffer, The God Who Is There (Chicago: Inter-Varsity Press, 1968), p. 27.

the soul a clue to meaning which has not been discovered outside of it.[31] The Good News for modern man is simply this—there is not this dichotomy between reason and meaning. God Himself has entered our tangible world of experience and made Himself known in the person of Jesus Christ. He has made it possible for man to touch God at the deepest level of his emotions, to have subjective experience which can be ascertained to be the product of Divine life on account of God's objective work in history.

The LSD experience, like all subjective experiences, is inadequate to justify religious truth claims because of the impossibility of translating psychological statements into God-language. The experience fails in its bid for credibility in the religious realm by reducing religion to psychology and by shifting truth to the subjective. It leaves the seeker, desperate for meaning and truth, with the chemical chimeras of his own brain. With Christianity it is otherwise. One early disciple put it this way: [32] "And we know that the Son of God has come and has given us an understanding, to know Him who is true; and we are in Him who is true, in His Son Jesus Christ. This is the true God, and eternal life. Little children, keep yourselves from idols."

---

[31] This is not to say that the LSD is in no way contact with reality. Francis Schaeffer (pp. 28f.) contends that in these experiences man touches neither nothing nor God, but rather the objective reality of the external world and the "mannishness" of man. "God has created a real, external world. It is not an extension of His essence. That real, external world exists. God has also created man as a real, personal being and possesses a 'mannishness' from which he can never escape. On the basis of their own world view often these experience-seekers are neither sure the external world is there, nor that man as man is there. But I have come to the conclusion that, despite their intellectual doubts, many of them have had a true experience of the reality of the external world that exists, and/or 'the mannishness' that exists. . . . Thus they have hit upon something that exists, and it is neither nothing, nor is it God. . . ."

[32] I John 5:20, 21 (RSV).

Part Five

LITERATURE
AND WORLD-VIEW

Absurdity and the Inscrutable:

The Agnosticism of Franz Kafka in THE TRIAL

Carole Fuester

In *The Trial* Franz Kafka's negative view of Christianity is reflected in the scene in which the protagonist, Joseph K., his life quickly drawing to a close, visits a Cathedral. Even in this sacred place, "there was no longer even a murky daylight; black night had set in. All the stained glass in the great window could not illumine the darkness of the wall with one solitary gleam of light." [1] *The Trial* exhibits the author's agnosticism in the dark chaos of a universe without divine light. From the infinite gap between a desire for meaning in life and the apparent absence of it, Kafka has drawn the conclusion that all is absurd, a conclusion which militates effectively against his acceptance of the Christian world view. Swimming in meaninglessness, man is alienated from man, and naturally, from any universal or absolute frame of reference. If "salvation" from this situation comes, it will be by inscrutable law, not by political action or ideology. [2]

The Trial admits no god in recognizable form. René Dauvin, observing that "God is dead or dying" for Kafka, offers as evidence the short story entitled "In Our Synagogue." In this tale the "Word" is embodied in a grotesque animal that haunts the synagogue at prayer time. No longer is a divine idea recognizable in it; the sexton wants to kill it. If God

---

[1] Franz Kafka, *The Trial*, transl. by Willa and Edwin Muir, rev. by E. M. Butler (New York: Modern Library, 1956), Chapter IX, p. 265.

[2] J. David Caute, lectures given at Indiana University, Bloomington, Indiana, July, 1967.

has not completely removed himself, He is still totally forgotten, silent, and unknowable.[3]

The Trial's Joseph K. is arrested one morning; he is never faced with his accusers or with the charges against him. Yet he pursues his case with vehemence, actually summoning himself to the Court of Law time after time. He finds that there is no way to reach innocence again; the lawyers are shams. Indeed, the Court is impervious to evidence; there is no final acquittal. Abandoning the usual channels of defense, K. turns to the supra-natural, but in the Cathedral he is told a parable of Non-Salvation. At last he quietly submits to execution "like a dog."

One is struck by how Kafka totters near the brink of theism. His proximity is evident in the nature of the "Court of Law" that confronts K. It depicts not merely an existential problem, but a theistic one as well. "The Court . . . springs from the consciousness that man has lost his way in the world . . . without having any link with the absolute and its standards. . . . The guilt . . . is not an isolated crime, but . . . a falling away from the eternal."[4] Joseph K. is caught in a vice of guilt from which he cannot extricate himself. He has a painful sense of having sinned against an inscrutable someone or something, as shown by the fact that he is not really surprised by his arrest: "K. has been brought to a conviction of sin."[5] Yet he protests his innocence continually: "I'm not guilty, it's all a misunderstanding. . . ."[6] He refuses to admit guilt resulting from sin against a divine essence.

A singular feature of *The Trial* is its view of life as absurd. Said Kafka: "Everything is illusion: family, office, friends, . . . all illusion, drawing nearer and further away; but the nearest Truth is merely that I push my head against the wall of a cell without doors or windows."[7] The book's irrationality and

---

[3] René Dauvin, "*The Trial*: Its Meaning," in *Franz Kafka Today*, ed. by Angel Flores and Homer Schwander (Madison, Wisconsin: University of Wisconsin Press, 1964), pp. 148-50.

[4] Herbert Tauber, *Franz Kafka: An Interpretation of His Works* (New Haven, Conn.: Yale University Press, 1948), p. 85.

[5] William R. Mueller, *The Prophetic Voice in Modern Literature*, Haddam House Books (New York: Association Press, 1959), pp. 103-104.

[6] Kafka, *op. cit.*, ch. IX, p. 264.

[7] Erich Heller, *The Disinherited Mind* (New York: Farrar, Straus, and Cudahy, 1957), p. 200, citing *Gesammelte Schriften*, ed. Max Brod (Prague, 1937), Vol. VI, p. 108.

incoherence reflect a fractured frame of reference. The work exhibits "the essence of non-plot." [8]

Although he will not admit into his universe either a righteous God or rational order, K. still looks with straining gaze for some sort of mediator between himself and the inscrutable Law. Such a seeking is revealed in the wishful depiction of the "Great Advocate," and in the "radiance that streams inextinguishably from the Door of the Law." [9] Yet all of K.'s attempts to gain acquittal through known means are doomed to failure. Even the many women, through whose influence K. tries to reach the High Court, prove illusory tools.[10] *The Trial* has no mediator: [11]

> As K. and his executors approached the quarry, his glance fell on the top story of the house adjoining the quarry. . . . The casements of a window there suddenly flew open: a human figure, faint and insubstantial . . . leaned abruptly far forward and stretched both arms still farther. Who was it? A friend? . . . Someone who wanted to help? Was it one person only? Or was it mankind? Was help at hand? . . . Where was the Judge whom he had never seen? . . . But the hands of one of the partners were already at K.'s throat, while the other thrust the knife deep into his heart and turned it twice.

In spite of his idea of a moral Law forcing itself upon him, Kafka does not seem to see behind it an opportunity for theism. Nevertheless he cannot cast out the sense of deep guilt within him. C. S. Lewis avers in *Mere Christianity* that this dilemma is universal: "Human beings, all over the earth, have this curious idea that they ought to behave in a certain way, and cannot really get rid of it." They also realize that they do not behave in that proper way. This fact cannot be dismissed by attributing it to mere educational or social convention: "We all do believe that some moralities are better than others," and this means we are using a third standard which is something different from those compared. As he examines "What Lies Behind the Law," he notes that we know ourselves better than we know anything else. "When I open that particular man called myself," Lewis continues, "I find . . . that somebody or something wants me to behave in a certain way." He concludes

[8] J. David Caute, *loc. cit.*
[9] Tauber, *op. cit.*, p. 113.
[10] *Ibid.*, p. 103. Cf. Mueller, *op. cit.*, p. 109.
[11] Kafka, *op. cit.*, pp. 285-86.

that "it is more like a mind than . . . anything else we know." However, "if it is pure impersonal mind, there may be no sense in asking it to make allowances for you and let you off." [12] K. constantly seeks such allowances, thus suggesting that he thinks or hopes that that for which he reaches is not simply impersonal mind.

The absurdity of life portrayed in *The Trial* is not even an internally consistent theory. As. C. S. Lewis noted in regard to his own former atheism: [13]

> In the very act of trying to prove that God did not exist—in other words, that the whole of reality was senseless—I found I was forced to assume that one part of reality—namely my idea of justice—was full of sense. . . . If the whole universe has no meaning, we should never have found out that it has no meaning.

Camus observed of Kafka's absurdity: "The absurd is recognized, accepted, and man is resigned to it, but from then on we know that it has ceased to be absurd." [14] Kafka would have probably looked both ways before crossing a street: there is indeed a core of rationality which one cannot root out of his humanity. How then can cosmic irrationality constitute a world view capable of militating against a rational, Christian world view?

Not only logically but pragmatically as well, Kafka's view of life presents problems. Can man live consistently, or even endurably, in Kafka's world? Surely Kafka did not find it satisfying. K. does not try to escape death, although he passes a policeman on the way to his execution. There is here devastating alienation: "I am divided from all things by a hollow space." [15] Kafka, instead of reaching outside of himself for a frame of reference, prefers the "absolute autonomy of man:" "solitary, gnawed at by death, forever causing suffering, for-

---

[12] C. S. Lewis, *Mere Christianity* (rev. ed.; New York: Macmillan, 1952), pp. 17-39.

[13] *Ibid.*, p. 45.

[14] Albert Camus, "Hope and the Absurd in the Work of Kafka," in *Kafka: A Collection of Critical Essays*, ed. by Ronald Gray, Spectrum Books (Englewood Cliffs, New Jersey: Prentice-Hall, 1962), p. 153.

[15] J. Hillis Miller, Jr., "Franz Kafka and the Metaphysics of Alienation," in *The Tragic Vision and the Christian Faith*, ed. by Nathan A. Scott, Jr., Haddam House Books (New York: Assocation, 1957), pp. 286-87, citing Franz Kafka, *Diaries, 1914-1923*, pp. 10, 180.

ever doing evil." [16] The results, then, of conceiving of life as meaningless are painfully evident in *The Trial.* In tracing the source of this meaninglessness, a more satisfactory world view may be found.

A comparison of two quotations will reveal the nature of this source. The first is from Kafka: [17]

> If I closely examine my ultimate aim, it turns out that I am not really striving . . . to fulfill the demands of a Supreme Judge, but rather very much to the contrary. I strive . . . [to] find favor in the whole world's eyes . . . that in the end I would openly perpetrate the in-inquities within me without alienating the universal love in which I am held—the only sinner who won't be roasted."

How striking this in in contrast with Helmut Thielicke's words: "Those who no longer fear God fear everything in the world." It is the separation of the world from its relationship to God, from absolute standards of morality and truth that results in the loss of meaning, the alienation, and the purely utilitarian value of man illustrated in *The Trial.* When there is no structure of reality in which to base the cosmos, "the world becomes a materialized absurdity." [18] The very inscrutability of God causes Kafka's framework of reality to be so fractured. Because of his agnosticism, he demonizes the Court and the Law.

The discussion to this point shows that the world view of *The Trial* contains elements of self-contradiction; nor is anyone able to live either happily or consistently within such a framework. There exists an irreconcilable tension between man and his external world on one hand, and the logical conclusion of such a world view on the other.[19] K. considers the universe meaningless, yet he desperately seeks to retain a meaningful

---

[16] Charles Moeller, "The Image of Man in Modern European Literature," in *The New Orpheus: Essays Toward a Christian Poetic,* ed. by Nathan A. Scott, Jr. (New York: Sheed and Ward, 1964), pp. 405-406.

[17] Miller, *op. cit.,* pp. 284-85, citing *Diaries, 1914-1923,* p. 10.

[18] Helmut Thielicke, *Nihilism,* trans. by John W. Doberstein, Vol. IV *Of Religious Perspectives,* ed. by Ruth Nanda Anshen (New York: Harper & Row, 1961), pp. 8, 97.

[19] Francis A. Schaeffer, *The God Who Is There* (Chicago: Inter-Varsity, 1968), pp. 12-23.

existence. Kafka has abandoned hope of a unified answer for knowledge and life.[20] He has relegated any extra-mundane source of meaning to inscrutability. Because all appears so absurd, he cannot muster a "leap of faith;" but, because the realm of the "Wholly Other" is so uncommunicative, he has no choice except to submit to chaos. He is in quest of the relationship outside himself which will give meaning.[21]

Kafka sees in Christ only "an abyss filled with light." He said, "One must close one's eyes if one is not to fall into it . . . ."[22] But it is evident that his own interpretation of life was largely an abyss of darkness. K. feels that he is lost, but fights against it: he dies "like a dog," but resents it. How strikingly this epitomizes the Biblical view of man: though man is lost, he is certainly far from nothing.[23] Christianity provides the *Weltanschauung* which deals with the dilemmas Kafka so vividly portrays. It may be apprehended with eyes wide open.

At this point, Francis Schaeffer's analysis of Christianity as the answer to the three basic needs of modern man is relevant. First, Christianity deals with the problem of the reality of individual personality. Personality cannot be derived from non-personal sources: Christianity reveals the personal God who created man in His own image. Second, Christianity deals with the truth question in God's propositional communication to men (whom He made to communicate in that way) in Scripture. His communication touches about all areas of life: there is no need to leap blindly into the unknown in order to find meaning. Finally, Christianity reconciles the paradox of man's simultaneous greatness and evil. God created non-determined man, as He Himself is non-determinded. Man, however, in exercising this attribute, has rebelled. Christianity teaches that man is now abnormal: he is separated from his only sufficient point of reference, his Creator. As a result he is also alienated from his fellow men. This is a moral problem, not simply a metaphysical one: man was not always rebellious (sinful), and a solution may therefore exist. God provided the solution

---

[20] Francis A. Schaeffer, *Escape From Reason* (Chicago: Inter-Varsity, 1968), p. 45.

[21] Thielicke, *op. cit.*, p. 141.

[22] Amos N. Wilder, *Theology and Modern Literature* (Cambridge, Mass.: Harvard University Press, 1958), p. 27, citing Gustav Janouch, "Conversations with Kafka," in *The Partisan Review*, XX (March-April, 1953), 178.

[23] Schaeffer, *Escape from Reason*, p. 90. Cf. Psalm 8:4-8.

by reconciling man to Himself when he himself took on human flesh—when he entered into the human situation—when he died a sacrificial death for His creatures. There is no dichotomy between the human dilemma and the interpretation and solution offered by the Christian world view.[24] Kafka rejected this world view, though it provides the meaningful explanation of the cosmos and existence for which he sought, because he did not see in Christ the perfect Mediator, the "Great Advocate," as God Himself, sustaining the punishment which the moral equilibrium of His universe demands of man (who is not, in spite of Kafka's objection, innocent).

Kafka's terrifying position is reflected with transfixing clarity in the following excerpt from the macabre "Dream of a World Without God," by Jean Paul Frederich Richter.[25] How reminiscent of the absurd, nightmarish world of *The Trial* this is: a universe where, if God were ever alive, only a distorted and inscrutable vestige of Him remains.

> And at this point a lofty, noble form, bearing the impress of eternal sorrow, came sinking down . . . and rested on the altar; whereupon the dead cried out, 'Christ! is there no God?'
>
> He answered, 'There is none . . .'
>
> And Christ spake on, saying, 'I have traversed the worlds, I have risen on the suns . . . there is no God. And I descended to whither the very shadow cast by Being dies out and ends, and I gazed out into the gulf beyond and cried, 'Father, where art thou?' But answer came there none, save the eternal storm which rages on, controlled by none . . .
>
> Then he, sublime, loftiest of finite beings, raised his eyes toward the nothingness and boundless void, saying, 'Oh, dead, dumb nothingness! necessity endless and chill! Oh, mad, unreasoning Chance! when will ye dash this fabric into atoms, and me too. . . ? . . . every soul in this great corpse trench of a universe is utterly alone! *I* am alone— . . . Alas! If every soul be its own creator and father, why shall it not be its own destroying angel, too? . . ."

This is the sort of world in which K. lives: the Cathedral is a museum, the book under his arm, a tourist guide, rather

---

[24] Schaeffer, *The God Who Is There*, pp. 87-142.

[25] Thielicke, *op. cit.*, pp. 129-30, citing *Wit, Wisdom and Philosophy of Jean Paul Frederich Richter*, ed. by Giles P. Hawley (New York: Funk and Wagnalls, 1884), pp. 196-98.

than a Bible. K.'s Christ is an unhelpful "abyss filled with light"; Richter's is a mere finite being. The result of both misconceptions is a "great corpse trench of a universe." Thielicke observes that the problem represented in this vision is related to the statements of St. Paul in I Corinthians 15. Here the Apostle deals with the Resurrection of Christ and faces the question: "What would be our situation if Christ did not rise from the dead?" The fact is that we would still be in such an awful world of death if "this *one* breach had not been made in the great, black wall." We should eat and drink "for tomorrow we die," if Christ was not raised from the dead.[26] It is in Christ that Kafka's idea of an inscrutable deity is corrected: He is the Logos, the Word, the ultimate communication; He shows that God has not emigrated from the world and thus left it without its sustaining bonds and supporting foundations.

How, Joseph K. might ask, is one to know that this breach in the wall has in fact been made? Paul suggests the evidence he accepts in I Corinthians 15:6: it is that of eye-witnesses to the Resurrection. It is empirical evidence. If the thought of putting trust in empirical evidence seems questionable, the reader might recall the discussion above regarding the fact that one must accept some sort of empirical data in order to function at all. As Edward John Carnell states, "If my understanding assures me that I cannot drive through the darkness ahead because a bridge has been washed out, I come to grief when I permit my inward passion for crossing to go in defiance of the evidence." [27]

What is the evidence for the breach in the wall? John Warwick Montgomery states the matter succinctly: [28]

> Christianity's claim to truth consists merely of a finger pointing back through time to an historical figure who divided world history into two parts—to Jesus of Nazareth—to His statements concerning Himself and true religion, and to the life He led attesting the state-

[26] *Ibid.*, p. 130.

[27] Edward John Carnell, *A Philosophy of the Christian Religion* (Grand Rapids, Mich.: Eerdmans, 1952), p. 475.

[28] John Warwick Montgomery, *The Shape of the Past: An Introduction to Philosophical Historiography* ("History in Christian Perspective," Vol. I; Ann Arbor, Mich.: Edwards Brothers, 1962), p. 328. Also included in this volume is a pertinent essay on "The Dependability and Value of the Extant Gospel Manuscripts" by Edward J. Barnes, pp. 241-50.

ments He made. An honest, historically accurate, scientific investigation of these data (involving chiefly a study of the documents collected in the New Testament) will show that Jesus claimed to be God incarnate, that He described the only true (but *not* the only *possible*) religion as consisting of fellowship with Himself, and that He attested His claims by a sinless life which profoundly affected everyone who crossed His path, and by a Resurrection which left no doubt in the minds of eye witnesses that He was in fact the true God.

Christianity offers Kafka the explanation for and the elimination of his feelings of despair, alienation, guilt, and meaninglessness. It holds forth a consistent world view. Its center is Jesus Christ: the Mediator whom Kafka seeks, and the scrutable God he needs. This Christ arose from the dead, an event which He offered as proof for His claims to Deity: He showed Himself to be God come into man's realm to help him. His mission was that of reconciliation, restoring man to his proper frame of reference in relationship with God. Men may again approach men in Christ's love. But one will have to decide to enter the Door of the Law through Christ's sacrifice, and not waste his efforts outside, as K., Block, and the Man from the Country in the Parable did.[29] Christ stated, "No man cometh to the Father but by me."[30] Kafka's opinion that "there is a goal, but no way; what we call the way is hesitation" will not bring an end to his despair and lostness.[31]

In the Cathedral, Joseph K. sees a picture of the Entombment of Christ. This indicates that all Kafka's characters are "condemned to endure permanently the terrible time between the death of Christ and his resurrection."[32] Let Kafka see on the cross the One who died sacrificially for him, and the One endured with the awful despair of K.'s lost situation: "My God, My God, why hast Thou forsaken Me?"[33] Let him find in the risen Christ deliverance from the death knell of the Law and from the mausoleum of meaningless existence. The promise of Christ is this: "I am the resurrection and the life: he that believeth in me, though he were dead, yet shall he live."[34]

---

[29] Miller, *op. cit.*, p. 95.
[30] John 14:6.
[31] Tauber, *op. cit.*, p. 90.
[32] Miller, *op. cit.*, p. 302.
[33] Matthew 27:46.
[34] John 11:25.

Hermann Hesse:

Novelist Against Man and History

Richard Kantzer

In the late sixties the Tolkien fad peaked. The hobbit world was assimilated into the average reading adult's literary horizon and exploited by the voracious American economy. Then literary critics began to discover the works of another author in the hands of American readers—especially younger readers who were participating in the American Counter-culture, or influenced by it. The rather unlikely discovery was that Hermann Hesse, a German author in exile writing chiefly during the period between the first two World Wars, a Nobel Prize winner in 1946, and dead in 1962 at age of eighty-five, was being read as a prophet of the new age dawning from the East (Japanese are reading him also) to the West.

Time, ever ready to join a crowd, admitted in October, 1968, that Hesse "in the past decade in the United States . . . has steadily risen to the status of a literary cult figure. College students rank him in the pantheon of literary genius with Dostoevsky, Tolkien, and Golding. In Hippie hovels those of his works already available in English . . . are family Bibles." [1] Exactly one year later, in *The Saturday Review* (Hesse's literary status is rising too, apparently), Henry S. Resnik surveyed the American college scene and discovered "evidence . . . that works of Hermann Hesse have replaced Tolkien's *Lord of the Rings* as a literary fad on the American campus." [2] He notes the christening of a Berkeley coffee house and a rock group after Hesse's anti-hero Steppenwolf, then rather sadly predicts the possible killing off of a new fad by the American mass culture overkill.[3]

---

[1] "The Outsider," *Time*, 92 (Oct. 18, 1968), 111.

[2] Henry S. Resnik, "How Hermann Hesse Speaks to the College Generation," *Saturday Review*, 52 (October 18, 1969), 35.

[3] *Ibid.*, p. 36. According to Kurt Vonnegut's figures, *Siddhartha*, originally published in 1922, has had nearly one million copies printed

A most amusing study could be made of the reactions of literary critics trying to give a serious evaluation of Hesse, and especially of his recent revival in the United States. In the 1969 Spring issue of *Symposium*, E. F. Timpe quotes a 1923 review of Hesse where the now incredibly antediluvian reviewer wrote:

> We are confused and perhaps exasperated by so much talk of soul forces, shaping destinies, realization of self. Whatever may have been the author's purpose, he gives us a nightmare of abnormality, a crazed dream of a paranoiac.[4]

Contrast this with Kurt Vonnegut's "easy explanation" for Hesse's popularity which, however, he rejects as too shallow:

> He is clear and direct and well-translated, and he offers hope and romance, which the young play hell finding anywhere else these days.[5]

Resnik also, in speaking of the *Glass Bead Game*, rejects a too-facile dismissal of Hesse's significance, arguing that:

> It is difficult to envision teeny boppers or sub-verbal hippies or sorority sisters ploughing through the *Glass Bead Game* for this is really a most challenging book, a triumph of imaginative power reminiscent in tone of late Conrad and just as hard to penetrate.[6]

Repeatedly one recognizes in such reviews the ambiguity which the works of Hesse present. They seem so simple and are so appreciated by "sub-verbal hippies" that it is always necessary to defend the effort to treat them as serious *oeuvres d'art*. When such effort is applied to Hesse's writings (done rarely in America, to be sure) one finds that "their subtleties make work. Their simplicity belies galaxies of knowledge in motion—history, theology, psychology, philosophy." [7]

If one is prepared to take the Hesse fad seriously (so I

in the United States since 1957, but 250,000 alone in 1969. *Steppenwolf*, issued in a $1.25 edition in September, 1969, sold 360,000 copies in thirty days (Kurt Vonnegut, Jr., "Why They Read Hesse," *Horizon*, XIII. [Spring, 1970], 29-30).

[4] Eugene F. Timpe, "Hermann Hesse in the United States," *Symposium*, XXIII 1. (Spring, 1969), 73-79.

[5] Vonnegut, *op. cit.*, p. 29.

[6] Resnik, *op. cit.*, pp. 35-37.

[7] Webster Schott, "A German Guru Makes the United States Again," *Life*, 65 (July 12, 1968), 11.

have tried to argue in this already lengthy introduction), then one has to go beyond the surface plot and action of Hesse's novels and examine his world-view. It is presented in self-interpreting comments embedded in the texts and in Hesse's unusual stylistic devices.

Perhaps, to be "honest to Hesse," one must not speak in terms of his view of reality as if he had one view of it. For in his writings Hesse purposely presents many views—even conflicting views. It soon becomes apparent that Hesse is portraying as best he can the breakdown of any traditional view of reality (or even of traditional willingness to talk in terms implying that one single view of reality might be correct). Reared by German Lutheran missionary parents in his pre-World War I years, he once indeed had an ordered view of the world, but personal experiences—especially the war— "placed him before the abyss" where he saw that he had only known the "appearances of things" behind which stands the reality of life.[8]

> The unmasking of reality can be precipitated by any sudden jolt in our lives—war, illness, misfortune—but when it happens, the shock of perception is severe enough to render questionable all order, all comfort, all security, all faith, all knowledge.[9]

This breakdown of Hesse's earlier view of reality parallels and partakes of those breakdowns in physics by the work of Planck and Einstein, in theology by Strauss, Renan, and Feuerbach (with their reduction of Christ to man, and of God to a projection of the mind), in psychology by Jung and Freud, and in anthropology by studies in comparative culture (treating all standards of morality as relative).[10] One notes this breakdown in Hesse's sharp condemnation of the ivory-tower scholar of Indian mythologies in Steppenwolf who "has not been through the war, nor is he acquainted with the shattering of the foundation of thought by Einstein (that, thinks he, only concerns the mathematicians).[11] No longer can Hesse accept

---

[8] Franz Baumer, *Hermann Hesse*, trans. John Conway (New York: Frederick Ungar Publishing Co., 1969), p. 51.

[9] Hermann Hesse, quoted in Theodore Ziolkowski, *The Novels of Hermann Hesse* (Princeton, N. J.: Princeton University Press, 1965), p. 6.

[10] Ziolkowski, *op. cit.*, pp. 15-17.

[11] Hermann Hesse, *Steppenwolf* (New York: Holt, Rinehart and Winston, Bantom Book, 1969), p. 90.

as real the picture of a world moving according to a purpose toward a goal which gives meaning to each of the events occurring on the way. Instead he becomes convinced of the irrationality of human conduct. He feels forced to admit that any other conclusion only covers up reality and separates real evil from consciousness.[12]

With this breakdown in his view of reality, Hermann Hesse also becomes trapped in an epistemological impasse in the quest for truth about any possible or all possible reality. He places reality—absolute reality—beyond the appearances of things, beyond rationality, meaning, and known values. Such a conclusion corresponds to what Francis Schaeffer describes as upper-storey/lower-storey systems of theology or art.[13] Hesse assumes himself freed to believe that all knowable, verifiable, empirical facts of experience are limited to the lower storey, but rejects as failures all thought systems which try to limit themselves to getting meaning and value for life from the contents of the lower storey. He plumbs to the depths of the lower storey and finds it gives him no hope, no reason to accept life or to go on living.[14] In despair of the lower storey, Hesse leaps to the upper storey, which he willingly admits is full of irrational content and is not knowable or communicable.[15] There, free from all rules of logic or ethics he wills into existence for himself new truths, new men, and new worlds for which he has no assurance of reality whatsoever. Even if purely mental constructs, the creations of his will help him through the life of appearances and so he accepts them.

Little hints and bold statements make very clear what Hesse has done. The reading material of Steppenwolf, for example, hero of the novel bearing the same title, includes

---

[12] Baumer, *op. cit.*, p.14, and Mark Boulby, *Hermann Hesse: His Mind and Art* (Ithaca: Cornell University Press, 1967), p. 82.

[13] Francis Schaeffer, *The God Who is There.* (Downers Grove, Ill.: Inter-Varsity Press, 1968), pp. 37-43.

[14] Hesse is so very right here! Without significance provided by the upper storey in actual relation with the lower storey, these lower storey thought systems are only for those atrophied "men without chests." This ought to lead him to despair. Cf. C. S. Lewis, *The Abolition of Man*, p.34.

[15] But why does he have to admit this? Here he admits more than is necessary, I believe. If it is not knowable, he couldn't know it to be irrational; if not at all communicable, he could not talk about its being there.

several well-worn books—including the titles of Goethe (of course), Novalis, Lessing (Hesse accepts the "ditch"), and Dostoevsky.[16] Hesse goes to the (absurd) length of explicating the purely fictional nature of his own fictional creation of Steppenwolf as a two-fold creature—torn between his wolf and his human nature.

> For the close of our study there is left one last fiction, a fundamental delusion to make clear. All interpretation, all psychology, all attempts to make things comprehensible, require the medium of theories, mythologies and lies; and a self-respecting author should not omit, at the close of an exposition, to dissipate these lies so far as may be in his power . . . So too, to come to the point, is the Steppenwolf a fiction.[17]

Of crucial significance to one who thinks his knowledge of ultimate truths and of God are founded on the Bible is Hesse's frank attack on that book. Words, much less its words, cannot communicate truth, reality, or divinity. In *Beneath the Wheel*, when young Giebenrath begins to learn Biblical Greek under tutelage of the State-church pastor, the Pietist cobbler Flaig warns him that the minister is not a real believer. Flaig fears that the pastor's critical ideas will destroy the pre-verbal faith of young Giebenrath.[18] Here Hesse is emphasizing that rational thought and learning (the pastor) are antithetical to the real yet non-intellectualized experience of the Pietistic believer (cobbler Flaig). Thus Hesse moves from the breakdown of traditional views of reality, and from the separation of meaning from reality, to involvement in a language crisis. One who experiences Hesse's absolute reality, beyond the appearances of conventional life, cannot communicate the content of his experience.[19]

In the *Journey*, the supposed narrator of the journey to the East (a timeless, placeless realm of the spirit) finds it impossible to narrate either the journey itself or his experience of the journey. The journey, belonging in the ideal realm, cannot

---

[16] Hesse, *Steppenwolf*, p. 14.

[17] *Ibid.*, p. 65. This is absurdity. To make the fundamental delusion clear, Hesse by his own confession is forced to lie, so that for him clarity is found in lies, insight becomes no sight or blindness, morality is having no morals.

[18] Ziolkowski, *op. cit.*, p. 80.

[19] Hermann Hesse, from *Unterm Rad, Erzahlung von Hermann Hesse* (Zürich: Fretz and Wasmuth Verlag, 1968), pp. 55 ff.

be expressed in the lower realm of life where people deal in words and meaning. Since the ideal realm (Hesse's Third Kingdom where totality is experienced simultaneously, i.e. erasure of the time-space categories) is without words, the narrator "is unable even to recall in full force his own experiences." [20] He only thinks: "The League aimed at quite definite very lofty goals during this journey (they belong to the secret category and are therefore not communicable) . . . ." [21] says Ziolkowski,

> At no point does Hesse, as narrator, attempt to portray directly the experienced Third Kingdom or magical thinking, for the direct rendition of totality and simultaneity exceeds the capacity of everyday language.[22]

With awareness of the philosophical implications such concepts have for the possibility of the Christian religion, the *Journey* can be considered the nightmarish trip to hell that life would turn out to be if Hesse were correct in his assumptions. In the story itself, after the "special document" of the journeying men disappears, the unity of the League which is making the journey collapses. Then the narrator seeks to tell of the unity which had existed at least for a while, but asks: "How can it be told, this tale of a unique journey, of a unique communion of minds, of such a wonderfully exalted and spiritual life?" [23] He answers his own question by a brief lecture on the difficulties of all historical writing. He cites the absence of a needed "center of events" to give them cohesion but admits that "there is no unity, no center, no point around which the wheel revolves." [24] Then most bitterly of all he confesses:

> Our Journey to the East and our League, the basis of our community, has been the most important thing, indeed the only important thing in my life, compared with which my own individual life has appeared completely unimportant. And now that I want to hold fast

---

[20] Ziolkowski, *op. cit.*, p.267.
[21] Hermann Hesse, *The Journey to the East.* trans. Hilda Rosner (New York: Farrar, Straus and Girous, 1956), p.46.
[22] Ziolkowski, *op. cit.*, pp. 80-81. Hesse knows too much! How does he know so much about the Third Kingdom that he knows it to be so radically different from normal experience that it cannot be verbalized?
[23] Hesse, *Journey, op. cit.*, p. 46.
[24] *Ibid.*, p. 47,48.

to and describe this most important thing, or at least something of it, everything is only a mass of separate fragmentary pictures which has been reflected in something, and this something is myself and this self, this mirror, whenever I have gazed into it, has proved to be nothing but' the uppermost surface of a glass plane. I put my pen away with the sincere intention and hope of continuing tomorrow or some other time, or rather to begin anew, but at the back of my intention and hope, at the back of my really tremendous urge to relate our story, there remains a dreadful doubt. It is the doubt that arose during the search for Leo in the valley of Morbio. This doubt does not only ask the question, "Is your story capable of being told?" It also asks the question, "Was it possible to experience it?" We recall examples of participants in the World War who, although by no means short of facts and attested stories, must at times have entertained the same doubt.[25]

This confession is the most bitter because it denies all, including the unity of the person. With no real self to experience the journey it is of course impossible that it could ever have been experienced. Not only is the journey now dead, but journeying man is dead also.[26]

So what does dead man do? Hesse replies:

Whatever happens, I have decided to exercise my will. Even if I have to re-commence my difficult story ten times, a hundred times, and always arrive at the same cul-de-sac, just the same I will begin again a hundred times. If I cannot assemble the pictures into a significant whole again, I will present each single fragment as faithfully as possible. And as far as it is now still possible, I will be mindful of the first principle of our great period, never to rely on and let myself be disconcerted by reason, always to know that faith is stronger than so-called reality.[27]

As had done Lukas, the historian of the war (is he possibly Luke the Evangelist?), the narrator is forced to create his

---

[25] *Ibid.*, p. 48,49. But this "I" who gazes into the mirror, who puts his pen away, and doubts his own capacity to experience is an "I" who can doubt and who is now experiencing. You can't live and be this skeptical. Didn't Descartes say something about this kind of thinking?

[26] Strangely, Hesse seems to have gone on living. He creates a "theory" of his death to which he does not commit himself in practice.

[27] *Ibid.*, p.52.

own history, regardless of its truth in relation to the real journey. This was the "only means of saving one from nothingness, chaos, and suicide. This book was written under this pressure and brought one the expected cure, simply because it was written, irrespective of whether it was good or bad that was the only thing that counted." [28]

Hesse's denial of the possibility for meaningful history strikes at the very possibility of meaningful history, and thus at the core of Christian belief. Hesse allows his reaction to the collapse of his pre-World War world-view, and to the Pietistic religion of his family to reject rationality and intellectually responsible religious beliefs.[29] (He rejects Pietism as intellectually unsuitable, though practically helpful in life, while intellectually responsible religion is seen as void of God and necessary personal warmth.) Does he have the right to do this? Has Hesse made a historical study of the life and claims of the One who claimed to be the Son of God, who promised to send the Spirit to guide his biographers "into all truth," and who rose bodily from the dead to show that his message from the ideal realm beyond was in fact worthy of belief in the actually-experienced world of cause and effect, space and time?

If Hesse chooses not to accept the world of experience as real, persists in viewing absolute reality as confined to a non-rational realm of which one can be aware but not knowl-

---

[28] *Ibid.*, p. 57. Only while a man remains unsophisticatedly oblivious (by lack of education, by choice, or by induced states of consciousness) does this solution satisfy. Yes, underwater basket-weaving does keep the body occupied. But when a person wakes up or is willing to consider his actual situation and to recognize that this occupation is only a panacea to keep the mind off reality, then the senseless practice becomes unbearable.

[29] Hesse would prefer not to have to do this, of course. He implies so in the following: "Our whole civilization was a cemetery where Jesus Christ and Socates, Mozart and Haydn, Dante and Goethe were but the undecipherable names on moldering stones; and the mourners who stood round affecting a pretence of sorrow would give much to believe in these inscriptions which once were holy, or at least to utter one heart-felt word of grief and despair about this world that is no more. And nothing was left them but the embarrassed grimaces of a company round a grave" (*Steppenwolf*, p. 88). Pietism, too, is only acceptable as long as the Pietist remains naively unaware that his warm feelings about God are, in fact, an illusion and do not correspond with reality. The pietist ought to recognize this, despair for his faith, then search for the good evidence for the true teaching about God and about the human experience of God in real life.

edgable, and so rejects the possibility of meaningful history, then he must be allowed this position only on the condition Hesse himself recognizes. Hesse can proceed to create his own histories. He can build his own universe in his works of art, he can experience aspects of his Third Kingdom in golden moments of sensual experience or drug-induced awareness where the totality of reality is experienced simultaneously, but he must always admit that such a life is "for mad men only!" [30] Trace the assumptions of Hesse to their practical conclusions and see what manner of ideal he creates and what manner of men his heroes become. Then compare this with the biblical and Christian view of man in all his evil but yet in possession of the dignity and hope of a creature who can experience God and know God in a way that can be verbalized. Hesse has neither sufficient reason for his despair, nor satisfying life in it.

For Hesse himself, attempted escape from despair in face of unattainable ideals led to the self-creation of an escape realm through art. Says the architect of the game of life in the *Magic Theater* (this is the dream world of Steppenwolf, the only place where ideals are attained) concerning his work,

> This is the art of life, . . . You may yourself as an artist develop the game of your life and lend it animation. You may complicate and enrich it as you please. It lies in your hands. Just as madness, in a higher sense, is the beginning of all wisdom, so is schizomania the beginning of all art and all fantasy.[31]

But even the Magic Theater fails: "This Magic Theater was clearly no paradise. All hell lay beneath its charming surface. O God, was there even here no release?" [32] Finally Hesse finds that the ideas he creates and the absolute reality of which he thinks he is aware (without knowing it since it is irrational) are all only variations on a view of his own self. On waking from the dream world of the Magic Theater, the hero, Steppenwolf, understood it all to be what it was—a dream in which the dreamer dreams himself under the illusion that the dream is something beyond himself. Still he determined, "I would sample its tortures once more and shudder

---

[30] *Ibid.*, p. 47.
[31] *Ibid.*, p. 220.
[32] *Ibid.*, p. 223.

again at its senselessness. I would traverse not once more, but often the hell of my own inner being." [33]

Moreover, Hesse's method is self-defeating, for by focusing on the self it ignores the message of hope coming from without. Another man also wrestled with his soul and asked questions similar to those of Hermann Hesse. He wrote of his experience, "Wretched man that I am! Who will deliver me from this body of death?" But the apostle Paul, for it was he, found an answer not in himself, but from outside, from God through Jesus Christ. He could go on to say "Thanks be to God through Jesus Christ our Lord. For the law of the Spirit of Life in Christ Jesus has set me free from the Law of sin and death" (Rom. 7:24-28). He had met a real person who had authority to speak the truth of God and to do the work of God. To come to this point, however, he had first to be willing to trust his sense experience of this Jesus Christ. He found it to warrant belief (I Cor. 15:13, 20) and to give hope by which he could make sense of the world and of its terminus in death.

Hesse's assumption about reality eliminates this possibility for his fictional characters. Perhaps only through the *rabies* to which consistent adherence to such an assumption leads them will the living antitypes of these characters be willing to test and taste the life of Jesus Christ. We pray they shall remain vulnerable to "the hound of heaven."

---

[33] *Ibid.*, p. 238. In doing this he repeats by choice his naive, self-deceptive, dreamy, but temporary satisfaction. Is this the only alternative open for man today? It is not; Hesse has no right to say "there cannot be" the absolute and knowable reality he dreams of. He ought rather to say "I do not know" of such a reality. If he would say this, then he must agree that "it is possible" that such a reality exists. But then for his own sake he should be looking for it.

Twentieth-Century Romanticism:
The World of Ayn Rand

Janet G. Porcino

Although she considers herself the "most creative thinker alive today,"[1] others consider her a philosopher "only in a generously accommodated sense."[2] Charles F. Schroder stated several years ago that he felt it was safe to say that her "attempt to formulate a philosophy of creative selfishness will make no great impact."[3] Furthermore, he claimed that both conservative businessmen and students would undoubtedly prefer more down to earth formulations, that the intellectuals would prefer more eloquent definitions (e.g., those of Russell Kirk, G. K. Chesterton and Hillaire Belloc), and that the academic world would not be expected to respond favorably to "gross oversimplifications of the lessons of the past and to her tendency to interpret history in terms of black and white."[4] Rosenbloom considers her analysis of the history of Western philosophy sophomoric.[5]

Yet Ayn Rand has gained a sizable hearing in the last decade. Sales of her major novels have exceeded the million mark. Ayn Rand discussion groups dot college campuses and more than 2500 people in cities across the United States attend courses given by the Nathaniel Branden Institute where her philosophy of objectivism is expounded.

---

[1] Excerpts from an interview with Ayn Rand by Mike Wallace in the New York *Post*, quoted in *Commonweal*, LXVII (January 3, 1958), 349.

[2] James Collins, "Ayn Rand's Talent for Getting Headlines," *America*, July 29, 1961, p. 569.

[3] Charles F. Schroder, "Ayn Rand: Far Right Prophetess," *Christian Century*, December 13, 1961, p. 1943.

[4] *Ibid.*, p. 1493.

[5] Joel Rosenbloom, "The Ends and Means of Ayn Rand," *The New Republic*, April 24, 1961, p. 28.

It is her fiction that has caused the greatest popularization of her views. Miss Rand has a true gift for creating suspense; yet her novel *Atlas Shrugged* strikingly resembles a fifteenth century morality play.[6] In the evaluation of one reviewer, the novel is a "cumbersome, lumbering vehicle in which characterization, plot and reality are subordinated to the author's expression of a personal philosophy. The book is a point of view stated and restated so often. . . ."[7] Her novels remind one of propaganda, but Miss Rand would neither deny nor regret this. Her explanation is that she has been forced to formulate her own philosophical framework since "my own basic view of man and of existence was in conflict with most of the existing philosophical theories." She has chosen fiction because it "made possible the integration of the widest abstract principles and their direct expression in application to man's life." An unashamed Romantic, she has written about life as she would like to see it and people whom she would like to know. She would like to create a world of free, joyously purposeful, active men. "My philosophy, in essence, is the concept of man as a heroic being, with his own happiness as the moral purpose of his life, with productive achievement as his noblest activity, and reason as his only absolute."[8]

Her romanticism and humanistic idealism may well be the cause of the admiration and the antagonism which her philosophy elicits. On the one hand, her views are no doubt accepted by some because they parallel popular existentialist thinking. While not recognizing the agony of life as do the existentialist thinkers, Ayn Rand agrees with a major tenet of existentialism in emphasizing the importance of the individual. She reacts violently against conformity and a depersonalized society. The individual willing and making decisions, acting and taking responsibility for his action is common to her thought as it is to Sartre's. In a predominantly "other-directed" society such an emphasis is sought and admired by men trapped in a meaningless existence. On the other hand, Miss Rand's overt rationalism and undying pessimism concerning the state of modern man has caused antagonism to her writings. Her anthropology

---

[6] Helen Beal Woodward, "Non-Stop Daydream," *Saturday Review*, October 12, 1957, 25.

[7] Patricia Donegan, "Atlas Shrugged," *Commonweal*, November 8, 1957, p. 155.

[8] Ayn Rand, *For the New Intellectual* (New York: Random House, 1961), 192.

conflicts not only with the optimistic humanism of those who think that man will rule the universe; it also conflicts with the prevalent Christian idea of human nature.

Miss Rand's determined purpose is to muster a band she has named the "New Intellectuals." She hopes they will lead her adopted country, America, from cultural and intellectual bankruptcy to a new era of productivity and positive leadership. The philosophical platform she provides these intellectuals is none other than her objectivism.

In attempting to enunciate an integrated, consistent, rational view of life, she has formulated an all-embracing dogma which touches virtually every area of human life and thought, ranging from economic theory (*laissez-faire* capitalism as the salvation of mankind) to personal ethics (the virtue of selfishness). Since however Miss Rand has not yet completed a definitive presentation of her philosophy (*For the New Intellectual* serves as an outline until such a presentation appears; it includes an introductory essay by Miss Rand and selections from her novels under appropriate headings), a thorough criticism of her position cannot be attempted. In fact, any criticism is difficult because Miss Rand has a talent for making "flat statements that have a certain shock value and a wide coverage, but convey very little definite content by which they can be tested. . . ." [9] "There is just enough truth about unprovable matters in [her] major assertions to make adherence by self-respecting persons possible for awhile. Best of all, like other similar systems, it supplies a coherent set of 'answers' which can never be shaken by mere argument (since every situation can be defined so as to fall within the terms of the system) and a stout forensic stick with which to beat fellow intellectuals who have not as yet seen the light." [10] Nevertheless, an attempt will be made to discuss the basic assumptions underlying her philosophy as they relate to the Christian faith.

Born in St. Petersburg, Russia in 1905, Ayn Rand wrote in her diary before she turned fourteen, "Today, I decided that I am an atheist." In a somewhat romanticised biographical essay, Barbara Branden writes, "there had never been a time when she was willing to accept an idea without proof . . . if she asked, 'Why?' about an adult's statement and was told that she must not expect to understand, that she must 'just

---

[9] Collins, *op. cit.*, p. 567.
[10] Rosenbloom, *op. cit.*, p. 28.

believe' or 'just feel it' or 'have faith,' her response was an astonished contempt." [11] Given no formal training in her parents' Jewish faith, she carefully considered the question of God's existence and wrote her conclusion in her diary: [12]

> First, that there are no reasons to believe in God, there is no proof of the belief; and second, that the concept of God is insulting and degrading to man—it implies the highest possible is not to be reached by man, that he is an inferior being who can only worship an ideal he will never achieve. By her view, there could be no break between conceiving of the best possible and deciding to attain it. She rejected the concept of God as morally evil.

As one might expect, this underlying atheism prejudices her interpretation of the history of western civilization. She divides history into trends of alternating creativity and mysticism. (The Middle Ages—or Dark Ages constituted a mystic period; the Renaissance, a creative period; nineteenth century America under capitalism was the most truly creative period in all history thus far.) Miss Rand sees contributing to the milieu throughout the ages the continuing conflict between a series of opposing ideologies. Two of these major antitheses are Reason versus Faith and Selfishness versus Altruism.

Her epistemological starting point is the principle "Existence exists," or "A" is "A," Existence is Identity, Man is "Man." The basic necessity of existence is to contribute to the continuance of life. The mind is man's tool for survival. Man *qua* Man has the faculty of reason which perceives, identifies and integrates the material provided by his senses. Reason integrates man's perceptions by means of forming abstractions and conceptions, thus taking man beyond the perceptual level of the animals to the conceptual level. The method reason employs in the process is logic, the art of non-contradictory identification. Reason is the only tool of knowledge; further, it is his moral faculty. "A rational process is a moral process." Therefore, it follows that "the vilest form of self-abasement and self-destruction is the subordination of your mind to the mind of another, the acceptance of an authority over your brain." Thus man lives on nothing but the work of his own mind, the merit of one's own ideas so as to rely on nothing but the Objective. To think is an act of choice.

[11] Barbara Branden, *Who is Ayn Rand?* (New York: Random House, 1962), p. 162.
[12] *Ibid.*

Mysticism or faith is but a short-cut to knowledge—or at best an attempt at knowledge. It falsely bases cognition on emotion or whim; it is the sixth sense that invalidates the other fives senses. Faith deals with the *un*earthly, the supernatural, the irrational which escapes the necessity of justification. "The morals of faith make you renounce the material world and divorce values from matter. . . . To renounce the material world is to surrender it to evil." Reason can answer the question "how"; faith can merely answer, "somehow." The issue of Reason versus Faith is the very issue of life or death, freedom or slavery, consciousness or unconsciousness. Hand in hand with this conflict is the issue between rational Selfishness and irrational Altruism.

Selfishness allows a man to have pride in himself and to admit that "he is his own highest value." The word "I" is the most important word in any langauge, as *Anthem* teaches. Selfishness allows a man to be truly man, to value himself, to choose what is best for himself and his survival, to produce and take pride in his accomplishments. Thus results joyous living. Selfishness does not require that one man have responsibility to another man. The characters of Miss Rand's novels exhibit this noble trait graphically. Unbending individuals, the heroes and heroines of her novels are extraordinarily endowed; there is not the slightest trace of dependency in any of these ideal men and women.

Altruism, says Ayn Rand, thanks especially to Immanuel Kant, is the greatest hoax ever perpetrated on society. The categorical imperative along with the Christian ethic has all but ruined civilization. The moral code of altruism is based on the principle that man has no right to exist for his own sake, that service to others is the only justification of his existence and that self-sacrifice is his highest moral duty, virtue and value. The self thus becomes the standard of evil while the selfless is the standard of good. It is not a case of whether one should give a dime to a beggar. "The issue is whether you do or do not have the right to exist without giving him that dime. . . . The issue is whether the need of others is the first mortgage on your life and the moral purpose of your existence. The issue is whether man is to be regarded as a sacrificial animal." [13] No earthly explanation has ever been given to the question, "Why must a man live for the sake

---

[13] Ayn Rand, "Faith and Force, The Destroyers of the Modern World," August 1, 1960, *Vital Speeches*, 631.

of others?" because there is no earthly reason for it; none has ever been given! Sacrifice makes people suckers and servants and not men. John Galt concludes in a speech in *Atlas Shrugged*, "I swear—by my life and my love of it—that I will never live for the sake of another man, nor ask another man to live for mine."

Ayn Rand clearly rejects Christianity and the ethic she associates with it. Christianity robs man of rightful dignity, of his rightful faculty of reason, and of joy. Reason is the antithesis of faith to Miss Rand. Anything which she does not perceive, she does not accept as part of reality. To this we simply ask on what basis she knows that her perceptions are true? She admits that the mind can make errors in thinking, but how does one become aware of error, especially if one rejects the thinking of others? What about the possibility of her senses misleading her? Further, logic is a limited endeavor. To Kenneth Pike, renowned scholar in linguistics, "The mind of man is not big enough to analyze all the world at once . . . when the components of a sample are separated for study, something may happen which destroys the whole." [14] To Pike, God's universe extends too far to be comprehended by the mind merely through the provisional, abstract mode of logic. And what of Miss Rand's claim that a thinking person must realize physical objects cannot act without cause? What omniscient perception led her to *this* grand, all-encompassing rule?

Ayn Rand's case against faith points out vividly the dichotomy she has made. She says that she desires men to see life whole, yet without faith in man's perceptive abilities one is doomed to solipsism. Without faith in the face of the inevitable fallibilities of human reason, there would be no reason at all. Faith—be it in God or in science—provides the framework in which reason operates. The fact that God has provided man with an objective revelation in Christianity is proof of this. Faith is not based on mere whim or emotion, but on the objective revealed character of God, available for investigation in the Scriptures. Every man should examine for himself the documents that reveal a God who cares enough about man to communicate with him. Faith in what he reads will secure the certainty his religious impulses crave.

Christianity, *contra* Miss Rand, does not rob man of his

---

[14] Kenneth L. Pike, *With Heart and Mind* (Grand Rapids, Mich.: Eerdmans, 1964), p. 7.

dignity, but crowns him with worth. Even a cursory examination of the Old and New Testament reveals this.[15] Though man has sinned in rejecting his Creator as his "ultimate concern," God still finds him infinitely valuable. Man, being a unique creation of God, has certain God-like qualities. The Old Testament indicates man is made "in God's image." Self-consciousness and self-determination make him a personality that can have fellowship with God. We have noted the significance of a revelation being given to man. This revelation explains that the sin of man in the beginning of time involved disobedience to a Creator who, on the basis of His Character, was entitled to obedience. The God revealed in Christian sources is not an unreasonable tyrant. Disobedience, as in human relations, estranged man from God, the One who created him for fellowship with Himself. The Bible records the history of the events God initiated to justly end the estrangement. In the Great Act, the central event of Scripture, man was infinitely dignified in God's decision to live with him as a man in Jesus Christ. God took on the full and complete experience of humanity to display to man what He is like and to demonstrate His love. God became man to enable man to become truly man. This involved a Death and Resurrection in man's behalf, in time and in space, in history. God himself, in love, took the penalty man deserves for his willful estrangement from Him. The man who believes that this is the case for him personally is restored in relationship to God, thus permitting him to be what God intended him to be.

Every individual is important to God. The distinctive self is not considered evil nor is self-improvement discouraged in Christianity. It is interesting to note that the apostle Paul was not a spineless whining person who made himself a doormat for opposing personalities! Rather in him one sees a man whom even the American sociologist Cooley judges to have no lack of an aggressive self.[16] His letter to the church at Philippi reveals a man strong enough to face both his weaknesses and strengths. He had a goal and a purpose in life and in death (Miss Rand says purpose is important). Like Jesus Christ Himself, Paul's humanity manifests itself in his statements of joy and sorrow, in a way that Miss Rand's characters never do. Christians through centuries have had intense self-feelings much

---

[15] See Luke 15; Matt. 10:31, 12:9-12.

[16] Charles Horton Cooley, *Human Nature and the Social Order* (New York: Schochen, 1964), p. 248.

as Luther. "Luther was a man of most intense self-feeling . . . what distinguishes Luther is not the quality of his self-feeling but that it was identified with sentiments and purposes that we look upon as noble, progressive and right." [17]

Christianity recognizes the need for proper self-love. Husbands are instructed to care for their wives *as they do their own bodies*, "for no man ever hates his own flesh but nourishes and cherishes it" (Eph. 5:29). Jesus told Christians to love their neighbors *as themselves*. Regard for self in Christianity is therefore not an end; it is related to our relationships with fellowmen. To love is to value, according to Miss Rand; it is thus totally consistent to love a God worthy of that love. It would then be possible to love other men because of God's love for them, because of their value to Him.

Sacrifice has always been the Christian ideal to two other Russian writers, Dostoevsky and Tolstoy. However sacrifice in the highest Christian sense is not unintelligent. Sacrifice to Miss Rand is unintelligent, unless it is done for a higher value. To the Christian every action is done out of love for Someone that is beyond himself and for others like himself whom he loves because God loves. When he does something for someone who does not deserve it, he is following the example of Jesus Christ who demonstrated His love and concern for man. Jesus was not weak in giving up His life; He has full control and power over His life and He chose to do the unexpected, from a human standpoint. Neither is the Christian a fool for following One who promised to raise him from the dead as he raised himself.

In spite of what Miss Rand says, man is already basically selfish. He acts in his own self-interest without her ethic. Perhaps what we have in America is a mass of "other-directed" people who spend much of their time worrying about what other people think of them, and whose actions are socially-conditioned to the extent that they are neurotic. This is not the fault of the Christian faith. Knowing Jesus Christ in a personal relationship in which He is Lord (because He is worthy of such rule) gives one a concern for, not a fear of others; knowing Christ frees him from acting out his life for a whimsical audience and places him before a just God. This is freedom.

---

[17] *Ibid.*, p. 212.

Part Six

CHRISTIANITY AND
PERSONAL COMMITMENT

THE NERVE OF THAT GUY CALLING ME A SINNER, AND ALL THOSE BIBLE VERSES..

I'D LOOK THEM UP...

BUT I'M AFRAID I'LL FIND THAT HE'S RIGHT!!

The Integrity of the Gospel Writers

Rod Rosenbladt

"Is it not possible that the Gospel writers were religious innovators, deifying their leader in the attempt to start a new religion?" This query is often posed by those who are acquainted with the genesis of any number of contemporary religious groups. The astute observer wonders whether the apostles and evangelists were not of the same stripe as those who today need a "holy book" or a "holy man" of some sort to "get their religion off the ground" and so proceed to manufacture one. This question is of no mean importance, as one who has looked carefully into the claims of Christianity realizes. Whereas other religions can survive the unmasking of their historical foundations (their important element is usually the universal "truths" or "teachings" of the founder), Christianity would dissolve under the same, since its truth is inextricably bound up with the events in the life of its Chief Figure. Therefore it is of prime importance both to ask and to answer the above question.

In an attempt to examine this question, several related and comparably crucial topics will necessarily be bypassed. These include the questions of the eyewitness character of the Gospel accounts, their authorship and date of composition, and the possibility of the miracles they record.

The reader has a right to ask if it is at all possible to answer the question of the basic integrity of the Gospel writers, seeing not only that we live more than nineteen centuries later but also that the question concerns the inner motives of the writers. Realizing that there is no such thing as absolute certainty in regard to factual questions, we shall examine the available evidence and draw our conclusions accordingly.

We begin our inquiry by noting the character of the New Testament writers as they are described in the documents. The early followers of Jesus seem to have been ordinary,

237

practical-minded people (tax collectors, fishermen, etc.). Far from being credulous, they appear to have possessed the skepticism of twentieth century positivists. One notes such examples as Thomas' disbelief in Jesus' Resurrection or Peter's return to fishing following the death of the One he had called The Christ.[1]

Though we may admit the possibility of collusion with intent to deceive, such an explanation is all but dissolved when we examine the Gospel writers' self-portrayal and descriptions of themselves and Jesus' disciples. For example, they describe in straightforward manner their own cowardice in collectively deserting their Master at the time of His arrest.[2] Peter is described in an especially unfavorable light, denying more than once that he was even an acquaintance of Jesus.[3] The writers describe their own impatience, recording their request that their Master call down fire from heaven upon an unrepentant town.[4] In another instance, Matthew describes the desire of some members of the group of disciples for power and glory beyond that of their cohorts.[5] Throughout the Gospel accounts, one is struck by the refusal of the disciples to face the evidence of Jesus' miracles.[6] These men are clearly not bragging of their impressive religious intuition!

In a similar vein, we notice what has been called the "nakedness" of the Gospel writings,

> the absence of all parade by the writers about their own integrity, of all anxiety to be believed, or to impress others with a good opinion of themselves or their cause, of all marks of wonder, or of desire to excite astonishment at the greatness of the events they record, and of all appearance of design to exalt their Master. On the contrary, there is apparently the most perfect indifference on their part, whether they are believed or not. It is worthy, too, of special observation, that though the evangelists record the unparalleled sufferings and cruel death of their beloved Lord, and this, too, by hands and with the consenting voices of those on whom he had

---

[1] John 21:3; John 20:24-29.

[2] Matthew 26:56b.

[3] Matthew 26:69-75; Mark 14:66-72; Luke 22:54-62.

[4] Luke 9:51-55.

[5] Matthew 2:20ff.

[6] There are multiple references such as Mark 4:35-41 and 6:51, 52 in the Gospels.

> conferred the greatest benefits, and their own persecu-
> tions and dangers, yet they have bestowed no epithets of
> harshness or even of just censure on the authors of all
> this wickedness, but have everywhere left the plain and
> unencumbered narrative to speak for itself, and the
> reader to pronounce his own sentence of condemnation;
> like true witnesses, who have nothing to gain or lose
> by the event or the cause, they state the facts and leave
> them to their fate.[7]

The accuracy of the above verdict can be checked by any
reader of the Gospels. One finds in these accounts very little
of what has come to be called "sensationalism," yet these
men claim that the events they record provide solid answers
for man's deepest existential problems. This fact is clearly
in favor of the integrity of the Gospel writers.

It has often been pointed out that the Gospel writers took
with utmost seriousness the historical, chronological and geographical details of their report.[8] Their honesty and competence in these matters have been vindicated again and again
against charges of error. This is not to say that all problems
in this area have been finally answered. But those who maintain
that the New Testament Gospels manifest shoddy historiography
have a very *tenuous case to support*. This accuracy of detail
is necessary to the truth-claim of the Christian faith (as we
pointed out above), but it does *not* establish *ipso facto* the
same. Why then speak of this question in connection with the
question of the integrity of the Gospel writers? There is a
particular reason why this point is integral to the case: the
very people to whom the apostles and evangelists proclaimed
the Gospel were those who were intimately acquainted with
the facts of Jesus' life. Many of those in the vicinity of Jerusalem
were intensely hostile to Jesus and His followers; they would
have been only too glad to have exposed the Gospels' message
as a colossal hoax. F. F. Bruce, Rylands Professor of Biblical
Criticism and Exegesis in the University of Manchester, has
this to say:

> It was not only friendly eyewitnesses that the early
> preachers had to reckon with; there were others less well
> disposed who were also conversant with the main facts

---

[7] Irwin H. Linton, *A Lawyer Examines the Bible* (Boston: W. A.
Wilde, 1943), pp. 43-44. Linton is here quoting the famous legal authority,
Simon Greenleaf, in his *Testimony of the Evangelists*.

[8] Luke 1:1-4 is typical of the attitude of the New Testament writers.

of the ministry and death of Jesus. The disciples could not afford to risk inaccuracies (not to speak of wilful manipulation of the facts), which would at once be exposed by those who would be only too glad to do so. On the contrary, one of the strong points in the original apostolic preaching is the confident appeal to the knowledge of the hearers; they not only said, "We are witnesses of these things," but also, "As you yourselves also know" (Acts ii.22). Had there been any tendency to depart from the facts in any material respect, the possible presence of hostile witnesses in the audience would have served as a further corrective.[9]

This point in particular is one of the strongest evidences of the integrity of the Gospel writers. The survival of the Christian faith in the midst of so hostile an atmosphere shows full well that its appeal to well known facts was irrefutable. Instead of transferring Christianity into the realm of transcendent, unverifiable "truths," the writers multiplied chances of criticism by stressing detail upon detail. No opportunity for cross-examination was bypassed, yet the enemies of the Gospel (including both Roman *and* Jewish authorities) were not able to produce evidence which would have effectively countered the claims of the apostles and evangelists.[10]

The possible motives for fabrication on the part of the Gospel writers must also be considered. It has always been possible to maintain that they manufactured their testimony for selfish ends, but this interpretation is highly unlikely. Instead of gaining money, honor, and power, they experienced poverty, scorn and imprisonment. They were exposed to all kinds of danger, held in derision by their own religious authorities, and looked upon as fools by the intelligentsia.

The laws of every country were against the teachings of his [Christ's] disciples. The interests and passions of all the rulers and great men in the world were against them. The fashion of the world was against them. Propagating this new faith, even in the most inoffensive and peaceful manner, they could expect nothing but contempt, opposition, revilings, bitter persecutions, stripes, imprisonments, torments and cruel deaths. Yet this faith they zealously did propagate; They had every possible

---

[9] F. F. Bruce, *The New Testament Documents: Are They Reliable?* (5th ed.; Grand Rapids, Mich.: Eerdmans, 1960), p. 46.

[10] Note the stress on common knowledge of the events of Jesus' life in passages such as Acts 2:22, 26:26.

motive to review carefully the grounds of their faith, and the evidences of the great facts and truths which they asserted; and these motives were pressed upon their attention with the most melancholy and terrific frequency.[11]

In the face of this evidence one can scarcely resist asking the obvious: "Can it really be that the early followers of Jesus submitted to such universal rejection in order to propagate a story *they knew to be false?*" It is one thing to suffer for a religious belief which is believed to be sound, but it is quite another to suffer for a self-conceived religious fraud.

Further doubt is cast upon any interpretation that posits fabrication by the disciples and the Gospel writers by their moral and doctrinal excellence. The ethical standards of their Master hardly encouraged dishonesty.[12] For example, if these men did not believe in a life after death where their testimony would be vindicated, they were certainly given "the short end of the deal" during their earthly life. Would they have opted for this, knowing full well that the Judgment spoken of by their Leader would probably never occur? Unless these men were some kind of "religious masochists," a notion for which we have absolutely no evidence, our knowledge of normal human nature militates against any interpretation which posits wilful fabrication by the Gospel writers.

Many have maintained that a "messianic fever" had captured Jewish thought in the first century, a fever that probably caused the followers of Jesus to deify Him. But there are several facts that make this interpretation as unlikely as the ones we have already examined. First, Jesus' teachings about Himself and His work were anything but hospitable to popular messianic expectations. The Jews of the first century were looking for a messiah who would take up the sword and free them from Roman dominion. The Pharisees and Sadducees were Jesus' strongest adversaries—hardly evidence that the religious community saw in Him the fulfillment of their expectations. If the disciples deified their leader, it was against the full force of their ethnic and religious surroundings.[13]

Second, the disciples would have been opposing their religious

---

[11] Linton, *op. cit.*, pp. 40-41.

[12] See especially John 8:44-46.

[13] For a fuller treatment of this area, see the chapter "Jesus Christ and History: Part 2" in John Warwick Montgomery's *Where Is History Going?* (Grand Rapids, Mich.: Zondervan, 1969).

heritage in deifying Jesus. When one examines the central tenet of that heritage, one wonders whether the disciples could have been psychologically capable of such a feat. That central principle of Judaism is, of course, "Hear, O Israel: the Lord our God is one Lord," and "You shall have no other gods before me." [14] Reviewing the history of idolatry in Israel (and the consequences for the followers of idolatry!), one doubts whether the disciples could have come to proclaim that the man Jesus was identical with the Lord of the Old Testament— that is, unless they had a compellingly good reason for doing so. Did such a reason exist? It did, and, seeing what evidence for the integrity of the Gospel writers has already shown, it is necessary that we examine this reason with utmost care.

Jesus Himself prophesied a single event which would, when accomplished, fully evidence His deity.[15] His sinless life and miraculous ministry, His fulfillment of Old Testament prophecy, and the authority of His words all evidenced His identity. But He pointed to one crucial event which would finally manifest His deity; that event was of course His Resurrection from the dead. Many scholarly studies have been made demonstrating the dependability of the reports of Jesus' Resurrection.[16] However, our purpose is not to examine the larger question of the evidence for this event, but only to view it in relation to the integrity of the Gospel writers. Is it possible that they fabricated the Resurrection accounts as final evidence for their proposed "new religion"? Here we think back to a point made earlier. The disciples proclaimed the fact of Jesus' Resurrection from the dead in a decidedly hostile atmosphere. Even if they had been able to pass off as valid numerous false reports of Jesus' miracles in other parts of the surrounding country, it is highly doubtful that they could have proclaimed His Resurrection to the people who had been gathered in the city of Jerusalem at the time! But this is exactly what they did. Anyone in the vicinity could have refuted their claim simply by producing the body of Jesus. But the disciples knew that this could not be done; He had risen and they had had prolonged eyewitness contact with Him. He, unlike other "messiahs" of the time, had substantiated His claim by conquering the powers of death.

---

[14] Deuteronomy 6:4; Exodus 20:3.

[15] Matthew 12:38-40; John 2:18-22.

[16] See Frank Morison, *Who Moved the Stone?* (London: Faber & Faber, 1944) and Merrill Tenney, *The Reality of the Resurrection* (New York: Harper & Row, 1963).

The evidence for Jesus' Resurrection eventually overcame the disciples' religious heritage, the opposition of the religious authorities, and the mockery of an incredulous world.

What have we discovered in this brief examination of the question of the integrity of the Gospel writers? We have discovered evidence which encourages us to opt for the integrity of the New Testament Gospels. The available data support the view that the writers did not fabricate their reports. But are we forced to bend our knee to this evidence? No, since this evidence is of a factual nature and as such cannot demand assent in the same way as deductive proof. On the other hand, deductive proof never offers a person knowledge of the real world. It is the nature of the case (for a religion which claims to be historical in the fullest sense of the word) that factual evidence must be central. Because this is so, the case may be at best highly probable rather than logically certain. This is the same kind of probability that leads us to make choices in everyday life; which of us refuses to eat because of the ever-present chance his food may be poisoned?

Anyone who finds himself offended by the evidence which has been uncovered here is advised to examine in depth the primary documents concerning Jesus of Nazareth. In doing so he will discover not only a Person who claims to be able to deal adequately with man's basic problems, but also offers objective support for this claim. He will discover in reading that there exist within all of us countless emotional reasons for rejecting Christianity. While many objections surely spring from honest intellectual doubts, some are revealed to have their source in the moral and volitional sphere. It is the wise person who is able to discern which is the case so that he may discover the One who has dealt with both problems.

The Resurrection—a Credibility Gap?

James F. Babcock

The truth finally leaked out. Jesus of Nazareth was just another nice guy whose luck ran out. Convinced that he was the Jewish Messiah, he set about to have himself arrested, drugged, crucified, and revived to fulfill the Jewish Scriptures as he understood them. Unfortunately for the comatose Jesus, a soldier jabbed a spear into his side before his henchmen could remove him from the cross. Later, all attempts to revive him were fruitless; his secret Jerusalem followers quietly reburied him in another spot unknown to his Galilean disciples, who soon repeatedly mistook the beloved disciple, a young priest from Jerusalem, for Jesus himself. Subsequently the eleven prominent Galilean disciples and others began propagating the incredible message that Jesus had risen from the dead. Christianity was born.

This is not of course the view of the New Testament writers. This is a sketch of the thesis of *The Passover Plot*, a recent bestseller by Hugh J. Schonfield. It attempts to bridge what Schonfield assumes is a credibility gap in the Gospels.

However the real problem for anyone interested in the New Testament is to determine whether in fact there is a credibility gap in the Gospels. This is exactly what Dr. Schonfield assumes without substantiation. Unlike some of his credulous readers who are dazzled by his erudition, his reviewers have detected a fundamental methodological error: Schonfield's argument depends on a chain of questionable inferences drawn from sources that he considers untrustworthy. Thus, in the opinion of the Jewish scholar Samuel Sandmel,

> Schonfield's imaginative reconstruction is devoid of a scintilla of proof, and rests on dubious inferences from passages in the Gospels whose historical reliability he himself has antecedently rejected on page after page.

245

In my view, the book should be dismissed as the mere curiosity it is.[1]

Though Schonfield's book is aberrant and error-ridden, it does have the virtue of showing that modern man is disposed toward accepting a radical reinterpretation of Christianity rather than the message of the Gospels themselves.

But is there in fact a credibility gap in the gospels? A common problem exists which has led to the supposition that a credibility gap is present. For many moderns this problem is the Resurrection, the heart of the New Testament message.[2] Perhaps it is a common problem because it seems incredible that Jesus of Nazareth actually solved the fundamental problem of life: death. Furthermore, to think of yielding one's allegiance to another who conquered this problem is devastating to twentieth century autonomy.

So the resurrection is a credibility gap. I can hear someone saying it now: "The miraculous. Yes, that is one problem. It is difficult enough to believe the fantastic accounts of the healing miracles and the nature miracles attributed to Jesus, but when the Gospels present this mythical Resurrection nonsense—why, that is too much for anyone to fall for today. Dead men don't rise from the dead. When a man is dead, he's dead."

Is that so?

What you say is plausible. You have never seen a corpse reanimated. Neither have I. What's more, neither had anyone in Jesus' time. Then rumors began circulating that one Jesus of Nazareth had restored life to a twelve-year-old girl soon after she had died; that he had stopped a funeral procession

---

[1] "Road Between Rome and Jerusalem," *Saturday Review*, December 3, 1966, 42. Another review by Joel Carmichael in *Book Week* (September 18, 1966), 15, points out that "what Mr. Schonfield has in fact done is to accept one of the various Gospel strands among all the others, in the complex palimpsest of the Gospels: the magnification of Jesus as the Jewish Messiah. . . . Quite arbitrarily, Mr. Schonfield assumes that this particular layer of tradition represents a geniune historical situation, and that the legendary accretions begin only later. But in so doing, he is merely swallowing the initial legend; this makes the arrogance with which he dismisses everything else look a little absurd." However in his book, *The Death of Jesus* (New York: Dell, 1967), Carmichael makes the same type of error that he accuses Schonfield of committing: he arbitrarily accepts certain passages and rejects others.

[2] In I Cor. 15:12-19, Paul has stated this most emphatically.

to tell a deceased young man to arise; and that he had restored life to a friend who had been buried in a tomb for four days.[3] Later it was reported that he himself had been crucified and buried, but that he too had returned to life.[4] This, without any "passover plot," is the report of the New Testament writers. It must be intelligently and critically evaluated before one pronounces on a *de facto* credibility gap in the New Testament.

EVALUATING THE NEW TESTAMENT REPORTS

Some begin their evaluation with the supposition that miracles are the least likely of all events. For Hume and for most moderns, it is always more probable that the witnesses of a "miracle" were deceived or deceiving than that a miracle occurred. Why? Because if something had occurred, it would not have been called a "miracle," which amounts to the specious affirmation that miracles are events which do not happen! Indeed this venerable verdict was served by Cicero two millenia ago:[5]

> For nothing can happen without cause; nothing happens that cannot happen, and when what was capable of happening has happened, it may not be interpreted as a miracle. Consequently, there are no miracles. . . . We therefore draw this conclusion: what was incapable of happening is not a miracle.

The fallacy should be apparent by now: the argument is circular. Of course miracles don't happen if they are so defined! In addition,

> we know the experience against them to be uniform only if we know that all reports of them are false. And we know all the reports to be false only if we know already that miracles have never occurred. In fact, we are arguing in a circle.[6]

There is no credibility gap necessarily attributable to the miraculous elements in the Gospels. On the contrary, if Jesus of Nazareth were God incarnate as he claimed, then

---

[3] Mark 5:22-43; Luke 7:11-17; John 11:1-46.

[4] For example see Acts 2:22-36.

[5] *De Divinatione* 2. 28, cited by H. van der Loos in *The Miracles of Jesus* (Leiden: E. J. Brill, 1965), p. 7.

[6] *Miracles* (New York: Macmillan, 1947), p. 123. Chap. xiii, "On Probability," deals at some length with Hume's arguments.

the unusual, the extraordinary, the miraculous—even a Resurrection—might be expected.

In evaluating the Gospel writers' reports one might also question the transmission of the records which purport to be eyewitness accounts from those who saw the resurrected Christ. Upon careful investigation, one finds however that the New Testament is much better attested than are other works of antiquity.[7] Though original manuscripts of the New Testament writings are no longer extant there are numerous copies, and in the days long before printing or xerography professional scribes transcribed these documents with astonishing accuracy. Today, with advances in textual criticism, scholars have substantially succeeded in restoring the text of the New Testament to its original form. The authenticity and general integrity of the New Testament documents has finally been established.[8] There is therefore no escape from the implications of the Resurrection because of a corrupted text.

Some have supposed that by the time the New Testament records were written, Jesus' message had become so corroded and encrusted with legendary elements that it could no longer be salvaged. This objection is highly improbable. The major problem for those who hold this position is expressed in one word: time. The New Testament was completed before the close of the first century, A.D.[9] In particular Paul's writings were completed before his death around A.D. 65, and I Corin-

---

[7] Thus in 1962, there were extant 76 papyri, 250 uncials, 2,646 minuscules, and 1,997 lectionaries of the Greek New Testament, according to Bruce M. Metzger in his monumental *Text of the New Testament: Its Transmission, Corruption, and Restoration* (New York Oxford University Press, 1964), pp. 32-33. By way of contrast, "for Caesar's *Gallic War* (composed between 58 and 50 BC) there are several extant MSS [manuscripts], but only nine or ten are good, and the oldest is some 900 years later than Caesar's day," writes F. F. Bruce in *The New Testament Documents: Are They Reliable?* (5th ed.; Grand Rapids, Michigan: Eerdmans, 1960), p. 16. The New Testament witnesses are more numerous and much nearer the time of composition, which, together, is what counts.

[8] Sir Frederic G. Kenyon, *The Bible and Archaeology* (New York: Harper, 1940), p. 288, 89, cited by F. F. Bruce in *The New Testament Documents*, p. 20.

[9] See recent texts on New Testament introduction. The two best are Paul Feine, Johannes Behm, and Werner Georg Kümmel, *Introduction to the New Testament*, trans. A. J. Mattill, Jr. (14th rev. ed.; Nashville: Abingdon, 1966) and Donald Guthrie, *New Testament Introduction* (3 vols.; Chicago: Inter-Varsity Press, 1961-65).

thians 15, his great chapter on the Resurrection, was written about A.D. 55. There simply was insufficient time for legends to develop. And if they had, they would surely have been refuted on the spot by eyewitnesses hostile to a new Christian teaching about a "risen" Jesus. Furthermore, "if the Primitive community created much of the material connected with its Lord, who then created the community?"[10] The period of oral tradition before the actual writing of the New Testament documents provides no escape from the factuality of the Resurrection of Jesus and its implications.[11]

Miracles, textual corruption, and legendary development notwithstanding, evaluation of the Gospels leads us to open minded consideration of the facts recorded there. When we trace through the accounts, we note the following points.[12] First, on at least five separate occasions up to several months before his crucifixion, Jesus predicted his death and Resurrection. Still his disciples did not understand the plain significance of his words.[13] When Jesus was arrested, his disciples fled for their lives. How different was their behavior several weeks later when they first preached the Resurrection to the crowds of pilgrims who had come to Jerusalem to celebrate the Jewish Passover.[14] Second, Jesus was unquestionably dead before

---

[10] H. E. W. Turner, *Jesus: Master and Lord* (2nd ed.; London: A. R. Mowbray, 1954), p. 84.

[11] "It is not the higher criticism but the higher credulity that boggles at a verse in Mark and swallows without a qualm pages of pure conjecture about the primitive Christians' psychology and its workings in the preliterary period." Cited by Turner, *ibid.*, p. 75.

[12] For a highly readable sketch of the events leading up to the trial and crucifixion of Jesus and an analysis of the evidence for the Resurrection, see Frank Morison, *Who Moved the Stone?* (2nd ed.; London: Faber and Faber, 1942). This remarkable little book was written by a lawyer who originally planned to write a short monograph stripping the last week of Jesus' life of the overgrowth of primitive beliefs and dogmatic suppositions which he assumed surrounded the Gospel accounts. His inquiry led him to become a Christian.

[13] Typical is Mark 9:31, 32 (RSV): "He was teaching his disciples, saying to them, 'The Son of man will be delivered into the hands of men, and they will kill him; and when he is killed, after three days he will rise.' But they did not understand the saying, and they were afraid to ask him." The other occasions can be found in Mark 8:31; 9:9; 10:34; and 14:28, as well as in the parallels in the other Gospels.

[14] Compare Matthew 26:56 with Acts 2:22.

he was placed in the tomb. Pilate was so surprised that Jesus had already died, that he asked a centurion to confirm it.[15] Finally, there is no question that the tomb was empty on the first Easter Sunday morning. The historical testimony is unanimous: check out Matthew 28:6, Mark 16:6, Luke 24:3, and John 20:3-7. But the amazing thing is that the disciples, the very ones who should have been expecting the Resurrection, refused to believe it at first. However their skepticism soon turned to faith. The difference, again according to our sources, came about as a result of several personal appearances of Jesus after his Resurrection. For example, the first appearance to most of the disciples at one time is recorded in Luke 24:36-43 (RSV):

> As they were saying this, Jesus himself stood among them. But they were startled and frightened, and supposed that they saw a spirit. And he said to them, "Why are you troubled, and why do questionings rise in your hearts? See my hands and my feet, that it is I myself; handle me, and see; for a spirit has not flesh and bones as you see that I have." And while they still disbelieved for joy, and wondered, he said to them, "Have you anything here to eat?" They gave him a piece of broiled fish, and he took it and ate before them.

This was neither vision nor mass hallucination. These and other chimerical explanations which have been proposed through the centuries do even less justice to the evidence than the straightforward historical interpretation itself.

It has been the continuing testimony since Peter's first ser-

---

[15] Mark 15:44,45. The classic answer to the so-called "swoon theory" was given by David Strauss, himself no believer in the Resurrection: "It is impossible that one who had just come forth from the grave half dead, who crept about weak and ill, who stood in need of medical treatment, of bandaging, strengthening, and tender care, and who at last succumbed to suffering, could ever have given to the disciples the impression that He was a conqueror over death and the grave,—that He was the Prince of Life,—which lay at the bottom of their future ministry. Such a resuscitation could only have weakened the impression which He had made upon them in life and in death,—or at the most could have given it an elegiac voice—but could by no possibility have changed their sorrow into enthusiasm, or elevated their reverence into worship." (*The Life of Jesus for the People*; English trans. [2d ed.; London, 1879], I, 412; cited by Wilbur M. Smith, *Therefore, Stand* [13th ed.; Natick, Mass.: W. A. Wilde, 1959], p. 383.)

mon on Pentecost (Acts 2) that Jesus Christ rose from the dead and solved life's basic problem. "Faith does not claw the air. It lays hold upon saving verities planted in the fabric of history." [16] The Crucifixion and the Resurrection are imbedded in the fabric of history as presented in the Gospels. Without the Resurrection, one is left with the tattered historical threads of unfulfilled promises and claims. But with the Resurrection, those same promises and claims speak forth Jesus Christ's incomparable greatness in conquering death.

In the final analysis, there was no reason acceptable to the risen Jesus of History for turning one's back on him. But perhaps you feel shortchanged. The men of Jesus' day had the opportunity to hear him, to see him, to look into his empty tomb. Yes, they had those advantages, but we have others. We have the evidence recorded in the New Testament. We can read Jesus' words to the once-doubting Thomas, " 'Blessed are those who have not seen and yet believe.' " [17] That Jesus did not mean a blind belief is made quite clear by the writer in the next sentence:

> Now Jesus did many other signs in the presence of the disciples, which are not written in this book; but these are written that you may believe that Jesus is the Christ, the Son of God, and that believing you may have life in his name.[18]

All the evidence that any man needs today is in the New Testament documents. For the present, according to these very documents, you have a limited opportunity to pass judgment upon them during this short life; after death, it is the resurrected Jesus of History and Eternity who will pass judgment upon you. It was he who declared, "He who rejects me and does not receive my sayings has a judge; the word that I have spoken will be his judge on the last day." [19] The stakes are exceedingly high. The choice is yours. Investigate Jesus' life and claims. Accept the eternal life he offers, the life-giving power he demonstrated in his Resurrection.

---

[16] Clark H. Pinnock, " 'On the Third Day,' " *Jesus of Nazareth: Saviour and Lord*, ed. Carl F. H. Henry (Grand Rapids, Michigan: Eerdmans, 1966), p. 153.

[17] John 20:29.

[18] John 20:30, 31.

[19] John 12:48.

The Two-Sided Game of Christian Truth

Michael Murphy

One must look both *along* and *at* everything.[1]

Let us not mock God with metaphor,
analogy, sidestepping transcendence;
making of the event a parable, a sign painted in the
    faded credulity of earlier ages:
let us walk through the door.[2]

I believe that historic Christianity offers man experiential certainty that God is, in fact, a reality. And I realize that this assertion may perplex and even anger you. For you probably suspect that sooner or later in this discussion I am going to say that Christianity demands faith, and faith just does not equal, or lead to certainty. Your reaction to Christianity may go even further: What does it *matter* whether Christ really claimed to be God or whether He actually came back from the dead to prove it? Well, I know what it is like to sit in on religious free-for-alls, to listen to people cooly debate the relative truth of this and that assertion, and finally to start screaming inside because all their coolness only sets them and their answers a million light years apart from me and my questions. I know what it is like to have people try to snare me in their theological-philosophical trivia when all I am trying to do is to make some sense out of myself and life. Nevertheless, I am still convinced that God is a reality and that it really does matter whether this thing, Christianity, is true.

---

[1] C. S. Lewis, "Meditation in a Tool Shed," *His*, XXVII (March, 1967), 32.

[2] John Updike, "Seven Stanzas at Easter," in *Telephone Poles and Other Poems* (New York: Alfred A. Knopf, 1962).

THE GAME AND HOW TO PLAY IT

There are two ways of looking at Christianity, two ways of answering the question of its truth: by looking *along* and by looking *at*. In an ingenious essay called "Meditation in a Tool Shed," [3] C. S. Lewis explains the difference between these two different ways of seeing. We see anything and everything either from the "inside" or from the "outside," either as participant or as observer. And each of these ways of seeing a thing yields a different experience of the thing, which fact forces us to ask which experience is the "true" or the "valid" one, which experience tells us most about the thing itself. Should we listen to people who live inside a thing, or to those who look at it as an object of study? Many people have naively and irrationally assumed that the external account of a thing is always superior to the account given from the inside, but in reality neither way of seeing is intrinsically better or truer than the other way. And in particular instances, we cannot know in advance whether one kind of looking gives a more correct account than the other, or whether both accounts are equally wrong, or whether both accounts are equally correct, but in different ways.

It is my contention that looking "at" Christianity and looking "along" Christianity yield experiences and accounts of the thing which are equally correct in different ways. Looking *at* the Christian faith is essentially preliminary to looking *along* it: looking at the thing helps us to see why we *should* look along it.

I am going to step outside the Christian framework for a moment, look "at" it with you, and outline some basic issues which must be faced in assessing its validity. Then I am going to ask you to step inside the thing for a moment, look "along" it with me, see how you might subjectively test the world-and-life view which unfolds as a result of answering the truth-question in the affirmative.

Like any game of merit, this one includes some qualifications and some warnings. First, the "rules" of the game may not be to our liking: the questions we are obliged to face in the process of looking "at," may very well not be the questions we find ourselves asking. But the "at" questions cannot be avoided (unless we are willing to pay the price of *irrational* commitment), and they are inextricably linked with those larger

---

[3] *Op. cit.*, pp. 31-32.

questions of meaning and purpose which haunt and intrigue us throughout our lives.

Second, the objective of the game demands personal involvement and self-examination; we cannot play *this* game with cool detachment. Our purpose in looking "at" Christianity is to see whether it is *true*, and whether it is *therefore worthy* of an "along" commitment. So we are forced to ask ourselves what we will *do* if we should discover that the thing is true, or that it isn't. The claim we are investigating for truth-value is not only that the God of interstellar space has entered our world in the person of Jesus Christ, but that our own identity and destiny are contingent upon our attitude toward that Person and toward the Truth which He proclaimed and manifested. We ourselves—and not merely the truth-claims—are at stake in the investigation.

Third, even though I will try to help you play the game, in the deepest sense this is a game which you must act out alone. You can and should seek the help of those who live inside the Christian view of things; the "along" account is as valuable and as necessary as the "at" account. But you alone know the questions, asked and unasked, which you bring to the game. Perhaps you bring specific questions about the validity of Christianity; perhaps only a vague distrust of it, or an inability or lack of desire to believe in it. Possibly you have been inside Christianity at some point in your life and now find yourself wondering how you could ever have done it, how anyone alive to the world as it is could ever stay there. Maybe you find yourself hooked to the idea of God, hooked to your own hopes that He is somehow *there* and wondering if there is any reason to hang on to those hopes. All I can say is—be prepared for anything. The game may suddenly become more realistic and more personal than you might expect or wish.

LOOKING "AT" THE THING

The "at" side of the game may best be played by following through a historical argument, for our objective is to determine whether Christianity is true, and the truth-claims of Christianity are historical in nature. I have chosen to present the argument in very brief outline form, not merely because of limitations of space, but because I want you to be able to view the argument as a whole and to see where it leads. So often we allow ourselves to become hung up on one point or step in an argument, thus destroying all possibility of understanding it in its totality, of "feeling" its cumulative force, of moving toward its logical implications. Accordingly, for the purposes of this essay, I ask that you approach the argument with the supposition that each point in it can adequately be established. Of course, should you decide to play the game for keeps within the context of your life, you will need to ask whether each point is actually sound. But the remainder of this essay will proceed on the assumption that the historical argument does lead us to the conclusion either that Christianity is true or that it might very possibly be true and thus does push us in the direction of existential, "along" involvement.

There are three main points in the argument:[4]

(1) The New Testament documents, which must be regarded as reliable sources of information,[5] portray the man Jesus as God-in-human-flesh.

(2) If Jesus was *not* God, as He claimed to be, He was (a) a charlatan or (b) a lunatic. Or (c) His disciples were charlatans, lunatics, or naive exaggerators. But none of these alternative interpretations fits the facts as the documents present them to us.

(3) All the primary source materials offer the Resurrection as definitive *proof* of Christ's deity and therefore, of His authority. Alternative naturalistic accounts of this event (and many have been offered) simply do not explain the historical facts and are all too often based on anti-supernatural presuppositions. Because the Resurrection event must be accounted for, we are driven to Christ's own explanation—that His Resurrection is the ultimate attestation of His deity and of His claims. Jesus Christ is God, and His claims are vindicated.

No, this line of reasoning does not offer us absolute deductive certainty that Christianity is true, that Jesus Christ is, in fact, God. But then absolute proof of any historical fact is never available to us; in reality all our knowledge is formed in terms

---

[4] I draw these points from John Warwick Montgomery's "History and Christianity" articles, which first appeared in *His*, December, 1964-March, 1965, and have been reprinted in his book *Where Is History Going?* (Minneapolis, Minn.: Bethany Fellowship, 1969) chaps. 2 and 3.

[5] Perhaps your mind reels a little at this statement and at its apparently dogmatic formulation. But notice that I did *not* yet say, ". . . which must be regarded as infallible sources of divine revelation." When dealing with the question of Christianity's truth, we need only approach the documents with the confidence that they are generally reliable sources of information concerning the life of Jesus of Nazareth. And this confidence is but a natural response to the evidence for the documents' integrity.

of probabilities. However this argument does throw the probability decidedly in favor of the truth of Christianity. The historical and logical evidence is formidable, and it is of the kind that compels assent.

But a person may be able to give intellectual assent to the claims of Christ, at least tentatively, and yet not be able to bridge the gap to volitional trust. For Christianity, if it is anything, is a compelling threat to our sense of independence and self-sufficiency: it pushes us to a drastic reevaluation of ourselves, both as individuals and as a race. It tells us that we are not alone in the universe, that we are not our own God and never have been, that we would not even have called to Him unless He had already been calling to us.

LOOKING "ALONG" THE THING

If, after looking at the historical basis for the Christian truth-claims, you should find yourself in this position—suspecting that Christianity might, after all, be *true*, and perhaps hoping both that it is and that it isn't—then one way out of the impasse might be to imagine what it would *mean* if it is true. I think I can help you to do this. I can't take your "leap" for you—the leap from historical probability to existential certainty—but I can help you to glimpse what it is like on this other side of that leap, inside the Christian vision of existence.

Before taking this intermediary step, if you feel you need to take it, consider the possibility, the remote possibility, that you yourself may have already, actually begun to slip inside. It happens that way in some people: they suddenly discover that, somehow, sometime, their knowledge of Christ-facts has produced intellectual assent, which has, in turn, yielded stirrings of inner conviction, propelling them toward full-orbed, gut-level commitment. Other people, like C. S. Lewis, are brought "kicking and struggling" to the other side by the sheer weight of the historical evidence. And others simply have to throw themselves into the wave, hoping and even believing that their feet will eventually find land.

Looking "along" Christianity, then, vicariously if not personally, imaginatively if not actually, we see that it is both a threat *and* a promise—a gracious, unmerited, unexpected promise of a whole new quality of existence. The announcement which may seem threatening when viewed from without, becomes increasingly tantalizing when seen from within. Yes, our egos and our categories are dealt a bruising blow, but we are bruised and crushed in order to be remade, in order to be set free. And the "freedom" which was so oppressive when we were alone, becomes truly liberating because we know we are *not* alone. We may still find it painful to admit that we cannot make it without Him and without our brothers, but somehow we learn to do this: we learn to live in relationship, in community, in love. And all our frantic struggles for meaning and purpose and value suddenly make sense, for by His coming Jesus Christ has said to us, Yes, you are valuable and, yes, there is meaning, real meaning. Life is quite other than you find it without Me. I bring you new facts and new possibilities. I bring you a word from Outside, the Word which you have sought and needed so long.

THE GAME ENDS—IN SADNESS OR IN JOY

The events of Christ's life—even His resurrection from the dead, biological death—can be validated apart from prior belief in them, but the effect, the *value* of those events, can only be realized as we place our trust in the Person about whom they center and to whom they point. The "at" experience is fulfilled and completed in the "along" experience.

And looking "along" Christianity, actually and not simply imaginatively, makes sense in light of the high degree of historical probability which confronts us when we look "at" the thing. This historical probability foreshadows the experiential certainty which is part of the "along" experience. And how do we move from historical probability to experiential certainty, from the "at" vision of Christianity to the "along" vision? By no more than a willing, willful "suspension of disbelief." For we have the word of Christ Himself that "whoever has the will to do the will of God shall know whether my teaching comes from God or is merely my own" (John 7:17). We are invited to test the Christian view of reality experientially, and such a test, though not without risk, is really no more than a logical response to the facts of history and experience.

But if you have examined the historical case for Christianity and concluded that it is probable that the thing really did happen, if you have listened to accounts from the inside in an attempt to test the "along" vision, and still find yourself unable to opt for the thing with your total being, should you not ask whether you are *willing* to do so? Could it be that long years of moral rebellion against God, of "freedom" from

His interference, are leading you to distort the data (historical, logical, and experiential) or to sidestep their implications?

Jesus Christ is a live option for our faith—our belief, our trust, our commitment—because of who He is, because of what He did. The door to existential, "along" relationship with Him has been opened for us by the evidence and by the events to which the evidence points: namely, His death and resurrection. But there is a warning attached to that second Event, addressed to any of us who would persist in ignoring or redefining it, to any of us who would hesitate to walk through the Door, to Joy:

> Let us not seek to make it less monstrous
> for our own convenience, or own sense of beauty,
> lest, awakened in one unthinkable hour, we are embarrassed
>   by the miracle,
> and crushed by remonstrance.[6]

---

[6] Updike, *loc. cit.*

APPENDICES

Appendix A

Passover Plot or Easter Triumph?
A Critical Review of H. Schonfield's Recent Theory

Edwin M. Yamauchi

"In another age, the author of this book would have been burned at the stake," reads an advertisement heralding Hugh J. Schonfield's *The Passover Plot* (London: Bernard Geis Associates, 1966) in the September 25th issue of the *New York Times*. The controversial book by the Jewish scholar raised a furor when published in England in 1965. Published in the United States in the fall of 1966 by Bernard Geis, it has received only cursory and unfavorable reviews thus far (cf. *Christianity Today*, December 9. 1966, pp. 29-30). Samuel Sandmel of the Hebrew Union College, author of *We Jews and Jesus*, writing in the *Saturday Review*, December 3, 1966, p. 43, says: "Schonfield's imaginative reconstruction is devoid of a scintilla of proof, and rests on dubious inferences from passages in the Gospels whose historical reliability he himself has antecedently rejected on page after page. In my view, the book should be dismissed as the mere curiousity it is."

Although the work will not convince scholars and will not appeal to Christians, it will undoubtedly attract many others because it is being sensationally publicized and will be issued in paperback. The book deserves some critical attention because it raises before the public the paramount issues of the death, the resurrection, and the deity of Jesus.

Schonfield Speculates That Jesus Was a So-Called Nazorean

Building on the speculative theories of Robert Eisler, the author holds that there existed in the time of Jesus a pre-

Christian Nazorean sect in Galilee with affinities with the Essenes of Qumran and the Mandaeans (p. 208). He even includes the Old Testament Rechabites and Kenites as elements in his North Palestinian Sectarians (pp. 38-39). He asserts, "We must therefore regard it as highly probable that for a time Jesus attached himself to a travelling body of sectarian craftsmen, and thereby came to be known as the Nazorean" (p. 64).

Although he does not fall into the error of identifying Jesus as an Essene, he argues that Essene influence was strong in Galilee since Damascus is mentioned as one of their centers in the Damascus Document of the Dead Sea Scrolls (pp. 38-39). (The distance between Galilee and Damascus is not taken seriously.) Some scholars had suggested that after the earthquake of 31 B.C. the Qumran community had temporarily abandoned their Dead Sea habitation for Damascus. But since we now have a manuscript of the Damascus Document dated long before 31 B.C., possibly to the early first century B.C., the literal interpretation of "Damascus" seems untenable—the references to the movement to Damascus are not prophetic. (Cf. Frank M. Cross, *The Ancient Library of Qumram* [Garden City, N.Y.: Doubleday Anchor, 1961], pp. 81-83).

The author suggests that the Mandaeans of Iraq and Iran—an Aramaic-speaking, Gnostic community—are the heirs of the so-called Nazoreans of Galilee (p. 208). There is indeed some indirect evidence to indicate that the Mandaeans may have had their origins in Palestine about the time of Christ. However, their literary texts, so widely used by R. Reitzenstein and Rudolf Bultmann in the 1920's and 1930's to interpret the Gospel of John, are medieval manuscripts. They may, it is true, contain some ancient traditions. But since most of the references to Christ are polemics against Byzantine Christendom, the uncritical use of such texts in New Testament exposition can hardly be justified. (See the present writer's article, "The Present Status of Mandaean Studies," *Journal of Near Eastern Studies*, XXV [1966], 88-96.) It is rather striking that critics who are often the most skeptical in their estimate of the New Testament can at the same time be quite credulous in the use of such late sources.

Schonfield Alleges That the Concept of Jesus' Resurrection Is Pagan, Patterned after the Rising-and-Dying Gods of the Near East

"It took a Nazorean of Galilee to apprehend from the Scriptures that death and resurrection was the bridge between the two phases (i.e., Suffering Just One and Glorious King). The very tradition of the land where Adonis yearly died and rose again seemed to call for it (p. 227)." The theory that there was a widespread worship of a dying-and-rising fertility god Tammuz in Mesopotamia, Adonis in Syria (note: not Galilee!), Attis in Asia Minor, and Osiris in Egypt—was propounded by Sir James Frazer in 1906. Schonfield rests his case on Theophile Meek's interpretation of the Song of Solomon as a liturgy of an Adonis-Tammuz cult, which is in turn dependent upon Frazer's hypothesis.

The theory has been widely adopted by scholars who little realize its fragile foundations. In recent years Samuel N. Kramer has made a thorough study of the Mesopotamian sources for the alleged resurrection of Tammuz by Ishtar, and has found that this popular belief was based on "nothing but inference and surmise, guess and conjecture." (*Mythologies of the Ancient World* [Garden City, N.Y.: Doubleday Anchor, 1961], p. 10.) In 1960 Kramer discovered a new poem, "The Death of Dumuzi (the Sumerian name for Tammuz)," which proves conclusively that instead of rescuing Tammuz from the underworld Ishtar sent him there as her substitute. (See the present writer's article, "Tammuz and the Bible," *Journal of Biblical Literature*, LXXXIV [1965], 283-90.) A line in a fragmentary and obscure text is the only positive evidence to indicate that after being sent to the underworld Tammuz himself may have had his sister take his place for half the year. (Cf. S. N. Kramer's note, *Bulletin of the American Schools of Oriental Research*, no. 183 [October, 1966], 31.)

The case is no less tenuous for the alleged resurrections of Adonis and of Attis. Pierre Lambrechts has recently shown that in the case of Adonis—the beautiful youth, beloved of Aphrodite, who was slain by a boar—there is no trace of a resurrection in the early texts or pictorial representations. The four texts which speak of his resurrection are quite late, from the 2nd to the 4th centuries A.D. (P. Lambrechts, "La 'résurrection d'Adonis,' " in *Mélanges Isidore Lévy* [1955], pp. 207-40.) He has similarly shown that Attis, the consort of Cybele, does not appear as a "resurrected" god until after 150 A.D.

The death and resurrection of these various mythological figures, however attested, would in all cases typify the annual death and rebirth of vegetation. This significance cannot be attributed to the death and resurrection of Jesus. A. D. Nock sets forth the most striking contrast between pagan and Christian examples of resurrection as follows: "In Christianity everything is made to turn on a dated experience on a historical

Person; it can be seen from I Cor. vx:3 that the statement of the story early assumed the form of a statement in a Creed. There is nothing in the parallel cases which points to any attempt to give such a basis of historical evidence to belief." (*Early Gentile Christianity and Its Hellenistic Background* [New York: Harper Torchbooks, 1964], p. 107; cf. also Bruce Metzger, "Considerations of Methodology in the Study of the Mystery Religions and Early Christianity," *Harvard Theological Review*, XLVIII [1955], 1-20.)

Schonfield Asserts That the Deity of Jesus Is a Pagan Concept, Influenced by the Roman Ruler Cult

He dismisses the subject of the deity of Jesus by that most disarming adverb—"obviously." "Obviously," he asserts, "we have to divorce the issue (of the Messianic Hope) from the paganized doctrine of the incarnation of the Godhead with which for Christians it has become intermingled..." (p. 21). He explains that this doctrine was intruded into early Christianity by Gentile believers who could not hold Jesus their true emperor inferior in dignity to Caesar (p. 200).

In 42 B.C. Julius Caesar was posthumously deified by the Senate. Augustus (27 B.C.-A.D. 14), his successor, accepted divine honors particularly from the eastern provinces. Technically speaking it was the emperor's genius or double who was being honored. After his death Augustus was also deified and introduced into the Pantheon.

It was a madman, Gaius Caligula (37-41 A.D.), who demanded worship of himself as a living god. Of a later emperor, Domitian (81-96 A.D.) Suetonius said: "With no less arrogance he began as follows in issuing a circular letter in the name of his procurators, 'Our Master and our God bids that this be done.' " Schonfield holds that these titles were inserted into the mouth of Thomas when he cried out to Jesus, "My Lord and my God" (p. 200).

Many scholars believe that the ruler cult was more the expression of political loyalty than of genuine piety. A. D. Nock points to the absence of *exvotos* to the emperor, i.e. dedications in which thanks would be given for prayers answered and sicknesses healed. In any case the situation of Jesus is quite unlike the above examples: (1) He was not a conqueror or an emperor with massive powers and a tradition of divine honors. (2) His followers who worshipped him in the first instance were not, as Schonfield assumes, Gentiles from a polytheistic background where heroes were readily assimilated to anthropomorphic deities but, as will be shown below, Jews from a monotheistic tradition.

Schonfield Ignores the Old Testament Foreshadowings of the Deity of the Messiah

We shall agree with Schonfield that the Jews at the time of Jesus were not expecting a divine Messiah. But it can be shown that Jesus and the early Hebrew Christians interpreted a number of Old Testament passages as indicating a Messiah who was one with God in a unique sense. Schonfield does not deal with such passages as Psalm 45:6 cited in Hebrews 1:8; Psalm 110:1 quoted by Jesus in Mark 12:35-37; Psalm 2:7 quoted in Acts 13:33, etc.

A telling testimony to the presence of such passages in the Old Testament is the way which Schonfield twice quotes Isaiah 9 (pp. 202, 223). In the first passage he notes that the message of the angels at Christmas "echoes the words of Isaiah ix: 'Unto us a son is born; and the government shall be upon his shoulder. . . . Of the increase of his government and peace there shall be no end, upon the throne of David, and upon his kingdom, to order it and establish it.' "

In the second passage in referring to a hymn from Qumran, Hodayot III, he notes that "the words of the hymn make obvious reference to Isaiah ix.6-7: 'Unto us a child is born, unto us a son is given: and the government shall be upon his shoulder: and his name shall be called Wonderful Counsellor. . . . Of the increase of his government and peace there shall be no end, upon the throne of David, and upon his kingdom, to order it, and to establish it with judgement and justice from henceforth even for ever."

The dots in Schonfield's citations represent a most eloquent silence. What has been omitted reads: "MIGHTY GOD, EVERLASTING FATHER, PRINCE OF PEACE."

Schonfield Assumes Rather Late Dates for the Gospels and Consequent Pagan Intrusions into Their Composition

Schonfield characterizes the Gospel of John as the work of a Greek author, the so-called elder John of Ephesus, who has introduced the picture of Jesus as "a posturing polemical figure with a streak of antisemitism," and "a pathological egoist" who claims to be the Son of God (p. 99). He dates the Gospel of John to A.D. 110-115 (p. 258).

The author does not take into account the revised estimate of the Gospel of John that the Dead Sea Scrolls have impressed upon many scholars, e.g. Bishop J. A. T. Robinson. W. F. Albright summarizes his personal views on John in *New Horizons in Biblical Research* (London: Oxford University Press, 1966), p. 46, as follows:

> All the concrete arguments for a late date for the Johannine literature have now been dissipated, and Bultmann's attempts to discern an earlier and later form of the Gospel have proved to be entirely misleading, as both of his supposed redactions have similar Jewish background. The date which I personally prefer is the late 70's or early 80's, i.e., not more than thirty or forty years after the composition of the earliest Pauline epistles.

Schonfield similarly adopts very late dates for the book of Acts, placing it in the time of Trajan, A.D. 98-117 (p. 197), and for Luke, dating it about 100 A.D. (pp. 169, 177). He bases these dates on the disputable dependence of Luke on Josephus' *Antiquities*, which was published in 94 A.D. But there are many cogent reasons for dating Acts prior to the Neronian persecution of 64 A.D. Acts 1:1 would further require that Luke was prior to Acts itself.

One of his arguments for the late date of Luke is the resemblance, pointed out by the mythographer Robert Graves (pp. 177, 254), between the incident on the Emmaus Road (Luke 24:13-32) and the first chapter of Apuleius' *The Golden Ass*. It is a glaring blunder for Schonfield to posit the Gospel of Luke about 100 A.D. on this basis, inasmuch as Apuleius was not born until 124 A.D. and did not publish his famous work until about 150 A.D.!

Schonfield Evades the Testimony of Paul to the Deity of Jesus

"Even the Hellenised Paul in his mystical philosophy never went as far as speaking of Christ as God, though his doctrine of the Messiah as the pre-eminent expression of God is so delicately poised in its terminology that it could be misunderstood by those unacquainted with its peculiar esoteric Jewish background of thought connected with the Archetypal Man" (p. 200). Schonfield's rather tortuous statement seeks to evade the full implications of Paul's testimony.

In a book which is about Jesus, Schonfield does not go into any detail about Pauline thought. But from his notes to *The Authentic New Testament* (New York: Mentor Books, 1958), a translation which he produced, we see that he does not question the fact that Paul was a Pharisaic Jew or that his letters were written before his death in the 60's. Paul's testimony on the issue of the deity of Christ is thus quite crucial.

Most scholars would not agree with Schonfield that Paul's language about Jesus is ambiguous. To quote a distinguished Jewish authority, H. J. Schoeps, (*Paul*, Philadelphia: Westminster Press, 1961):

> In Phil. 2:6 Paul speaks of an *isa einai theō* of Christ, which can only mean that 'Christ was and is equal with God. In 2 Cor. 11:31 Paul relates the Jewish formula of benediction, the word *eulogētos* (blessed) . . ., which applies to God, to Jesus Christ and no doubt feels no scruple in so doing (p. 152).
>
> The equation of the *Christos* with God Himself, which cancels the line of demarcation between the God of the Old Testament and the Messiah, leads logically to the fact that Paul transfers all the Old Testament statements about God to the exalted *Christos Iēsous* (p. 153).

Schonfield Distorts the Testimony of Jesus

He maintains that "Jesus as much as any other Jew would have regarded as blasphemous the manner in which he is depicted, for instance, in the Fourth Gospel" (pp. 21-22). When the high priest Caiaphas adjured Jesus to declare under oath whether he was the Messiah or not, Jesus answered, "I am, and ye shall see the Son of Man on the right hand of power, and coming in clouds of heaven" (Mark 14:62). The high priest thereupon rent his clothes and said, "Ye have heard the blasphemy." Schonfield guided by his preconceptions interprets the rending of the garments merely as "a formal sign of sorrow." He holds that "Jesus had committed a 'blasphemy,' not of God in Jewish law but of Tiberius Caesar in Roman law" (p. 148).

This is a most unconvincing interpretation of what the high priest regarded as blasphemy. The rending of the garments was a protest against a *gidduf*, a blasphemy against God, according to Mishnah Sanhedrin VII:5; according to Mishna Kerithoth I:1 this was worthy of death. To quote the Jewish scholar Schoeps:

> In the scene of Jesus' trial at night He is asked by the high priest with a solemn oath to say whether He is the Son of God. According to Mt. 26:63 and Mk. 14:61-62, the question is put directly by the high priest, and ac-

cording to the older tradition contained in Mark, is answered by Jesus in the words *egō eimi* (I'am').

E. Stauffer has carefully investigated traces of the liturgical theophany formula *Ani* (*we*) *Hu* (literally "I and He" but meaning "I am He") in Jewish writings. It seems to me to be proved that this lies behind the *egō eimi* statements, and that in the mouth of Jesus it implied that He predicated of Himself divine nature, while in the ears of the high priest it sounded, of course, like a horrible blasphemy (op. cit., p. 161).

Schoeps points out that the mere claim to have been the Messiah would not have been adequate reason for the Sanhedrin to have condemned Jesus to death. In A.D. 132-35 when Rabbi Akiba proclaimed Bar Kokhba the Messiah, the rabbis who disagreed did not persecute the latter. In the Jewish view history would be the judge of messianic claims. (Cf. Gamaliel's speech in Acts 5:34 ff.)

Schonfield objects that if Jesus were guilty of blasphemy he would have been stoned (Lev. 24:16). He recognizes, however, the fact that the Jews at this time were deprived of the right of capital punishment, a fact confirmed by the Talmud. They were indeed tempted to stone Jesus when He said, "I and the Father are one" (John 10:30, 31; cf. Luke 5:20 ff.).

On two occasions they evidently took advantage of the temporary absence of a Roman governor to take the law into their hands. In 37 A.D. when Pilate had been recalled they stoned Stephen for blasphemy (Acts 6:11 ff.). In A.D.61 between the terms of Festus and Albinus they stoned James, the brother of Jesus. (See Josephus, *Antiquities* XX:200; Eusebius, *Church History* II:23.)

Schonfield Contrives an Implausible Plot
to Explain the Circumstances of Jesus' Death

The author conceives of Jesus as a sincere but astute messianic pretender, whose intimate knowledge of the Old Testament prophecies enabled him to manipulate people and events so as to achieve the fulfilment of those prophecies. Toward the end of his ministry he took certain people into his confidence —Joseph of Arimathea, Lazarus, a Judaean priest (John 18:15), and an anonymous "young man." It may be asked why Jesus did not confide in Peter, James, and John—his closest disciples.

His accomplices were to give Jesus a drug so that he might feign death on the cross. He would then recover and after three days reveal himself as the resurrected one. According to Schonfield the drug was given in the "vinegar," i.e., the cheap wine, offered to Jesus when he said, "I thirst." He nowhere mentions the fact that Jesus had earlier refused wine mingled with gall or myrrh as an anodyne (Mark 15:23; Matthew 27:34).

As evidence of Joseph of Arimathea's participation in such a plot, Schonfield argues: "It has been noted by scholars that Joseph asked for the body (sōma) of Jesus, which could indicate that he did not think of him as dead. It is only Pilate who refers to the corpse (ptoma)" (p. 168). No doubt scholars have noticed the difference in the synonyms, but only someone with Schonfield's imagination could argue that in this context sōma means a living body and not a corpse; in Homer this is always the case. (Cf. Josephus, Antiquities XVIII:236 to cite but one of numerous possible cases.)

After the body had been laid in Joseph's tomb, the plotters came on Saturday night to revive Jesus. The setting up of a guard at the tomb is dismissed as "a late reply to allegations that the body had been stolen by the disciples . . ." (p. 170). Unfortunately for the plot Jesus had received a spear wound and could not be revived. The plotters then disposed of the body somewhere, leaving the riddle of the empty tomb (p. 172).

Schonfield Explains Away the Appearances of the Risen Christ as Cases of Mistaken Identity

Schonfield recognizes that the early Christians became convinced of the resurrection of Jesus not primarily because of the empty tomb but because of the appearances of "the risen Christ." He also concedes that "Christians are surely right in protesting that the Church could not have been established on the basis of deliberate falsehood on the part of the apostles. . ." (pp. 170-71). He admits that "we are not dealing in the Gospels with hallucinations, with psychic phenomena or survival in the Spiritualist sense" (p. 159). He further remarks, "What emerges from the records is that various disciples did see somebody, a real living person. Their experiences were not subjective" (p. 173; italics are the author's).

According to Schonfield, Mary Magdalene, who was after all unbalanced, did not see Jesus in the garden but simply the gardener (pp. 171, 174). The angel at the empty tomb (Matt. 28:2-5) was simply a "young man" (cf. Mark 16:5), perhaps the same as the gardener. The two disciples on the road to Emmaus mistook a stranger for Jesus, possibly the same "young man" (pp. 177-78).

Commenting on the rendezvous with Jesus by the Sea of Galilee (John 21), Schonfield quotes vs. 12, "None of the disciples dare ask him, 'Who are you?' knowing it was the master," and then gratuitously adds, "but this was just what they did not know" (p. 179). The same ubiquitous young man was mistaken by the disciples on the mountain of Galilee (Matt. 28:17). He does not mention I Cor. 15:6 which probably refers to this incident. There St. Paul says that more than 500 at one time saw the risen Jesus. (In Schonfield's *The Authentic N.T.*, the qualifying phrase, "of whom the greater part remain until now," is strangely omitted.)

Schonfield dismisses the two appearances of Jesus to the apostles in Jerusalem, the first week without and the second week with Thomas. He argues that this is a Judean tradition followed by Luke and John (not noting the allusion in Mark) which is at variance with the Galilean tradition in Matthew. He explains this story as a Jerusalemite response to the Galilean story (John 21) since "in both there is an eating by Jesus of broiled fish" (p. 178).

It is commonly agreed that there were ten appearances of Jesus after his death to the disciples. Of these Schonfield does not allude at all to: (1) the early appearance of Jesus to the women returning from the sepulchre (Matt. 28:9, 10); (2) the appearance to James (I Cor. 15:7); nor (3) the final appearance to the disciples on the Mount of Olives (Mark 16:19; Acts 1:4-9). (4) He mentions without comment the appearance to Peter (I Cor. 15:5; Luke 24:34). (5) & (6) As seen above he dismisses the two appearances in Jerusalem as conflicting Judean traditions (Mark 16:14; Luke 24:36-43; John 20:19-25; I Cor. 15:5).

In the four appearances that he does seek to explain: (7) to Mary Magdalene (Mark 16:9-11; John 20:11-18), (8) to the two disciples on the Emmaus road (Mark 16:12, 13; Luke 24:13-5), (9) to the disciples fishing on the Sea of Galilee (John 21:1-23), and (10) to the disciples gathered on the mountain of Galilee (Matt. 28:16-20; I Cor. 15:6), Schonfield capitalizes on certain statements of hesitation or of initial failure to recognize the risen Jesus. He does not apply his ingenuity to the cases where there are no such statements.

The Alternatives

Schonfield seeks to maintain that neither Jesus nor his apostles were guilty of any fraud. Yet he does not explain how the plotters—Lazarus, Joseph of Arimathea, the mysterious "young man"—can be regarded as innocent of deception. The latter is mistaken for the risen Jesus on the four occasions of "appearances" admitted by the author, but never quite manages to correct the misapprehension of the disciples. He is supposed to bear a message from the dying Jesus "that the Messiah had risen" and "that they would see him in Galilee" (p. 179), knowing full well that he was quite dead, since according to Schonfield (p. 175) he had assisted in the second burial of Jesus. We are asked to believe that the skeptical disciples were confused by the appearance of this young man into believing that Jesus had arisen and that they were so transformed by this confusion that they turned Jerusalem upside down with their preaching.

Schonfield asserts that it is not his intention to denigrate Jesus. He professes admiration for Jesus as a "dynamic personality" who worked and plotted to accomplish God's will (p. 185). But the level of that admiration is revealed in his concluding comparison of Jesus with the flamboyant British prime minister Disraeli, "another famous schemer" (p. 187).

We are left with the following alternatives: Was Jesus the Son of God or was he a "pathological egoist"? Was the empty tomb the result of an elaborately contrived Passover plot or of an eternally decreed Easter triumph? Is Christianity based on the mistaken identity of an anonymous "young man" or on the recognition of the risen Christ?

Appendix B

A Sample of Scrollduggery *

Joseph A. Fitzmyer, S. J.

The "Battle of the Scrolls" resumes—at a time when most people had come to believe the issue was more or less settled. Its latest phase appears in an article by John Marco Allegro in *Harper's Magazine* for August, 1966, entitled "The Untold Story of the Dead Sea Scrolls." The title on the cover of the magazine—"The Dead Sea Scrolls: A Threat to Christianity?"— reveals the article's tenor. Couched in the form of a question, it makes its point by implication and insinuation. This is just what much of the article does; its purpose is to upset the assurance about the scrolls in "both layman and clergy" created by pronouncements "from the seminaries" offering "comfort to the anxious reader."

The article's main allegation is that "Christian scholars," unable to "deal with such distasteful material sufficiently disinterestedly," have been exercising a boycott and withholding the texts. Only a "new generation of uncommitted scholars" will be able to probe "the significance of the scrolls without fear or favor, undeterred by religious or academic pressures." Such statements imply that the international team of eight scholars called together in 1952 is incapable of handling the material of Qumran Cave IV, because they are committed Chrisians—all save Mr. Allegro, who is "of no religious persuasion." He says: "Half [of them] were Roman Catholics—three seculars and one Jesuit."

Being the only Jesuit ever associated with the team—and in a very minor capacity, in 1957-58—I may be permitted to rise to the occasion, play the sinister role that my title implies, and tell a little more of the "untold story." The picture of

---

* Specially revised by the author for book publication in this volume; the essay appeared originally in *America*, September 3, 1966.

myself in the "scrollery" of the Palestine Archeological Museum in Jordanian Jerusalem that graces the article (p. 52) does me a dubious favor, for it serves to enhance the negative impression made by the article and helps to build up in the reader's mind the idea of the Christian "boycott" of the scrolls. How cleverly it feeds the "niggling fears of the anxious inquirer"! (It is, of course, just possible that Mr. Allegro is not thinking of me as the "Jesuit," and has wrongly identified one of his "Roman Catholic" teammates in this way; in the *New Statesman* for Dec. 17, 1965 [p. 970], he erroneously gives the title to Msgr. Patrick W. Skehan. If this be so, we have a classic example of Mr. Allegro's disregard of the facts—or of his misinformation.)

Mr. Allegro is an accomplished popularizer. Though many of his publications of scroll texts are of dubious merit, he has written widely on popular aspects of the scrolls. Serious readers have learned that his little Pelican book, *The Dead Sea Scrolls*, contains a good account of the discovery of the scrolls and of their contents; in this area he had the benefit of ample consultation with his learned teammates in Jerusalem. But when he attempts to assess their significance for the origins of Christianity, Mr. Allegro moves in a dream world of unreality, where free association replaces logic.

Being a clever writer, Mr. Allegro knows how to exploit the impression shared by many today that a committed Christian cannot be an objective scholar. Even this present attempt of mine to answer some of his allegations will be brushed aside as coming from a "committed" Christian, a "Roman Catholic"—and worse still a "Jesuit." Hence it should be recalled that on a former occasion, when Mr. Allegro expressed similar views on Christian origins, five of his teammates reacted by sending a letter from Jerusalem to the London *Times* charging him with either misreading the texts or building up a "chain of conjectures which the materials do not support" (see *Time*, April 2, 1965 [p. 71], where his picture is captioned: "Philologist Allegro: Inference Is Not Evidence"). His one-time teacher, the eminent British scholar H. H. Rowley, of Manchester's Semitics department, likewise deplored his unscholarly presentations. *Time*'s caption hits off well much of what Allegro has written in *Harper's*.

To insinuate that there has been a Christian "boycott" of the Cave IV materials, Mr. Allegro asserts: "Fourteen years after the discovery of the Wounded Partridge cave, not a single volume dealing with this material has appeared." This is unfortunately true. Along with Mr. Allegro, many scholars interested in the scrolls, who have not had the privilege of being "editors" of the Cave IV material, feel strongly about the delay in its publication. Israeli scholars who have been privileged to publish similar material have given the scholarly world a commendable example with their rapid publication of texts— as did the American editors of the Cave I materials.

In the main, two factors account for the delay in the publication of Cave IV texts. First of these is the complicated "jigsaw puzzle" that initially faced the editors of the tens of thousands of Cave IV fragments. No complete scroll was found in this cave; from the fragments, they tediously pieced together, identified and deciphered over four hundred different texts. Only on the day before I left Jerusalem (July 9, 1958) were "the last"(?) of Cave IV fragments brought to the museum. This reason for the delay in publication was valid, certainly, up to that time—but since then one could say that Mr. Allegro has a complaint.

Secondly, a peculiar desire obsesses some of the members of the international team to say the last word on every text entrusted to them. This is the real reason for their delay—not the calculated boycott that Mr. Allegro implies. Instead of yielding to this desire, they should publish the texts with brief notes, and do so quickly.

But strangely enough, Mr. Allegro himself, one of the privileged editors of the material, had not yet published his own volume in the series, *Discoveries in the Judaean Desert of Jordan,* when he wrote the article in *Harper's Magazine.* He was one of the first to arrive in Jerusalem in 1952 to work on the newly discovered material. At that time the now famous *pesher,* or Essene "commentary," on Habakkuk from Cave I had recently been published. It revealed exciting details about the history, tenets and practices of the Qumran sect. It also illumined in an extraordinary way the manner in which New Testament writers quoted and interpreted the Old Testament. Of the different types of literature represented in the Cave IV fragments, similar *pesharim* and the Essene cryptic texts were entrusted to Mr. Allegro for publication. But as it turned out, the significance of these texts was overrated; with one exception (the *pesher* on Nahum), they have proved to be rather tame stuff in comparison with the material assigned to other editors. There was little that was sensational, and Mr. Allegro should certainly have been able to complete the definitive edition of his relatively uncomplicated material in the 14 years that elapsed between 1952 and the *Harper's* article—or at least in the period since 1958.

(Toward the end of 1968—after 16 years since the material was first entrusted to him—Allegro finally published it in *Qumrân Cave* 4: I (4Q158-4Q186), as volume 5 of the series *Discoveries in the Judean Desert of Jordan* (Oxford: Clarendon). But how did he publish it? From the scholarly point of view, it is a very shoddy piece of work; it is regretable that the handsome volume of the Clarendon Press had to be wasted on such a publication. Of the 29 texts now definitively published in it, 15 of them had previously been offered to the scholarly world in preliminary form. Many scholars had subsequently written on these preliminary publications of Allegro; yet almost without exception he has omitted all reference to them. If one wants to get some idea of the extent of this omission, he can consult the thirteen-page bibliographical aid that I published in the *Catholic Biblical Quarterly* for January of 1969. A full review of Allegro's volume can also be found in the same publication (31 [1969] 235-38).)

By contrast, volumes by "Christian scholars" entrusted with material from other caves, as well as that of Cave IV, have already appeared. The texts of Frs. D. Barthélemy, O.P., J. T. Milik, P. Benoit, O.P., R. de Vaux, O.P. and M. Baillet, and of Prof. J. A. Sanders, are available for everyone to scrutinize in the definitive form. I have yet to see a book review that criticizes their interpretations for a religious bias or an inability to deal "sufficiently disinterestedly" with the "distasteful material" that Mr. Allegro claims is emerging from the scrolls.

Mr. Allegro refers to the "limited preliminary publications" of Cave IV texts permitted to the team by Père de Vaux, the editor-in-chief, who restricted "prior publication of our documents to no more than one per year." But he does not explain that this restriction was made lest all the choice pieces should appear in this preliminary form and render the "definitive series" of little value. After all, an agreement had been made with the Clarendon Press of Oxford, which has been issuing the texts with its well-known meticulous care and handsome format. The decision ascribed to Père de Vaux was not an effort to withhold material allegedly "distasteful" to Christians.

Mr. Allegro has published a number of his texts in preliminary form. But how has he done so? Writers in scholarly publications have complained about the piecemeal, unscholarly way in which he has presented his texts, releasing them in confusing order, misnaming them and reconstructing them to suit his pleasure (see A. Dupont-Sommer, *Semitica* 13 [1963], pp. 55-56; H. Stegemann, *Revue de Qumran* 4 [1963-64], pp. 235-70; W. R. Lane, *Journal of Biblical Literature* 78 [1959], pp. 343-46; S. B. Hoenig, *Jewish Quarterly Review* 55 [1964-65], pp. 256-59).

In the later part of his article, Mr. Allegro insists that there is "far too much that does not ring true in the New Testament in the light of the new comparative material." In other words, there is "much in the New Testament that is authentic Essenism . . . perverted in some way, robbed of its exclusivity, its political import, and given a new direction." And the New Testament, he says, is "so much at pains to disguise and reformulate this sectarian prehistory that the informed observer is left with a strong sense of unreality about the whole story."

The last sentence implies that Mr. Allegro is an "informed observer." But what puzzles me most in such statements is his understanding of the New Testament. Has he ever read it? Wandering around in the never-never land of Mr. Allegro's fantasies about what the New Testament is saying, I feel like Alice in Wonderland. To take up each point he tries to make in this part of his article is impossible here. Let us examine a few of the more preposterous statements.

"The New Testament," he avers, "is, of course, full of references to healing, and to *magoi*, 'wizards.' " We shall allow him to translate *magoi* as "wizards" for the sake of the argument. But a glance at a New Testament Greek concordance reveals that the word occurs six times (Matt. 2:1, 17, 16, 16; Acts 13:6, 8). Even to count in the abstract noun *magia*, "wizardry" (Acts 8:11) and the verb *mageuô*, "practice wizardry" (Acts 8:9), scarcely fills the New Testament with references to it. And even adding the admittedly more numerous references to healing by no means fills the New Testament with them— much less makes of Jesus an Essene.

That the name "Essene" may mean "healer" has been seriously argued by reputable scroll scholars; it is a possible though not wholly convincing explanation. But that it has anything to do with "diviners," or that the word *khārash* ("to divine") has anything to do with Jesus, "the son of a carpenter" (*khārāsh*), or with John the Baptist, "the son of a deafmute" (*khērēsh*)—even by changing the vowels—these are free associations of Mr. Allegro's.

Another mode of Mr. Allegro's argumentation must be detailed. He says, for instance: "It now appears that the name

Jesus itself means 'Essene.' " To whom does it so appear? Apparently only to Mr. Allegro. He does not give us any basis for such a meaning. What is the evidence for such an interpretation of the name? No reputable New Testament scholar will deny that the explanation given in Matt. 1:21: "You shall call his name Jesus, for he will save his people from their sins," is a popular etymology. It exploits the similarity of the late form of the name Joshua (*Yeshua'*) with the abstract noun for "salvation" (*yeshû'ah*). But that it is the name being explained in Acts 13:8 ("Elymas the magician, for that is the meaning of his name") violates all the canons of interpretation.

Again, no one will deny that there is a certain amount of punning on the names of persons in the New Testament, and that therefore an effort must often be made to understand what the name means. Apropos of Peter's name, Mr. Allegro says: "A newly deciphered document refers to one administrative official by a Semitic word which must underlie the nickname Cephas given to Simon Peter. The Essenes clearly deemed it a rather 'special' word, since it signifies one having the ability to read men's minds through their faces. This gives us the clue to the origin and purpose of the story in Matt. 16, where it is Peter who recognizes the Messianic calling of Jesus." I suppose we shall have to take Mr. Allegro's word for it that there is such a "newly deciphered document." But why does he not publish this text to which he refers so obscurely? Or at least give us the form of the Semitic word, so that we ourselves can judge whether it has indeed the meaning he assigns to it?

(Further information about this "newly deciphered document" has been made available in the second of three articles that amateur-Scrollman, Edmund Wilson, recently wrote on "The Dead Sea Scrolls, 1969," in *The New Yorker* (29 March 1969). On pp. 46-48 he gives part of a taped conversation in which three or four reputable scholars (Y. Yadin, G. Vermes, F. L. Cross, and E. F. Carpenter) challenged Allegro to show them the document, or at least describe it and give the form of the name *Kephas* that allegedly appears in it and is the basis of his interpretation. They were put off by Allegro, and even Edmund Wilson, who feels a certain affection for Allegro as a "man of historical imagination," was constrained to paint Allegro in his true colors and to acknowledge that "his utterances are coming to sound more and more fanciful" [p. 48]).

Mr. Allegro continues: "Furthermore, since Peter is here

and elsewhere being designated an 'Inspector, Overseer' on a pattern with the Essene administrative functionary, we can now see that many of the other stories related about him, speaking with tongues, relating the wonderful works of God . . . are simply demonstrations of the supervisory work required of the Essene administrator." In this statement, "here" obviously refers to Matt. 16:16-19. And yet neither in this passage nor "elsewhere" in the New Testament is Peter ever called a "bishop" (*episkopos*). Etymologically, this Greek word means "overseer, inspector," and in the Septuagint it translates the Hebrew word *paqîd*, "commissioner, deputy, overseer." The latter is the name in the scrolls for an Essene administrator, who is sometimes called by an even more closely related word, *mebaqqer* ("inspector"). But Mr. Allegro is apparently unaware of the fact that there is no New Testament evidence that administrators in the Jewish Christian communities of Palestine were ever so designated.

The *episkopoi* emerge first in the Hellenistic local church founded by such wandering apostles as Paul. In Acts we read of them only once, when Paul summons the "elders" (*presbyteroi*) of the Church of Ephesus to Miletus to address them on his last return to Jerusalem (Acts 20:28). The name of the Christian "bishop" may indeed reflect that of the Essene functionary; it may even be a "takeoff" on it, robbing it of its exclusivity and giving to it a new direction—but so what?

We could obviously go on to many other points in Mr. Allegro's discussion. In much of his presentation there is utter lack of logic. Often it goes like this: If A is like B, than A *is* B; if Christianity resembles Essenism, then Christianity *is* Essenism. Or, if A is influenced by B, then A is B; if Christianity is influenced by Essenism (and who would deny it?), then Christianity is Essenism. And sometimes the conclusion is given a further twist: then Christianity has perverted Essenism.

"The very scholars who should be most capable of working on the documents and interpreting them," Mr. Allegro contends, "have displayed a not altogether surprising, but nonetheless curious, reluctance to go to the heart of their matter." I hardly think, when readers realize he is referring here to a questioning of "the source and originality of Christian doctrine," that many of them are going to be persuaded his charges are just.

Time magazine for April 15, 1957 (pp. 38, 43), carried an estimate of the scrolls that is still valid: "Only lately have scholars accumulated enough facts to be able to settle down to a sober appraisal of the scrolls' significance. The majority verdict: the scrolls do not shake the foundations of Christianity, but they greatly contribute to the understanding of those foundations. . . . The only Christians whose faith the scrolls can jolt are those who have failed to see the paradox that the churches have always taught: that Jesus Christ was a man as well as God—a man of a particular time and place, speaking a specific language, revealing His way in terms of a specific cultural and religious tradition. For Christians who want to know more of that Matrix in which their faith was born, the People of the Scrolls are reaching a hand across the centuries."

Appendix C

Computer Analysis and the Pauline Corpus:

A Case of Deux Ex Machina

James R. Moore

T. H. Huxley is alive and well in Scotland. Or so it seems, for in the latter half of the twentieth century the evangelical church is again being twitted by self-appointed "bulldogs" of science in the persons of A. Q. Morton and his lesser compatriot, James McLeman. Beginning with an article in *The London Sunday Observer* on November 2, 1963, followed by a popularization of their research, titled *Christianity and the Computer*, and concluding in *Paul, the Man and the Myth*, [1] Morton and McLeman have scandalized the unsophisticated and rather amused the learned by publishing a computer revelation of a "five letter Paul." Their basic technique was exceedingly simple: count the number of times the Greek word *kai* ("and") appears in each of the Pauline epistles; average each sum over the number of sentences in its epistle; and compare the averages. They found a consistent average in Romans, First and Second Corinthians, Galatians and, practically, in Philemon: The averages derived from the other epistles were quite different, proving that they could not have been written by the apostle.

Laymen for the most part had never questioned the authen-

---

[1] London: Hodder and Stoughton, 1964; and New York: Harper and Row, 1966, respectively. Other writings include Morton's articles: "The Integrity of the Pauline Epistles," *Journal of the Manchester Statistical Society* (March, 1965); "Computer Criticism: A Reply" (to H. K. McArthur, "Computer Criticism," *The Expository Times*, LXXVI [1965], 367-70), *The Expository Times*, LXXVII (1966), 116-20; "Dislocation in I and II Corinthians," *The Expository Times*, LXXVIII (1967), 119 ff; and, with M. Levinson and W. C. Wake, "On Certain Statistical Features of the Pauline Epistles," *The Philosophical Journal*, III (1966), 129-48.

ticity of the epistles bearing the apostle's name. Radical biblical criticism was for them only a dim memory passed on from great-great-grandfather's day, when Colenso, *Essays and Reviews*, and *Lux Mundi* agitated English orthodoxy. To scholars, on the other hand, aware of the speculations of F. C. Baur and the "Tübingen school" which reached generally the same conclusion over 100 years ago, the "revelation" of Morton and McLeman seemed not a little anachronistic, especially since the view that Paul had written only the so-called *Hauptbriefe* had come into considerable disrepute in recent years. However, for both parties, the use of a computer in advancing the view was plainly unsettling: it became, alternately, the supreme accreditation or the *deus ex machina*.

Which way shall we have it? An answer will emerge as we consider Morton and McLeman's argument and the attitude which has attended its promulgation.

'YOND MORTON HAS A LEAN AND HUNGRY LOOK'

In 83 pages Morton and McLeman make the rather pretentious claim to integrate their research with "a contemporary view of the Bible, the church and personal religion" (p. 7). Whether or not this task has been accomplished there is little doubt that in *Christianity and the Computer* the authors snuggle up to the lay reader in the familiar second person and attempt to pick his evangelical pocket. He is told, "you must conclude" (p. 12), "you see it for what it is" (p. 16), and "you will always have the uncomfortable feeling" (p. 18). Thus personally involved, he reads of "the typical figure of the evangelist clutching his Bible to his breast" (p. 14) and of "the sentimental view of the origins of Christianity" (p. 35). He is asked to conclude, "whether we like it or not" (p. 12), that "the traditional conception of a scriptural authority is in ruins" (p. 44). Any lesser view, he discovers, can be called "bibliomancy" (p. 57). Moreover, the few with temerity to examine Morton's *Paul, the Man and the Myth* will find that it, too, comes laced with tendentious assertions on page after page: for example they are told that "the true believer [sic] in the twentieth century has still not shaken off the fascination of verbal inspiration" (p. 132) and that the more open-minded approach to the work of Schweitzer which their research requires must be swallowed, "however bitter a pill it may be in some quarters" (p. 108).

Though Morton and McLeman might be accused of *odium*

anti-theologicum, it is probably safe to say that their unfortunate attitude is "more than a problem of personal relation." [2] One feels certain that there is a larger design, perhaps like that of Huxley, to collapse the traditional church by inveighing against Scripture in the name of science. What Caesar said of conniving Cassius may find its contemporary application here:

Such men as he be never at heart's ease
Whiles they behold a greater than themselves,
And therefore are they very dangerous.

ATTITUDE AND ARGUMENT

One must admit as a matter of principle that even great hostility does not preclude sound scholarship. However in the present case there may be some relation between the two, for one needs not read long before he finds Morton and McLeman creating oversimplifications, sweeping generalizations, and either/or extremes where issues are more complex.[3] Before taking up some of the technical problems which underlie these deficiencies, we would do well to check the suspicion they engender regarding the relation between argument and attitude in *Paul, the Man and the Myth.* An absolute judgment is admittedly impossible. But comparison of the book with results from another computer enterprise will at least offer an illuminating contrast.

In his *Audience Criticism and the Historical Jesus*, J. Arthur Baird offers an entirely new approach to the Synoptics through a computer analysis of the logia, their audiences, and their speaker-audience relationships.[4] His conclusion, if correct, is

---

[2] Reinier Schippers, "Paul and the Computer," *Christianity Today*, IX (December 4, 1964), 223.

[3] Cf. John W. Ellison, review of *Christianity and the Computer*, by A. Q. Morton and James McLeman, *Journal of Biblical Literature*, LXXXIV (1965), 190; and *Paul, The Man and the Myth*, pp. 18, 20-21, 42-44, 101 ff.

[4] Philadelphia: Westminster, 1969. Here is Baird's opinion of his forerunner in computer analysis: ". . . when Morton sticks to his scientific method in researching the authorship of the Pauline corpus, his statistics come as welcome relief into a discussion long befogged with the mists of debate, homiletics, and special pleading. It is unfortunate, however, that this first significant use of the computer for New Testament study was marred by Morton's own special pleading for a Biblical skepticism that had nothing to do with the evidence of his scientific study" (pp. 28-29).

in this writer's judgment many times more revolutionary for modern theological scholarship than anything Morton and Mc-Leman or any other computer scholar has yet published. That is, if there were ever a cause for ostentation, this would be it. Says Baird: "In this complex and limited manner, it would seem highly probable that we can indeed break through the *Geschichte* barrier and talk of the authentic, historical Jesus. Basic to all stands a body of logia possessing a rare stability and integrity, reflecting a church deeply concerned from a very early period to preserve the exact words and ideas of Jesus, and uniquely successful in doing so." [5] Significantly, this very modest conclusion is reached only after the computer technique and its pertinent data are laid bare on page after page, and its limitations frankly acknowledged. In the sharpest possible contrast, Morton and McLeman are practically paranoid in attempts to anticipate and fend off criticism in *Paul, the Man and the Myth*. All dissent is rifled down mercilessly; to them it is a manifestation of an "instinctive defense of the old against the new" (p. 102). Only 32 pages of the book's 217 relate directly to their techniques (pp. 65-97), and all data (presumably their best evidence) is arranged in 54 tables at the back of the book. Only two-thirds of these tables are interpreted in the text and most are unintelligible to all but the professional statistician. We may conclude in this case that argument *is* dulled where the axe is ground.

SOME TECHNICAL PROBLEMS

What can be said critically about Morton and McLeman's techniques? To begin with, it would take a professional statistician to evaluate the intricacies of sampling and significance testing employed by them. Since this writer makes only the mildest pretense to being a mathematician, he must defer to better authorities. John J. O'Rourke, one who has himself done work on statistical aspects of the *kai* criterion employed by our authors, thinks the fact that *Paul, the Man and the Myth* was ever published "is a mystery unless the mere tossing about of statistical terminology gives authors some special privilege." [6] He isolates one "monstrosity from the standpoint of one with only an elementary knowledge of statistics" on

[5] *Ibid.*, p. 173.

[6] Review of *Paul, the Man and the Myth*, by A. Q. Morton and James McLeman, *Journal of Biblical Literature*, LXXXVI (1967), 110.

page 84 [7] and allows himself to "hope that this work will not discredit statisticians in the eyes of biblical scholars;" O'Rourke adds, ". . . statisticians may be able to resolve certain questions of concern to the biblicist, but Morton and McLeman have not helped to do so." [8]

More important though is the fact seemingly ignored by Morton and McLeman: statistical conclusions are mute concerning authorship. "Statistical inference," Nieboer has recently emphasized, "allows no more than the conclusion that . . . differences exist. . . . causes are an extrapolation beyond the statistical tests." It is one thing to suggest multi-authorship or non-Pauline authorship (a scientifically reasonable hypothesis); it is quite another matter to claim on the basis of computer analysis that this is the *only* acceptable explanation (a product of *deus ex machina* scientism).[9]

Moving into the more familiar realm of philology and Biblical studies, we can facilitate analysis of Morton and McLeman's research by expressing concisely its premises:

> *Major Premise:* All ancient writers of homogeneous continuous Greek prose manifest unconscious characteristics of style which occur with the same average per unit frequency throughout each writer's works.[10]

> *Minor Premise:* A discriminating characteristic of all writers of homogeneous continuous Greek prose is the average per sentence frequency of *kai*.

The major premise prompts several important questions. First, unless the statement is some kind of metaphysic, it is necessary to account empirically for its universality. Professor

---

[7] *Ibid.*

[8] *Ibid.*, p. 112.

[9] Maynard C. Nieboer, "The Statistical Analysis of A. Q. Morton and the Authenticity of the Pauline Epistles," *Calvin Theological Journal*, V (April, 1970), 73. In his valuable article, "A Reconsideration of Certain Arguments Against Pauline Authorship of the Pastoral Epistles" (*The Expository Times*, LXX [1958], 93), Bruce M. Metzger presents four critical questions for the statistical scholar of the New Testament to consider. Question two reads: "How *different* can the results of a particular analysis of the two texts be before they throw serious doubt upon the theory that they have a common author? That is, what facts must the statistician have before he can say what statistics mean?" Adds Metzger: "None of these questions can be answered *a priori*, and several of them involve aspects that elude objective criteria."

[10] See *Paul, the Man and the Myth*, pp. 49-50.

G. H. C. MacGregor and Morton consulted classical scholars to obtain a "representative selection of writers of Greek prose" which finally consisted of ten classical representatives and four authors from the *Koinē* period. One cannot, however, desist from asking whether the data obtained from analyzing the unconscious literary habits of these few writers is in fact adequate underpinning for an all-inclusive major premise. Was a truly representative cross-section of Greek prose, extending from the pre-Socratics to the Byzantine period, really employed? In the second place, one must ask whether unconscious literary habits were in fact continuous from classical to *Koinē* Greek. The representative selection of writers does include Philo, Josephus, and Clement of Alexandria, but can these writers really furnish significant data in light of Morton's observation that "when you turn the single page from the Old Testament to the New Testament you are passing in time from the world of Shakespeare to the world of Queen Victoria, or from the age of the Pilgrim Fathers to the age of the atom"? [11] Yet even if their data were blessed with continuity of literary habits, it is by no means certain that the characteristics of such writers parallel those of a Roman Pharisee who was, in all likelihood, trilingual.[12]

Finally, one must know what "homogeneous" means before he can rely on Morton and McLeman's conclusions. It is *said* that homogeneous means "all the parts of the work are consistent with each other and with the whole work" and implies that the prose "is made up and set down by one man." [13] However the researchers then proceed to overlook Old Testament quotations, liturgical, creedal, and sermonic materials in the epistles. True, Hebrews is recognized as heterogeneous, in part because of its extensive Old Testament quotations, and Romans is found heterogeneous in its first 150 sentences.[14] But perhaps this should prove the point: namely, that other epistles, like Hebrews, may in fact be heterogeneous because

---

[11] *Christianity and the Computer*, p. 17.

[12] Schippers, *op. cit.*, p. 225. Morton and McLeman admit the fact that Paul was a Jew writing in Greek "no doubt . . . does make some differences in certain respects;" but instead of learning which respects reveal the differences we are simply given the raw data from Philo and Diodorus Siculus to show that "there is no detectable difference as far as sentence length distributions are concerned" (*Paul, the Man and the Myth*, p. 58). Thus endeth the matter!

[13] *Paul, the Man and the Myth*, p. 50.

[14] *Ibid.*, p. 91.

of Old Testament quotations whether or not the tests reveal homogeneity; and (perhaps even simultaneously) they may be heterogeneous, like Romans, because another literary form was employed by the author (as the "Wisdom of Solomon" may have been used in Romans one[15]). Specifically one can mention the confessional element in I Corinthians 15, or that ten percent of Romans is composed of Old Testament quotations,[16] or that Philippians 2:5-11 was almost certainly composed in Aramaic and used in corporate worship before Paul adapted it into his discussion on humility,[17] or even the conjectural analysis of Ephesians which makes the book a composite of Paul's sermon notes assembled with the help of his friends. Morton and McLeman should be prepared to answer why the 335 words of Philemon are significant enough to receive a Pauline designation when the contribution to heterogeneity made by passages such as these can be completely ignored.[18]

Regarding the minor premise, the question of sentence length immediately arises. Sentence length might be used as a test of authorship, but since *kai* will inevitably occur with greater average frequency in long sentences than in short, one needs to know whether Morton and McLeman's word-test is a second and confirmatory test or merely the same test in disguise.[19] In any event, sentence length is an elusive characteristic, for our texts came to us without punctuation. Since editors have used different conventions of punctuation it would be naive for one to consider a sentence a "given" phenomenon throughout the literature employed. Morton and McLeman's rather

---

[15] See F. F. Bruce, *The Epistle to the Romans* ("Tyndale New Testament Commentaries"; Grand Rapids, Michigan: Eerdmans, 1963), pp. 82, 88.

[16] See E. E. Ellis, *Paul's Use of the Old Testament* (Grand Rapids, Michigan: Eerdmans, 1957).

[17] See Ralph P. Martin, *An Early Christian Confession* (London: Tyndale, 1960), and *Carmen Christi* (Cambridge: C.U.P., 1967).

[18] Questions one and three posed by Metzger (see n. 9 above) read: "1. How long must a treatise be in order to provide a sufficient sample of an author's style?" and "3. What allowance should be made, in assessing specific texts, for differences in the two works as regards (a) subject matter and (b) literary form? If the subject and the form *are* different, can the investigator devise a set of tests which are least likely to be disturbed by this?" Regarding the former query, Metzger mentions that G. Udney Yule, in his fundamental work, *The Statistical Study of Literary Vocabulary* (Cambridge, 1944), considers a solid basis for statistical analysis to be about 10,000 words.

[19] G. B. Caird, "Do Computers Count?" *The Expository Times,* LXXVI (1965), 176.

vague and defensive discussion of this important point tends to deprive one of any confidence he previously had in their scholarship.[20] In addition, O'Rourke finds it "most unusual that no mention is made of the criticism of sentence length as a criterion for determining unicity of authorship made by Gustav Herdan, himself, a statistician, at the time of the appearance of W. C. Wake's studies upon which our authors depend; if anything their tables would support Herdan's critique." [21] Another writer declares that "other authorities in the statistical field have produced evidence to demonstrate . . . that sentence length and the occurrence of common words are two of the less reliable statistical tests." [22]

Beyond the criticisms just presented there is one which, in a single motion, undercuts both premises. Many scholars consider it the *coup de grâce* for Morton and McLeman's computer revelation. Clark Pinnock, for example, puts it concisely:

> [Morton] ought to have taken time to read Otto Roller's thorough study of the literary characteristics of Paul's letters [*Das Formular der paulinischen Briefe*, 1933]. This scholar established, among many other points, that Paul employed a secretary in the composition of his correspondence. Tertius wrote the letter to the Romans (16:22). The style of Silvanus, the amanuensis, may account for the similarities between I Peter (5:12) and I Thessalonians (1:1), just as Luke may be the link between the Pastorals (2 Timothy 4:11) and Acts, whose affinities we often noticed. Morton, by grandly ignoring this fact, has deprived his readers of a critical third factor. For the alternative to simple Pauline authorship of a letter is not forgery, as he contends, but may equally be a dual authorship.[23]

---

[20] *Paul, the Man and the Myth*, p. 54.

[21] O'Rourke, *op. cit.*, p. 110.

[22] K. Grayston, "Paul and the Computer," *The Expository Times*, LXXVIII (1967), 334. On the difficulties inherent in statistical methods applied to literary works see Yule (*op. cit.*) who employs the characteristic mixture of rare and common vocabulary elements as a criterion for authorship.

[23] "Honest to Computers?" *Inter-Varsity*, Spring, 1964, pp. 16-17. In the judgment of W. F. Albright, "Since St. Paul's Greek was dictated to different amanuenses at different times and in different places, we could not possibly expect uniform quasi-literary style or

Morton responds to this criticism almost disdainfully. Without even mentioning Roller's study (which he had surely heard of by the time *Paul, the Man and the Myth* was published in 1966), he simply declares that "we do not know" about Paul's use of amanuenses. Several sweeping statements later the real revelation comes: "But would anyone argue thus unless he felt that the Pauline authorship had to be defended? Why should it be defended? It has never had any better foundation than the accretion of centuries of acceptance as the least troublesome assumption to make." [24]

Now it appears we have here, not so much a computer revelation of a "five-letter Paul," as a revelation of a foregone conclusion through a computer. *Deus ex machina* indeed. With this revelation, asserted in a truly Huxleyan spirit, one can counterpose an admonition given by none other than T. H. himself:

> Now, when those who put their trust in scientific methods of ascertaining the truth . . . find themselves confronted and opposed on their own ground by ecclesiastical pretensions to better knowledge, it is, undoubtedly, most desirable for them to make sure that their conclusions, whatever they may be, are well founded. [25]

---

vocabulary in his letters. For this reason attempts to determine the authorship of the Pauline Epistles by statistical data obtained with the use of computing machines prove little except the kind of literary Greek preferred by different amanuenses" (*The Teacher's Yoke*, ed. by E. J. Vardeman and J. L. Garrett [Waco, Texas: Baylor University Press, 1964], pp. 28-29). I am indebted to Professor Richard Longenecker's mimeographed critique of the Morton-McLeman enterprise for this quotation.

[24] *Paul, the Man and the Myth*, pp. 94-95.

[25] "The Lights of the Church and the Light of Science," *The Nineteenth Century*, July, 1890, p. 11.

The Contributors

James F. Babcock: University of Michigan, B.S., Electrical Engineering, 1966 (Eta Kappa Nu, Tau Beta Pi, Phi Kappa Phi); Trinity Evangelical Divinity School, M.Div., magna cum laude, 1970 (Teaching Fellow in Hebrew); Instructor in Biblical Languages, Trinity Evangelical Divinity School.

Clark Eugene Barshinger: The King's College, B.A., Psychology, 1967 (Pi Gamma Mu); DePaul University, M.A., Psychology; Trinity Evangelical Divinity School; McCormick Theological Seminary, M.Div.; Assistant Professor of Psychology, Trinity College (Illinois).

Ronald J. Behm: Nyack Missionary College, B.A. cum laude, Philosophy, 1965; Trinity Evangelical Divinity School, B.D. cum laude, 1968; M.A., Philosophy of Religion, 1969; co-author with Columbus Salley of *Your God Is Too White* (Inter-Varsity, 1970).

Gregory W. Best: Stanford University, B.A., East Asian Studies, 1971; Trinity Evangelical Divinity School, M.Div.

Joseph Blasczyk: Moody Bible Institute; Northern Illinois University, B.A. with honors, Sociology, 1968 (Alpha Kappa Delta); Trinity Evangelical Divinity School, M.Div., cum laude, 1972.

Bruce E. Bonecutter: Michigan State University, B.A. magna cum laude, Social Science, 1971; Trinity Evangelical Divinity School, M.Div.

Rev. Joseph A. Fitzmyer, S. J.: Professor and Head of the Biblical Section, Department of Theology, Fordham University.

Douglas Frank: Wheaton College, B.A., History, 1963; State University of New York at Buffalo, Ph.D., History, 1969; Trinity Evangelical Divinity School; Assistant Professor of History, Trinity College (Illinois).

Carole Fuester: Muskingum College, B.A., History, 1966 (Valedictorian, Phi Alpha Theta, NDEA Title IV Fellow 1966-67, Fulbright Fellowship Alternate 1966, Woodrow Wilson Fellowship Honorable Mention 1966); Indiana University, M.A., History, 1967; Philadelphia College of Bible, 1968; Trinity Evangelical Divinity Schools; Assistant Professor of History, Westmont College.

Ronald A. Iwasko: University of Minnesota, B.S., Civil Engineering, 1957; M.S., 1959; Trinity Evangelical Divinity School, M.Div. magna cum laude, 1971.

Richard F. Kantzer: Trinity College, B.A. summa cum laude, History, 1969; Trinity Evangelical Divinity School, M.A. summa cum laude, Biblical Studies, 1972.

Esther (Yue) Lo: University of Hong Kong. B.Sc. with second class honors, 1968; Wheaton College; Trinity Evangelical Divinity School, M.A.

Mel Loucks: Westmont College, B.A. cum laude, History, 1967; Trinity Evangelical Divinity School, M. Div. cum laude, 1970; Princeton Theological Seminary, Th.M., 1972.

James R. Moore: University of Illinois, B.S. with high honors, Electrical Engineering, 1969 (Edmund Janes James Scholar 1965-69, Sigma Tau, Eta Kappa Nu, Tau Beta Pi, Phi Kappa Phi); University of North Dakota, Summer Institute of Linguistics, 1968; Trinity Evangelical Divinity School, M. Div. summa cum laude, 1972; Ph.D. candidate in Ecclesiastical History, University of Manchester, England (Marshall Scholar).

Michael Murphy: Oakland University, B.A., English, 1967; University of Michigan; Trinity Evangelical Divinity School; Instructor in English, Trinity College (Illinois).

Janet G. Porcino: Wheaton College, B.A., Christian Education, 1967; Trinity Evangelical Divinity School, M.A., Biblical Studies, 1969; Staff, Inter-Varsity Christian Fellowship.

Rod Rosenbladt: University of Washington; Pacific Lutheran University, A.B., Psychology, 1964; Capitol University, B.D., 1968; Trinity Evangelical Divinity School, M.A. cum laude, Philosophy of Religion, 1972.

Robert Sabath: Moody Bible Institute; Baylor University, B.A. magna cum laude, Psychology, 1970; Trinity Evangelical Divinity School, M. Div.

Arnold D. Weigel: Waterloo Lutheran University, B.A., Philosophy, 1961; Waterloo Lutheran Seminary, B.D. with honors, 1965; Pastor, Christ the King Lutheran Church, Thornhill, Ontario.

Loren Wilkinson: Wheaton College, B.A., Anthropology, 1965; Johns Hopkins University, M.A., Anthropology, 1966; Trinity Evangelical Divinity School, M.A. cum laude, Philosophy of Religion, 1971; Syracuse University, Ph.D., Aesthetics; Instructor in English, Trinity College. (Illinois).

Edwin M. Yamauchi: Associate Professor of History, Miami University, Oxford, Ohio.

* * * * * * * * * * * * * * * * * * *

To use C. S. Lewis' words, *John Warwick Montgomery* was brought over the threshold of Christian faith "kicking and struggling." The year was 1949. The place, Cornell University, Ithaca, New York. Herman John Eckelmann, a persistent engineering student, succeeded in goading Montgomery into religious discussions. Montgomery, a philosophy major disinterested in religion, found himself forced to consider seriously the claims of Jesus Christ in the New Testament in order to preserve his intellectual integrity. After no mean struggle he acknowledged his rebellion against God and asked his forgiveness.

Having found new life in Jesus Christ, Montgomery chose to remain in the humanities in order to apply new insights gained there to the propagation of the Christian faith. After graduation with distinction in philosophy from Cornell, he sharpened his bibliographical skill with two degrees in library science from the University of California at Berkeley. Theological training was important, too. Montgomery had earned two degrees in theology at Wittenberg University, Springfield, Ohio by 1960. Then, with characteristic zeal, he plunged into doctoral studies with the result that in 1962 he was granted the Ph.D. in Bibliographical History from the University of Chicago. And, as if six degrees in ten years were not enough to exhaust a married man with three children, Montgomery mastered the French language and wrote in the year 1963-64 a 1,000-page dissertation for the degree of *Docteur de l'Université, mention Théologie Protestante* at the University of Strasbourg, France.

Dr. Montgomery is currently Professor of Church History, Chairman of the Division of Church History and History of Christian Thought, and Director of the European Program at Trinity Evangelical Divinity School, Deerfield, Illinois. Because of the European Program (in which students spend the spring quarter studying at the Protestant Theological Faculty of the University of Strasbourg and touring the Continent) he lives six months each year in the United States and six months in France. In America he is a well-known lecturer on university campuses across the nation; in Europe he serves as Executive Director of European Operations of the Christian Research Institute.

When Montgomery is not teaching or travelling, he is writing. Author of twenty books—the best known of which are *The Shape of the Past, Where Is History Going?,* and *The Suicide of Christian Theology*—and numerous scholarly articles in American, British, and Continental journals, Montgomery, a Lutheran clergyman, has become known in recent years as the foremost American theological spokesman for "confessional" Protestantism. In 1968 he was chosen to represent this position, over against fundamentalism, liberalism, and the death-of-God viewpoint, in *Spectrum of Protestant Beliefs,* edited by Robert Campbell, O.P. His "Ninety-Five Theses for the 450th Anniversary of the Reformation" created a considerable stir in Germany, where they were published alongside Luther's in 1967.

Montgomery is a member of numerous societies, including the Tolkien Society of America, the American Historical Association, and Phi Beta Kappa. He is honored by inclusion in ten biographical dictionaries, among which are *Who's Who in America, Who's Who in France, Who's Who in Europe,* and the *Dictionary of International Biography.*

James R. Moore

Index of Names

292